Praise for Patrice Vecchione's

STEP INTO NATURE

"Wise and full-hearted advice on blurring the boundaries between inner and outer nature. Patrice Vecchione guides us into deeper, freer levels of imagination and creativity."

—**David George Haskell**, author of *The Forest Unseen*, Pulitzer Prize finalist

"Patrice's sense of joy and spirit of inquiry inspire me to live in nature more and to honor the creativity often buried beneath the 'business' of life. Her writing is seamless as she navigates the depth of provocative insights about both nature and art-making. *Step into Nature* instantly becomes an old friend, urging us oh so gently to wake up to the wonder around and within us."

—**Tandy Beal**, artistic director and choreographer

"Patrice Vecchione masterly weaves a tapestry between the natural world around us and within us in this collection of simple and accessible stories filled with wisdom that holds a full field guide for anyone who is interested in the muse, art, or creative process and how nature can feed our internal fire."

—**Jon Young**, author of *What the Robin Knows: How Birds Reveal the Secrets of the Natural World*

"After reading Patrice Vecchione's book and supplementing it with a nature walk, I realized the value of her work at a basic, human level. Even though I lived on the Central Coast of California most of my life, where much of Patrice's inspiration for *Step into Nature* comes from, I never had time to chart the names of flowers, the trees and weeds, and until reading Patrice's book, I never appreciated not having this knowledge. Unless we become aware of our surrounding nature, we will be unable to sustain its existence. Vecchione sets us straight and enriches our lives."

—**Gabriella Gutiérrez y Muhs**, first editor of *Presumed Incompetent: The Intersections of Race and Class for Women in Academia* and author of *Rebozos de Palabras: An Helena María Viramontes Critical Reader*

"*Step into Nature* is a gift for all of us who spend too much time inside four walls! Patrice Vecchione's enthusiasm is infectious and her stories, reflections, and art-making suggestions are inspiring. Quoting everyone from Darwin to Dickens, from Kafka to Lorca to Liszt, she has chosen memorable and moving passages that are a treasure chest in themselves."

—**Ellen Bass**, author of *Like a Beggar* (poetry)

"A practical guide on how to access the inspiration available everywhere and in everything, *Step into Nature* is a necessary and extraordinary book. With useful examples, detailed packing lists, and stimulating prompts, this book will open you to the many creative influences that are right outside your door."

—**Camille T. Dungy**, author of *Smith Blue* and editor of *Black Nature: Four Centuries of African American Nature Poetry*

"In an era of cascading ecological crises, what could be more important than reconnecting people to the wonder and beauty of nature? Patrice Vecchione's elegant paean to the wild world, *Step Into Nature*, accomplishes its vital mission with a poet's eye and ear.... an enchanted map linking inner and outer worlds, guiding us through the marvels of nature to discover our own innermost artistic visions."

—**Tai Moses**, author of
Zooburbia: Meditations on the Wild Animals Among Us

"The subject matter is more important than any other, so it is my pleasure to recommend *Step into Nature*."

—**Elizabeth Marshall Thomas**, author of *A Million Years with You*
and *The Hidden Life of Deer: Lessons from the Natural World*

"*Step into Nature* shows that in nature your imagination will embrace you with a feeling of happiness. Patrice Vecchione reminds us of the importance of caring for the places we love and how every step you take in the natural world will make you want to return again."

—**Erick Higuera**, marine biologist, conservationist,
and underwater cinematographer

"If you take Patrice's hand she will take you on a walk with mountain lions and aspens, over ice and through fire, among your fears, empathies, and imaginings. Then she'll deposit you back in your comfortable chair with a kiss on your head. And only later will you find that your pockets are quite full of turquoise and in your hair, feathers."

—**Wallace J. Nichols, PhD**, author of *Blue Mind*

"In words carried as lightly in hand as a newfound robin's egg, Patrice Vecchione invites readers into a warm and ranging conversation—one that's held with the natural world and its many plants and creatures, with her own thoughts and life, with an array of the world's great writers, scientists, and artists, and, finally, within their own hearts and minds. *Step into Nature* illumines the intimate connection between inner and outer, contemplative and wild, and shows the reasons these connections matter."

—**Jane Hirshfield**, author of *The Beauty* (poems) and *Ten Windows: How Great Poems Transform the World*

"Patrice Vecchione has given us a true workbook for the senses, full of beautiful methods and exercises for getting ever closer to our surrounding world. Read it and your travels into nature will be enhanced and changed. I shall never head for the woods without a ladder and a hammock again."

—**David Rothenberg**, author of *Bug Music* and *Why Birds Sing*

STEP INTO
NATURE

Also by Patrice Vecchione

Nonfiction
Writing and the Spiritual Life: Finding Your Voice by Looking Within

Poetry
Territory of Wind
The Knot Untied

As Editor
Fault Lines: Children's Earthquake Poems (coeditor)
Catholic Girls (coeditor)
Bless Me, Father (coeditor)
Storming Heaven's Gate: Spiritual Writings by Women (coeditor)
Truth & Lies: An Anthology of Poems (for young adults)
Whisper & Shout: Poems to Memorize (for children)
The Body Eclectic: An Anthology of Poems (for young adults)
Revenge & Forgiveness: An Anthology of Poems (for young adults)
Faith & Doubt: An Anthology of Poems (for young adults)

PATRICE VECCHIONE

STEP INTO NATURE

Nurturing Imagination and Spirit in Everyday Life

WITHDRAWN

ATRIA PAPERBACK
New York London Toronto Sydney New Delhi

BEYOND WORDS
Hillsboro, Oregon

ATRIA PAPERBACK
A Division of Simon & Schuster, Inc.
1230 Avenue of the Americas
New York, NY 10020

BEYOND WORDS
20827 N.W. Cornell Road, Suite 500
Hillsboro, Oregon 97124-9808
503-531-8700 / 503-531-8773 fax
www.beyondword.com

Managing editor: Lindsay S. Brown
Editors: Sylvia Spratt, Anna Noak
Proofreader: Michelle Blair
Design: Devon Smith
Composition: William H. Brunson Typography Services

First Atria Paperback/Beyond Words trade paperback edition March 2015

ATRIA PAPERBACK and colophon are trademarks of Simon & Schuster, Inc.
Beyond Words Publishing is an imprint of Simon & Schuster, Inc., and the Beyond Words logo is a registered trademark of Beyond Words Publishing, Inc.

For more information about special discounts for bulk purchases, please contact Simon & Schuster Special Sales at 1-866-506-1949 or business@simonandschuster.com.

The Simon & Schuster Speakers Bureau can bring authors to your live event.
For more information or to book an event, contact the Simon & Schuster Speakers Bureau at 1-866-248-3049 or visit our website at www.simonspeakers.com.

Manufactured in the United States of America

10 9 8 7 6 5 4 3 2 1

Library of Congress Cataloging-in-Publication Data
Vecchione, Patrice.
    Step into nature : nurturing imagination and spirit in everyday life / Patrice Vecchione.
        pages   cm
    1. Imagination. 2. Inspiration. 3. Creative ability. 4. Human ecology. I. Title.
    BF408.V323 2015
    153.3—dc23

                                                                    2014037669

ISBN 978-1-58270-500-2
ISBN 978-1-4767-7293-6 (eBook)

The corporate mission of Beyond Words Publishing, Inc.: *Inspire to Integrity*

In memory of my beloved father-in-law, Roy Stark,
who loved the natural world;

for Charlotte Cecil Raymond,
in gratitude for the sustenance of her support;

and for Michael Stark,
who has my love, and takes my hand, and into the forest we go.

All the leaves of the earth
are an alphabet in my hands.

—Marjorie Agosín

There is only a single, urgent task:
to attach oneself someplace to nature . . .

—Rainer Maria Rilke

Poetry comes to me
like water coming to a river,
like a river coming to the sea.

—Jeremy Millburn

CONTENTS

INTRODUCTION

YOU COME TOO

I only went out for a walk, and finally concluded to stay out till
sundown, for going out, I found, was really going in.
—John Muir

My infatuation with the woods began with the most basic act:
I bent to tie my shoes and placed one sneaker-clad foot in
front of the other. I walked into the forest, along narrow poison-
oak–bordered paths and on former logging roads, up hills, around
bends, past trees and more trees, into sunlight and more often into
shadow and dappled darkness. I didn't set out to revive my imagination, didn't think my spirit would be restored, and had no idea that
joy and inspiration would overcome me.

I went into the woods near my Monterey home for exercise—
enjoyed the air filling my lungs when I walked up hills, felt my head
clear, became enchanted by the views. Over time, I became newly and
deeply curious about the earth. Nature began working on me, and I
began to change and grow. My perspective on the world and my own
life shifted. I found possibility where there'd been none. I wanted to
learn about that which had never held my attention before—from
butterfly habitats to mountain lion hunting tactics.

From that, art came. It was a natural progression inspired by the conversations I was having with the earth. Making art felt less effortful, the call to it more true. Though art has been a primary part of my life for as long as I can remember, time in nature gave it a greater platform.

The creativity of the natural world validates my own endeavors. The earth's bounty and beauty infuse my work. Returning home from a walk, pictures form in my mind that I rush to put on paper. The earth's ways of doing things make me want to try them out too: How might a poem make the staccato of raindrops? Could I layer hues in a collage like leaf mulch layered on the ground? Nature has turned my writing upside down. Noticing connections between things makes leaps of imagination nearly effortless. Attention to detail and nuance have grown in me, both in the art I make and in my whole life. The boundaries of my curiosity have dropped away.

Out in the woods one day, for seemingly no reason, I stopped, mid-step. It's odd how the eyes see before the brain knows what's being seen. Or was it a mystical occurrence—had nature called my name? In the midst of the thick green foliage and twig-crossed brush: a single, cobalt blue, five-petaled flower. It was the end of winter, but there, exactly when I needed a sign that spring was on her way.

Being in nature has deepened my belief in the unexplainable. Magical, spellbound thinking, which is so much a part of artistic process, may serve us more than we know. One day I saw a cluster of bees gathering along a trail, making a soft collective buzz. I spotted their hole-in-the-ground hive, but kept walking. Then, curiosity nabbed me and I turned around to get a better look. Both hive and bees had disappeared. I doubled back many times, but never saw a single bee. Had they slipped into their hive, buttoned it up, and flown off in it to a safe place? The experience ruffled my thinking with wonder.

We've become people who place utmost faith in the rational mind at the cost of the creative mind. We won't find all the answers we need via a linear and pragmatic route; certainly not the most beautiful, unpredictable solutions. For the imagination to blossom, we need to think afresh. To learn how to best care for the earth and how to find the will to do so, we need to ask previously unasked questions, be more wholly aware, engage our senses and our spirits, honor our emotions, and put stock in the earth's wisdom.

I used to think that artistic inspiration came only rarely, striking like a lightning bolt. Outdoors, I discovered, it's everywhere—in the furrows and burrows, caves and treetops, atop that far hill, on the undersides of leaves, and, my favorite, in the sounds that small creatures make traveling through the brush. Outdoors, imagination expands more easily. The stimulation we receive from the earth is far more varied than most anything found between four walls, a floor, and a ceiling. Out on the land or at sea, our senses become easily engaged. The mind responds to the bends and twists of nature. Even on days when my imagination feels drier than a desert, somewhere along the way what I see intrigues me, and my mind becomes supple again.

When I began walking in the forest it would have never occurred to me to make the universe my companion, as the seventeenth-century Japanese haiku master, Basho, suggested, and that by doing so, my art might grow. Nor would I have considered that trees are the lungs of the world; that's what a grocery clerk named Jamie told me when I mentioned I was writing this book. I used to feel a firm distinction between human affairs and nature's. We are disconnected from the idea of being a part of the planet, as my friend Janet says, by the "topsy-turvy tenor of life." The pull of work and family can isolate us from both nature and our own imaginations. The more time I spend outside, the less conviction I have in a division between me and the earth.

Noticing that the simple act of walking allows my thoughts to shift and that I think differently when my feet are in action, I consider my great-grandfather Alphonse. When he was twelve, he fled the orphanage in Rome's Jewish ghetto and stowed away on a ship bound for America. He was heading to New York City and the community of fellow Italians there. But the ship deposited him in, we think, Charleston, North Carolina. From there, he walked to New York City by himself, where he worked hard, married my great-grandmother, and years later became a champion pinochle player. He told his grandson, my father, "I had a long walk. Lucky for me, it was autumn and the apples were ripe." Walking itself is part of our shared lineage; once upon a time, that's how everyone got around. If we return to ambling amongst the trees might our spirits get wind of it and feel free? Might the art we make find its wings? Alphonse walked his way into a new world, and we might also.

The natural world has inspired artists, seekers, and thinkers for millennia, but in recent times, the pace of life has sped up and its demands have moved us indoors. Yet nature's capacity to lead us to important truths, to invigorate and restore our imagination and equilibrium, is infinite and within reach. Taking a walk, who knows where you might end up? You might fall in love with the call of one particular bird and walk toward her song; I've certainly gone far afield doing so. Or the desert may whisper long-hidden secrets, show its subtle colors and rattle-bearing snakes. Does the rhythm of the waves mirror the determination of your footsteps? The wide-open plains, do they set your feet to walking? Alone in a gully, what's that darting behind the rocks? It can be as simple as a startling slice of blue sky that you catch outside your kitchen window that draws you outside and into the imaginative beyond.

In determining the scope of this book, I made list upon list, asking myself certain questions over and over. How does walking on the earth influence imagination, increase its breadth and depth? What is it about the way art speaks to me that makes me listen? Why does my spirit feel a primal resurgence? How is it that nature can draw one simultaneously inward and outward? Why do I feel a greater sense of emotional balance when I walk? What makes me want to know the planet, as I never cared to before? It is my hope that we may traverse these questions, their answers, and more together in the chapters to come.

To support you on your journey, each chapter contains a few items for inspiration and inquiry from an imaginary cupboard—the Cabinet of Curiosities. You'll find a compendium of suggestions, activities, and resources within the text. These inspirations are designed to entice you outside, allay any hesitation, and delight and surprise you.

Step Into Nature is a book designed to strengthen trust in spirit, invigorate the imagination through the wall-less rooms of nature, and deepen our love of the earth. If we want to care about the earth, don't we need to know her? Can we express ourselves fully by finding new ways to explore our creativity? What's the link between nature, imagination, and mystery? The practical aspects won't be left behind—we'll discuss what to bring and what to leave, how to get lost, and when to be found.

Throughout this book, you'll notice that both nature and the earth are referred to in the feminine, as in Mother Nature. I continue this familiar tradition to keep nature close, as a child stays close to his mother.

Being in nature is a way to go the distance that requires nothing fancy—no new boots, no suitcase. Just open the door and walk outside—into the air and, simultaneously, into your self. May this book be your companion. Dog-ear the pages. Let sand get in the binding. Mark the pages with mud. Nature accepts us exactly as we are—bedazzled or bedraggled, lonely or lively, willful or wistful. Your imagination and your spirit will grow alongside your joy, and a love for the earth will flower.

1

THE ALLURE OF THE EARTH

AN ANCIENT AWARENESS

Landscape was here long, long before we were even dreamed.
It was here without us. It watched us arrive.
—John O'Donohue

We come from the earth. The deserts, forests, and plains are our ancestral home. Once upon a time, our floors were dirt and our stoves were open fires; water was sipped from a stream. There was nothing to separate us from the land. People believed that their power came from the earth. Though we've drifted away from that ancient awareness, our cells have not forgotten, nor have our spirits. It's the modern mind that has gone astray. But it hasn't traveled so far that reclamation isn't possible. Now is a good time to rediscover our roots. Our imaginations and our bodies, to say nothing of the earth herself, will benefit from our return.

Beyond any single thing, nature's appeal comes from her aliveness and from the fact that we're a part of her. It's alluring to return to the place we once knew as well as our own names. How could it be otherwise? As much as we love a bed at day's end, or a kitchen with hot running water, the natural world is still our home. If we seek liberty from walls, a plaster firmament, and swept floors, we might find that freedom from one thing can provide freedom into another.

The difference between inside and out isn't just a variation of containment, though that's part of it. As we will see in this chapter, the power and presence of the earth is significant.

Brandon Stanton's book of photographs, *Humans of New York*, captures a wide array of personalities. Some pictures are accompanied by a subject's comments. One caught a gray-haired elderly woman smiling beatifically at the camera; she said, "Every time I force myself to go outside, something wonderful happens!"[1] I know just the feeling. It can be a matter of forcing myself sometimes because of inertia or a frightfully long list of things to do, but getting out the door is always worth it. On a similar note, Charles Montgomery's book, *Happy City: Transforming Our Lives Through Urban Design*, documents that people in cities are happier when they pass by small parks. Montgomery writes, "Green space in cities shouldn't be considered an optional luxury. It is a crucial part of a healthy human habitat."[2]

If an attraction to the natural world is something you've been asleep to, as I was for most of my life, it can be startling once it awakens in you! I have to wonder: Didn't I live just fine before I was enthralled by sunlight breaking through fog, the humping crawl of caterpillars, the redness of wild raspberries? The conversations between unseen birds have become as interesting to me as my conversations with friends. Wasn't life just as good before I began walking in the open air alone?

WAKING UP TO NATURE

Shortly after college, my sister signed up for a several-month-long backpacking expedition. The leader took the group into California's High Sierra for study and exploration, where they would be incommunicado for weeks at a time. I thought she was crazy. That was the furthest thing from this city girl's idea of fun. Why don hiking boots if I could slip on a pair of heels? How could walking in the mountains lead to poetry or anything except for blistered feet and a profound longing for the comforts of home? My sister has always had an affinity for nature and for the animal kingdom, in particular. She knew the call of the earth when I was entirely taken by Manhattan's art museums and used bookstores. So didn't I live just as finely before discovering the great outdoors? No, actually, I didn't. Not as finely as I live now, connected to, communing with, and infatuated by the earth. My younger sister knew something important a long time before I caught on.

Elizabeth Marshall Thomas, in her book *The Hidden Life of Deer*, remembers her father telling her that the chemistry formulas for hemoglobin (a component of our blood) and for chlorophyll (which allows plants to take in carbon dioxide and release oxygen) were almost identical. Thomas writes, "Both had the same amounts of carbon, hydrogen, nitrogen, and oxygen, and only one difference: right in the middle where hemoglobin has iron, chlorophyll has magnesium. That a plant and a person shared something so basic seemed awesome. It gave a sense of the oneness of things."[3] We truly are part of this planet, as certainly as any other creature. We are nature. There's liberation in that thought, and comfort; our restored connection with the earth makes sense—it's our birthright.

Roaming the plains, running after waves, wading in the river, and standing at the edge of cliffs, we're interacting with aspects of the essence of who we are. These are our spiritual and alchemical, nascent, elemental selves. In the forest, every growing thing contributes to the environment's well being—from the freshness of the air to the physical space that surrounds our bodies. There, no bank teller insists I'm overdrawn. The traffic light doesn't take forever to change. I'm never running late to get to the next hilltop. The trees don't point their branches at me and tsk, tsk because I've been away too long. The rocks never try to sell me a single thing.

Over the decades, necessity has pulled us farther and farther from our source. Most of us now make our livelihoods unconnected to nature and live removed from her. Our separation from nature has developed a need that earlier generations didn't have. When people lived close to nature and worked there, too, a relationship with the earth was a part of life, even if it wasn't easy. The longer a person is away from the earth, the greater the call may be to return. Even if, like me, you're numb to the craving—until you're not.

Consider the parts and places of nature you feel connected to. Is it the deep darkness of many-roomed caves or the lushness of a rainforest? Perhaps butterflies' ability to flit resembles your own? You might jot down a list of those aspects of nature that feel like "family."

WHERE IS NATURE?

Nature's not far away, really. No rabbit holes to squeeze through, no boulders to heave out of the way. You don't need to hightail it to Alaska's Kenai Fjords or the Mojave Desert to set your feet upon concrete-free earth. A taste of nature may be no farther than right outside your door or at the neighborhood park. Even on a day when a short walk in the open air is impossible, you can open the window and lean your head out, inhale the breeze and take in the sky, the absolute expanse of it.

Every Tuesday, some of Monterey's homeless women gather for a lunch prepared by local volunteers. Once a month I come and offer a writing workshop. In her poem, one woman wrote, "I'm not homeless; my roof is enormous; it's the sky!" There you are, too, a part of it. The earth isn't far away; it's just under your feet. The sky surrounds your skin.

Mostly, I walk at a park ten minutes from my home. I'm extremely lucky it's there. It wasn't till years after moving here that I was aware the park existed. There are closer natural enclaves—the frog pond a few blocks away, where a symphony can be heard at the wettest times of year; a swath of field where neighbor kids play; a beach in front of the big hotel. However, the kind of nature that puts trucks, school buses, billboards, crowds, and shopping malls at a distance is the place for me. I am comforted when surrounded by green and brown, with a sky roof overhead, far from a car-studded street. To be in a place that's shadowed, deep, and wide revives my spirit and stimulates my mind. If I can't get to my woods, I'm damn happy with that frog pond!

Sometimes I go a bit farther afield, wanting to see something new. I remember one day when my husband, Michael, and I went south from our home along the coast road to a hiking area called Sobranes Canyon, in the Santa Lucia Mountain Range. From our front door to the trailhead, the effort was minimal, a mere half-hour drive. We walked inland from the coast. Large prickly pear cactus, tall grasses, wildflowers, and scrub brush bordered the open path. Quickly the landscape transformed into a dark redwood forest canyon with ferns, nearly as tall and far wider than I am, and a rushing creek. We climbed up and up. We could have walked the full four-hour loop but hunger for the lunch we didn't bring got the best of us.

Chances are, where you live there are similar opportunities—ways to reach a hunk of nature without having to go too far. Truly, a city park or any body of unfettered land will do just fine. Someone I know frequents the dump on the outskirts of town because that's the closest place he can go for some wide open space to feel dirt under his feet. There are spots in New York's Central Park that feel very far away from the city.

Begin to research natural areas near you. These are places that may be hidden in plain sight. Look for locales where you can get your feet on some earth and be close to trees, rocks, and bushes.

Nature isn't only in sublime, untouched-by-human-hand places. In fact, cultivated spaces that resemble unblemished ones can be enormously satisfying. In the heart of San Francisco, in the Tenderloin neighborhood, a change is taking place. In the midst of the former red-light district, there's a sanctuary of green called "The Tenderloin National Forest." Surrounded by residential buildings, instead of the drug paraphernalia that previously littered the sidewalks, is an oasis where cherry, cypress, and even a couple of redwood trees grow. Two ponds make homes for goldfish. There's a garden with aloe cactus too. Residents reclaimed the land; they took it back from concrete and stucco.

Artist Topher Delaney's medium is the land itself; she designs gardens. In a garden created for the Marin Cancer Center, Delaney included plants from which certain chemotherapy drugs are developed. She said, "Nature heals the heart and soul, and those are things the doctors can't help. That's what the garden is all about—healing the parts of yourself that the doctors can't."[4] There are fewer dividing lines between the human-made world and the non-human-made one than we sometimes think. The earth is what everything else stands on—below the street and sidewalk, holding up house, school, and office. Where the corner store now stands, there were once trees, a field, or even a river. When invited, nature rushes in.

Most of us don't live lives that offer easy access to unfettered, abundant wilderness. My friend Robin is the exception. Having moved from a coastal city, she can now touch the High Sierra because it's right outside her door. When asked what she misses about urban life, she replied, "Well, truthfully, I don't miss much. Sometimes, certain people. When I go back, I enjoy the food, going to restaurants, hearing live music." She traded those things to be up close and personal with the earth. We don't have to, though. Where are the places in your area that the ground makes a carpet of green or brown and you can kick off your shoes and feel earth between your toes?

ALLURING, ISN'T IT?

Nature is never boring. It's not ho-hum or redundant. Nothing vague or general about it. Though some people may say "if you've seen one tree, you've seen them all," don't believe it for a minute. No one tree is the same as another any more than one person duplicates another. This tree is as wide as it is tall and its leaves are red, and that one's over one hundred feet tall, unwavering in its upright posture.

The earth is dynamic, resplendent, and ever changing. There is only this tide pool, *this* dry canyon, this dark-eyed junco. A leaf shimmers in the sunlight; a lion opens her mouth; the rain squall comes as if from nowhere, and all of a sudden you're drenched. Near my home, people line up every evening to catch the sunset with its banners of pink, yellow, and orange. Of course, the earth's magnificence can also be terrifying and destructive—such as when an earthquake threatens the ground you're standing on, when a tornado wrecks your town. But boring? Never.

One experience in the natural world doesn't duplicate another. I've never walked the same trail twice, no matter how often I place my feet on the same path. The day is different, and the light is too. Last night's wind knocked that tree down. There's more pink and purple vetch vine in bloom. Today you need a sweater, yesterday you didn't. In her memoir, *The Turquoise Ledge*, Native American author Leslie Marmon Silko writes about how she takes a familiar walk each day and is occasionally surprised to find bits of turquoise beside the trail that weren't there the day before.[5] Lots of walks I take are circular. If I begin my walk in the opposite direction from the way I usually go, it's as if I'm in a different place; such a small change too.

INFECTIOUS INFLUENCE: HOW NATURE CHANGES US

Nature is transformative. Lots about us—our outlook and our behavior—can change as a result of just being on the earth. Breath comes more easily. In nature, it's difficult to rush. When I go out for a fast walk, it's never fast the whole way. The earth forces me to slow down, because I'm captivated by what I see, and both my body and mind benefit from that adjusted pace. My curiosity is awakened; there's more that I don't know or understand about the woods—the behavior of its creatures, how the wind moves, why that tree's fallen but not the one beside it. As never before, I'm interested in the details of the natural world. Although I avoided science courses in school, now biology, botany, geology, and physics intrigue. The art I make these days often includes bits of lichen, moss, dead bees, and some kind of seed pod I don't know the name of. Even when my work doesn't include nature's detritus, its subjects are determined by my experience observing and engaging with the earth.

My understanding of what it means to pay attention has changed. The idea of paying attention used to feel like a duty. Now, I experience it as a privilege—I *get* to pay attention, to notice where I am and what surrounds me. The "how" of paying attention is also new.

I don't hurry. I practice observing slowly, using most all of my senses. This isn't always possible—not because I've got somewhere else to be, but because I feel distracted. When I can absorb the world around me, I don't only notice the essence of where I am; I experience all life more intensely, often in alliance with spirit.

Take a hike. You may walk farther than you thought you could, stay out longer than you thought you would. Your gait will influence your thinking, and vice versa. As your behavior changes, the way in which you see yourself may change too.

My compassion has grown. Since the earth's come close, I care about the natural world in a less abstract way. Even when people thwart her, nature does her damnedest to revive and survive—the river finds a new path, the bird adapts to its polluted environment. Being out in the air motivates me to be adaptive, too, less rigid. I want to do all I can to support the earth—from picking up litter to campaigning for the earth's welfare. Wanting others to have access to the park I love, I volunteered to open the gates a few mornings a week, since the park system is underfunded.

After spending time in the forest, I began to do things that were definitely out of character. Mud is no longer my enemy. Never had I liked to get dirty without a sink and towel close at hand, but there I was one day, crawling across a meadow for a close-up view of an autumn-colored moth, unbothered by the burrs that stuck to my socks and unaware my hair was flecked with dried grass. I once stuck my hand inside an almost deserted beehive. Rainstorms only mean I reach for a slicker; no longer a reason to stay inside.

Have I discovered my inner Pippi Longstocking? You may find your own such alter ego awaiting birth or rebirth. I bet you'll be pleased with how nature influences and changes you. You might see yourself and the world differently, and such a transformation may serve your life.

NATURE AND OUR EMOTIONAL LIVES

When my father came for a visit, we walked together at Jacks Peak Park, a place I love and where I mostly walk. He did what I never would in a forest: he yelled at the top of his lungs. He was angry and fearful about what life comes down to when its end draws near. The boom of his voice made me feel protective of the forest, made me want to shelter it from his gruff sound. I tell you, the tree branches quivered. Why hadn't he saved his rant for my kitchen table? Though I wish he'd chosen another location, the boundless space gave him the room he needed to let go of a bit of his fear, for that is what his anger hid. After leaving the park, my father's spirit was a whole lot lighter.

Take your sorrow outdoors and watch it change. A meadow is a good place to give in to tears—I know. The grass hasn't shriveled up from my sorrow's salt. "The heart, when it is too much alive, aches for that brown earth," wrote Willa Cather.[6] Yesterday afternoon, a couple sat on a bench before one of the most impressive views at Jacks Peak Park, overlooking Monterey Bay; you could even see individual boats sailing on the water. When I said hello as I walked by, the woman kept her face turned away from me but the young man halfheartedly returned my greeting. His eyes were two dark pools of grief. Whatever their trouble was, they chose to bring it into the woods. Though the trees can't undo what made them sad, I'll bet that, like my father, they felt lighter when they left. Author of the book, *The Nature Principle: Reconnecting with Life in a Virtual Age,*

Richard Louv said, "Although we may not understand exactly how or why it works, as little as five minutes spent in nature has been shown to improve mental health."[7]

In a writing workshop, a student shared: "This is a small story, but of a difficult time, so it mattered a very lot to me, and I've never forgotten it. When I was quite young, my husband was off at war, on a tanker somewhere in the Pacific. I was home alone with a one-year-old and another in the oven. Oh, I was lonely. I went to my parents' home for an extended visit and while I was on my way my father had an awful car accident. Then, the day before her wedding, my best friend was killed in a car accident.

"One evening I went outside for some air, just to catch my breath, to be alone for a moment. I stood on the porch looking out at the night. For the first time, I saw the brilliant Northern Lights. I felt as if those magical lights were shining for me; I was uplifted, able to imagine myself carrying on, saw my life as possible again." Up in the barren country of eastern Washington, she saw the magic of light during a dark time, just when she needed it. In medieval Europe, the aurora borealis was believed to be a sign from God. This writer certainly imagined it that way. Nature has a way of infusing our lives like that.

Rory Stewart, in his book *The Places in Between*, writes about walking across Afghanistan, shortly after the tragedy of 9/11: "The pace of my legs began to transform the rhythm of my breathing and thinking . . . I began to take longer and faster strides, half racing along the dirt track. My anxiety faded and I reveled in the movement of my muscles."[8] A difficult feeling may not evaporate but, given fresh air, time, and space in which to shift, emotions can ease like loosening knots. The actual abundance of physical space provides release, but also the emotional space you can get when you put some distance between yourself and what's troubling you. In a desert with its millions of sand grains, the self comes down to size.

Abundance is restorative. On a prairie, how many blades of grass could there possibly be? If you stand at the end of a long valley and look ahead, it seems to go on forever. There's a comfort in that. Though we may not all have enough of everything we need in our lives, knowing that there are certain places where the multitudes thrive does something for a person. This can put us at ease and help us to feel safe—I won't die of lack, not while I'm surrounded by this enormous sky, watching thousands of leaves caught by the breeze. Of course, if we want to support the earth's enoughness, it's important to get out there and do what we can to preserve it.

Daily, moment by moment, the earth makes and remakes herself—aiming always toward her own growth, her own survival. Each spring the same flowers—California poppy, prettyface, pearly everlasting—return. They remind me of my own resilience, my ability to revive after what can feel like a personal winter. Every growing thing contributes to our well-being. In a forest or out at sea, there are numerous hearts beating along with ours. Being surrounded by so many plants and animals, even those we never see, affects us. How can it not? Even alone, we're never in isolation when out in nature. There, it's indisputable—we're part of a larger world that's made up of many beings.

IN THE PRESENCE OF BEAUTY

I've walked through untrammeled beauty with my mouth hanging open and, chances are, you have too. Often it's the littlest things—a fleck of mica, rolling tumbleweeds—that get me. The other day I discovered that when a leaf drifts downward, if the angle of the sun is right, you can see the leaf's approach not only by looking at it but by watching its shadow as the leaf nears the ground. On a walk one early spring day, Monterey naturalist Nikki Nedeff bent down to a little low-growing vine, snapped off a leaf, crushed it between her fingers, and held it up to my nose. Yerba buena. I was shocked. How could this low-lying plant have escaped my notice all these years? It's got the scent of cinnamon mixed with mint and a hint of chocolate. Yerba buena—"good herb"—was California's original name. Nature reels us in this way with subtle and grand enticements. No accident, either. In a variety of ways, nature does this on purpose. Just as flower nectar lassoes the bees, we are too drawn to the scent. That's how all the parts of nature continue—by drawing in that which they most need for survival.

Alan Watts wrote that the beauty in Chinese calligraphy "is thus the same beauty which we recognize in moving water, in foam, spray, eddies, and waves, as well as in clouds, flames, and the weavings of smoke in sunlight."[9] Much of the art we make is a mirror of nature mixed with our human creativity, individual inclinations, and desire to see what we can create too. Being in the presence of the earth's magnificence, it's not surprising that we want to respond. Making art is one way to have a relationship with the beauty of the natural world.

Where do you find the beauty that reels you in—in nature, art, and life? Some artists find that the blank slate of working in an austere environment inspires their work. Others, like me, surround themselves with shape and color. What conditions inspire you?

WAYS OF BEING

In French, the word journey, *journé*, refers to the distance you can walk in a single day. Walking is my favorite way to be in nature. But rarely do I have the luxury of an entire day to wander. Usually, it's an hour or two, and even that can feel like time I've stolen from something "important." Ha! My feet know better. For years, I spent most of my outside time on a bicycle, which is great for the distance that can be covered. Because it's so much slower than a car, you see more.

On a bike, you're bare to the air, which helps to destroy the illusory divisions between self and nature. But walking is far slower, and far better for observing the earth and the self, and for developing a creative relationship with nature. Walking, you change your scene but not quickly. You get to witness every part of the landscape—from the grandness of sunset to the minutia of slow-ambling bugs.

In her memoir, *Bird Cloud*, Annie Proulx, known for her writing about Wyoming and the West, writes, "Walking induces a trancelike state that allows the mind freedom and ease and encourages exploration of odd possibilities and improbable connections."[10] Many of our great minds—writers, artists, scientists—have found that walking enhanced their thinking. Darwin began his day with a short walk. Charles Dickens wandered the London streets late at night. Einstein was a walker. The poet Wallace Stevens put it this way: "Perhaps the truth depends on a walk around the lake."[11]

A couple of weeks ago while walking on Jacks Peak's Lower Ridge Trail, a former logging road, I heard a sound coming from the low, trail-side bushes, and stopped. It was a small animal sound, kind of a peep, but not birdlike. A few feet farther along I faintly heard the same sound. Curiosity lit, I placed myself between the two sounds and stood looking, listening, and waiting. One gray mouse darted out from the brush, wiggling around, flicking the ground with his long tail. A little ways down the trail, I heard another squeaky voice. Two mice were talking to each other! I think one mouse said to the other, "Here I am." And his companion responded with something like, "Oh, great! I'm on my way over." As I listened to the chatting mice, a poem written by a first grade student of mine played through my mind:

> "I am the wind,
> quiet like a mouse
> singing to his brother."

If I'd been riding in a car or even on my bike, this conversation, and so much more, would have been lost to me.

Imagine "translating" a conversation between two parts of nature—between a tree and its leaves, the mountain lion and her cub, the rain and the soil. Or a conversation between you and a part of the natural world.

There's a place on the trail where once I found a near-perfect eggshell. Each time I walk by that spot, I remember the surprise of finding it and carefully carrying the tiny egg home. Sometimes even what's long gone can be returned to us when strolling along a path. Being in a kind of abeyance, letting the mind roam, clears out the cobwebs. Antonio Burgos wrote, "'Can you smell the jasmine?' 'What jasmine? There isn't any.' 'The jasmine that used to be here in the old days.'"[12] Walking in the woods returns my life to me over and over again.

The best way to be in nature, to really take in the ten thousand things of it, may be to stay still. Easier said than done. When I was a child, if my mother caught me sitting quietly for more than a few moments, perhaps a crayon suspended in my hand, she'd say, in her most exasperated voice, "Don't just sit there, do something!" Obviously, my mother was no meditator. Each time she pulled me out of my reverie, I lost a bit more of my ability to linger in the place between doing one thing and doing another. Years later, I'm still relearning how to not rush out of the suspension of activity. The forest and the beach are my favorite classrooms. I used to pack a book. No longer. Never can I bring myself to open one. I'd rather read the butterflies, the lace of the spiderwebs suspended between tree branches.

NOT TO FORGET THE OTHER SIDE OF NATURE

Of course, not all of nature is idyllic. If nothing bad happens to you in the natural world; if you steer clear of the evening news; if you live in a place that hasn't been struck by any of nature's destructive behaviors, you might be swayed to believe that the natural world is benevolent. The forest where I walk isn't a haven for all the beings there. Though I may tilt a bit too far in the direction of romanticizing nature, I'm not ignorant of its realities and perils. Nature may often offer me respite, but not so for the bee pedaling on her back, unable to right herself, the dueling hawks, or the badly wounded dusky-footed woodrat I met trailside one day.

There's a word in Spanish for something or someone not quite right, something's twisted: *chueco*. Because of global warming, that's often how the weather feels these days. When the weather is thrown off, some of us get thrown off too. Are you one of those people? How have you been affected by the changing climate?

Nature is neither kind nor unkind. Nature is just nature—no more, no less. Sometimes it actually is a jungle out there. The snake may bite; the cliff edge may crumble; a gale may knock you down. You don't have to go far to know the other side of earth's bounty and peace—from drought to flood to volcanic eruption. Global warming, rivers diverted, roads placed where they never should be, and other human behavior have resulted in the earth behaving as we wish she wouldn't.

The philosopher Jean-Jacques Rousseau said, "Nature never deceives us; it is we who deceive ourselves."[13] When threats to the earth become paramount, people respond. Then, we recognize that our home is truly in peril. Isn't that such a part of human nature? Take something away and we recognize its value. This is certainly one of those times when the crisis is more critical and more pervasive. We know that our home place cannot be taken for granted, that we must honor and attend to what we love. And what a calling that is—just to feel the soil beneath your feet is truly something worth celebrating and protecting.

GOING FORWARD BEFORE TURNING BACK

If you give in to the call of nature, loosening the strings that confine you, you'll feel the earth's call. Your shoes may grow wings like those of Mercury, the god of poetry. You'll be led to the destination of that breeze, the one that's pulling you, along with whatever gleaned flotsam it's picked up along the way—fallen leaves and flower petals, gum wrappers, a lost dollar. If you're a contrarian, like me, you might prefer to take the chill air in your face and head toward its source, your shirt pressing to your skin and your eyes stinging in the wind. Some of us are drawn to take to the sea—eager to do more than just stand at its shore.

We don't have to be gone for days, weeks, or months at a time to lay claim to being in nature, stimulate the imagination, and revive the spirit. Sometimes a short tour is all we need. No matter the duration of your adventure, heed a word of warning: sometimes it's hard to turn back—to trade the fresh air for the inside stuff. I tell myself, "I'll walk to that next bend, the one I can't see past." Once there, "Well, how about to where the hill crests instead?" And so on. Even when I start out tired, walking reinvigorates me before too long. The approach of darkness can speed me home. Mostly, I head home before I get to the place from which I can't turn back—that magical location that would propel me only forward. I know there is such a place, and that I could walk past the reach of the familiar. This does have its appeal, especially when the day ahead is full of things I'd prefer to ignore. But considering the scope of my life and those I love, it's not something I'll choose to do, not now, anyway. When my cats are hungry or my husband is, or the living room is about to fill with students, I walk back to where I started and return to where the door opens, takes me in, and shuts safely behind me. By the next morning, though, I'm ready to step out into the day and onto the earth once more.

If you're ready, put your hand around the doorknob and pull the door open. Step over the threshold. I always quicken my stride along windowless hallways and skip lightly down the last few steps. Once all walls are behind you, turn your face toward the breeze, feel it run though your hair. Look up to morning's blue sky or evening's starry display. Just as the flowers lasso in the bees, so will you be taken in by the allure of nature.

2

A JOURNEY

NATURE, SPIRIT, AND IMAGINATION

The man who has no imagination has no wings.
—Muhammad Ali

This morning, I took the hill hike into the forest. The trail starts out steep and continues, without reprieve, till the summit—a good choice when I'm feeling energetic or frustrated. I was both. The climb, canopied by sheltering oaks and pines, cleared my mind of the frustration and gave my body an ideal outlet for its energy. There are no views until the top, at which point there's an award-winning one of the city and the bay. On the way home it's easy, a nice break from my typical walk, which lulls me with its ease until the homeward stretch slams a series of hills upon the trail.

The up-from-the-start walk has something else that keeps me coming back. It's the trail where I'm most likely to catch a glimpse of the red-shafted northern flicker. Even the briefest sighting of this bird is rewarding because it's rare—they are very shy. Since I first saw one speed away and found a black-and-white-spotted feather with an orange spine, I've been eagerly waiting to see a flicker up close. This bird beguiles me. I love coming upon the bright orange arrow of one of his feathers in a forest that's mostly muted brown and green. If a flicker is up in a nearby tree, she lets me know I've come too close with her loud, single-note *kyeer* call. After only the briefest peek of her white bottom, that bird is gone. As elsewhere, the elusive lures the imagination into its net.

Flickers are good for the forest. They make roosting holes in trees that other small animals, who aren't skilled house builders, move into after the flickers have gone. And flickers are good for startling humans with their laugh-like cry. Today there was one in a nearby oak and for the first time he didn't hurry away before I could get a good look. He just sat there—absolutely gorgeous—and I got to see for real what I'd only seen in books. The creamy body is flecked with brown-black dots, a red-spotted face, and a long, pointed beak—this bird is a member of the woodpecker family.

Knowing I was heading home to write, I took the flicker sighting as a good sign for the work ahead. My imagination asked, "Why not?" and as if in confirmation, another flicker came! It sat down on the branch beside the first bird. And again, a little farther down the trail, gift of gifts, I saw a second pair of flickers. I felt certain the writing would come well, if not easily.

What if we were to give precedence to enlivening our spirits, to furthering our vigorous imaginations? What if we followed our subtle inklings, walked barefoot through the fish-flush stream of nature? Life—from the common to the rare—in its infinite variety and complexity invigorates innovative thinking. In places full of non-human-made things—lizards, reclusive mountain lions, so many flocks of birds, whole contingents of insects, and more, there's plenty to excite us. An outing into the woods is a perfect way to see things not only for what they are but for what they might be. New sensibilities may arise. I've felt my innate knowing revive and have experienced access to levels of awareness my pragmatic mind can only be jealous of. Gore Vidal said, "It is the spirit of the age to believe that any fact, however suspect, is superior to any imaginative exercise, no matter how true."[1] Here's our chance to change all that—a chance and a venue through whichever forms call your name. We'll look at nature, spirit, and imagination, and the intersection between them, and how strengthening that connection can be a way to hold them up to the sun.

NATURE, IMAGINATION, AND THE INEXPLICABLE

The Spanish poet Antonio Machado wrote,

"Spring has come.
Nobody knows how."[2]

The American poet Theodore Roethke penned the words,

"Light takes the Tree; but who can tell us how?"[3]

Two poets from two different continents and two different, though overlapping, times. Machado was born in 1875 and died in 1939, and Roethke was born in 1908 and died in 1963. An awareness of nature's magic can be found all over their poetry—each takes something explainable and puts it beside that which is beyond explanation.

Why does this stone glimmer in the moonlight but not the one beside it? Wind swishes the branches of that tree but not all the others nearby. Once, as it was getting dark, Michael and I were walking back from a hike at Pinnacles National Monument. Close to the ground beside the trail we saw something surprising—a tiny shining light. "What on earth?" When we bent down and moved the brush away, the light disappeared. We pulled our hands back and the light shone. After trying this a couple of times and finding ourselves unable to explain it, we opted to believe in mystery. This was early in our courtship. Had our infatuation with each other spilled over?

I wondered if a little gnome had lit that light and then blown it out just before our discovery.

In the "actual" world we're not going to encounter Thumbelina or Mrs. Tittlemouse. But the imagination says, "I can make your dreams come true." Consider any daring thinker or inventor. In part, their imagination is what took them further than they or others had gone before. Had Michael and I been walking with a knowledgeable someone who could have explained that light, we'd have been relieved of the mystery. I'm glad no such person was anywhere around. The moment would have been ruined.

Jot down a list of inexplicable things—those from your own life, and those you've dreamed of, heard about, or read. Consider your reactions to that which you can't explain and don't understand.

It's not that I want to remain ignorant. Hardly. The more I'm out in nature, the more my curiosity gets piqued. I want to know the why and how of it all. As I walk, I want to know the facts and be in the presence of the mysterious truths. It's a matter of timing. I don't want the facts to cut off my questions, creative investigations, and curiosity at the pass. Questions are often a lot more compelling than answers. They keep me on the edge of my seat in wonder.

SQUASH BLOSSOMS AND SEA CREATURES

The other morning I went out into the garden to pick some of the large blossoms opening on the volunteer squash plants, having just learned that once the fruit is on the vine, there's no harm in picking the flowers. While rinsing them carefully, so as not to tear their delicate yellow petals, I caught a whiff of something sweetly floral. Had Michael put a bouquet in a nearby vase? Nope. Squash blossoms are fragrant! I'd never known.

The best art is that which outwits the artist first, long before a viewer gets to be startled. No longer a youngster, I know pretty well how I'll behave in most situations. But when I sit down before a blank page, what I write always surprises me. Even with a clear idea of my subject, the process of engaging the imagination leads me to say things I hadn't intended. Often, I write something I wasn't even conscious of knowing, or I put ideas and images together for the first time. Few things are as astonishing as life itself—save for art and art-making, that is. My best work comes out of writing with a willingness to go where I've not gone before. If I know just what I'm going to say and how I'll say it, why bother? That one phrase comes to me instead of another is a small mystery, and that makes me feel connected to the concept of mystery itself.

The earth is infinitely imaginative and resourceful. If there's something blocking her path, nature tries her best to find a way over, through, or under. Watch how water behaves and you'll have a perfect example. If the tree bars its way, water goes around. And nature is phenomenally varied and inventive. Every day, she's new. The basic facts make me swoon: Did you know that the strongest muscle in your body is your tongue and that a crocodile can't stick his out? During the course of a year, your heart pumps enough blood to fill an Olympic-size swimming pool. Mosquitoes don't bite; they stab. Butterflies taste their food with their feet.

Never have I been more charmed by nature than on a recent visit to the Monterey Bay Aquarium. This is when I was first introduced to the leafy sea dragon, *Phycodurus eques*. An animal? Couldn't be. Sea dragons look more like rare orchids or gorgeous, flowing seaweed.

They appear to be fairies floating gracefully in the water. The inventiveness of their form is, not surprisingly, a form of protection. The leafy sea dragons are another example of nature's creativity.

What's blocked your path? How have you responded in the past? What technique might you incorporate from nature for the next blocked moment?

Consider the genetic code that mutates to adapt to new environments. According to evolutionary biology, all the earth's living organisms are descended from a common ancestor—bacteria, actually. What a very lot of shifting and changing and redesigning has created the infinite variety on the earth today. Various beings will find their own adaptive solutions in order to thrive in the same environment. The human imagination possesses these qualities too. It changes form with ease. You can just as well use it to make dinner as sing a lullaby. If you're late and need a creative excuse, your imagination will supply you with one. If you can't remember the correct answer, given a chance, your imagination will give you an inventive, and likely more interesting, one. The imagination is responsive to being tickled behind the knees.

A SKY-TRAVELING PARADE

Since I was nineteen years old, I've taught poetry to children, guiding them toward finding words to express themselves. Children have a need, desire, and uncanny ability to speak their inner truths deeply through poetry. If I asked a class of thirty second-grade students to describe, in a nonrhyming poem, what was at the bottom of their hearts, fifteen minutes later there would be many original poems. I've been amazed, humored, and moved by the children and their poems. But until the last few years, I've never been disappointed.

It used to be if we went out to the playground on a sunny day, got down on the ground and looked skyward at the clouds, the kids would see elephants parading, a dragon biting its own tail, a tall man singing to a crowd, and countless other combinations. Then we'd go inside and write poems about the elephants, the dragon, or the singing man. Nowadays, it's not like that. The children are still there. The sunny day still is, too, and the white clouds billow in the sky. We lie down, look up, and I ask, "What do you see?" It's quiet, till someone calls out, "Clouds, Miss Patrice. I see the clouds."

It's not that the children don't want to see the sky-traveling parade. And it's not like they can't. It's that they don't. Sad and simple. In fact, my young students have a hard time actually seeing the clouds themselves, so compelled are they to jump into the next activity. Children's once-upon-a-time vibrant imaginations have been swallowed and spit out by the many changes in how young people access creativity, technology, education, and the physical world itself.

If a person sits on the couch too long, the hard bulk of the calf muscle shrinks and the gluteus maximus becomes flaccid and increases its, well, maximusness. The same is true for the imagination muscle. Unused, it becomes useless—might as well not have one. An imagination that's neglected forgets itself, and then the world of dreams and wishes and infinite possibility shrinks. Not only is art-making a deeply personal experience that enriches those who practice it, but if we become a culture without the capacity to create, we'll be lost at sea.

However, the imagination never entirely abandons us. Like our physical muscles, the imagination muscle is responsive and willing. Given the opportunity, it will flourish, able to invent more, pretend further, and create infinitely finer, more elaborate constructions.

A limber imagination enables people to make things up, to create pictures in our minds, to solve puzzles, to find cures for new diseases, to invent, and more. To make art, we follow the inkling of an idea that we have no road map for. We just need to tear ourselves away from what holds us back—put down the spatula, the heavy briefcase, the laptop, and head to a place in nature. Within view of a few trees, the imagination can prosper.

On a blue-sky day, take a short return trip to childhood and lie back on a soft spot of ground. Look up at the clouds. Who's traveling there? What appears out of the billowing white?

THE PAINTED HANDS

There are those who are inclined to make art from nature, those who make art in nature, and those who make art with nature. On a few rock walls deep in the dry and rugged Santa Lucia Mountains, in the Los Padres National Forest, are the most unusual painted handprints that have been left by any culture. According to authors Gary S. Breschini and Trudy Haversat's article, "Hands: A Unique Esselen Indian Artform," "When you study the Esselen handprints, you begin to realize that they are not just casually smeared on the cave walls, nor are they simple, crudely-drawn figures. Rather, they were very carefully painted—the unique signatures of the individuals who painted them."[4] Some are of right hands but many are of left hands too. Unlike other ancient cave hand paintings, these hands weren't dipped in color and then pressed against the walls but were painted and then filled in with vertical lines, so they have a striped look, and one hand has swirling lines painted within it. The hands vary in size. According to Breschini and Haversat, it's unknown why the Esselen people painted these hands; the hand may have been a clan symbol or painting them might have been part of initiation rites.

In his poem, "Hands," Robinson Jeffers, a poet who built his home at the edge of the Pacific, writes about these paintings,

> . . . like a sealed message
> Saying: "Look: we also were human; we had hands, not paws . . ."[5]

The impulse to make art to say, "I had an imagination; I was a life-effecting being, I was here," is very old, indeed. Behind each of those handprints, there is an unknown story that draws us in. We are rooted in art and story. People have been turning to art-making for a very long time. We come to it naturally; art is in our blood.

Make several tracings of your own hand on paper. Enter into each one via a different route—words or paint. You might make a map from the lines in your hand, color the actual lines, or consider writing about what you hold in the palm of your hand. Can you, like a fortuneteller, read your own palm? Might a poem be hidden there?

THE LANGUAGE OF FLOWERS: EXTRAVAGANCE AND DARING

What would spring be without daffodils? How many shades of yellow are there—from sunflower to marigold, from nasturtium to lupine? There must be a hundred pink blossoms on just one hairy honeysuckle bush. The earth's prodigious production reminds us of our own ability to blossom. Given every advantage, not a single one of those buds will hold back an iota of its unfurling.

The earth and imaginative, spirit-infused people alike possess determination and resilience, and both respond to a sense of the imperative. According to *Smithsonian* magazine, just after the 2010 earthquake in Haiti, artist Frantz Zephirin said he needed to paint, "So I took my candle and went to the beach. I saw a lot of death on the way. I wanted to paint something for the next generation, so they can know just what I had seen." Zephirin continued, "Each day, twenty ideas for paintings pass in my head, but I don't have enough hands to make all of them."[6] He daringly found inspiration even in chaos and despair, responding to difficulty through art.

"Take chances," my friend Elliot writes in an email. "That's the only way to get anything worthwhile done." Without taking the risk, there's no way to get there. I've written my way into new territory, said something in a way I'd never considered before. And suddenly, I don't know where I am. Part of what defines an artist is that person's acceptance of the process—which isn't always the same as an enjoyment of it. It's a willingness to take chances and to do what hasn't been done before. It's trying familiar things in not quite the same way as before, even in small ways.

Up in Desolation Wilderness in the Sierra Nevada Mountains, alone in a cabin for a week, I sat in a rocking chair facing Echo Lake and wrote and wrote, sometimes terrified by what I was able or unable to say. One day, as if from nowhere, this line came forth: "It is so quiet my mother could be alive." But after writing it, I questioned myself, felt uncertain. The line was entirely illogical; no matter how quiet it was or will ever be, my mother will remain dead. A voice in my head said, "Keep it," and that voice was friendly, so I did. Years later, I'm glad. The resonance of that line, not based in fact but in emotional truth, holds firm.

Along the bluffs at Point Reyes in Northern California, a herd of elk are running, kicking up the dirt as they go, unconcerned that one small human watches from the sidelines. When it snows on the plains, the falling crystals don't clothe only a tiny patch of earth in white. Snow, generous in its delivery, covers miles and miles of ground announcing, "Winter is here," surprising the children come morning. Nature is exuberant, unhesitant, unrestrained. It's neither paltry nor parsimonious. In *Pilgrim at Tinker Creek*, Annie Dillard put it this way: "After the one extravagant gesture of creation in the first place, the universe has continued to deal exclusively in extravagances."[7] This connotes confidence—nature's not going to make so many of this and so much of that for no reason. Nature shows her hand and gives over the loot freely. Where else do we find such qualities of generosity and daring? In visionaries, artists, explorers, inventors, scientists, entrepreneurs, those who fall in love, anyone who dares.

Consider this: the world's largest flower, called *Rafflesia arnoldii*, is found only in the rain forests of Indonesia. It can grow to three feet across and weigh up to fifteen pounds! Think of coming upon one of those unawares, though that's pretty unlikely, since *Rafflesia arnoldii* gives off the scent of rotting flesh. Along the same lines: somewhere in the depths of the Redwood National Park is the world's tallest tree. Photographs verify its existence, but, in an effort to preserve the tree, its exact location is being kept secret. This redwood is said to be 379 feet, 4 inches tall. Nobody told the tree, "Hey, getting a little too tall for your bark, don't you think? I mean, take a look at your sisters." When the Datura lilies open at night and flood the garden with perfume, nature doesn't think maybe she's overdoing it a bit. If the earth doesn't hold back, why should we? Nothing and no one is served when we are less than all of who we are.

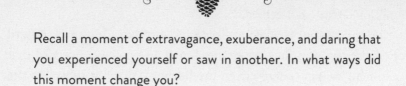

Recall a moment of extravagance, exuberance, and daring that you experienced yourself or saw in another. In what ways did this moment change you?

CONTAGIOUS ENTHUSIASM

Not long ago, I arrived at a high school to teach poetry to a group of restless kids. Some of nature's extravagant enthusiasm has, over the years, rubbed off on me, and I know that if I hold back anything, the young writers do the same, and that's not how good writing happens. Restraint is not the key that opens the door to creativity, especially not in the initial process of inception, when the writer is rooting around to find what's hiding in the dirt.

Working with kids, I use everything I've got—poems and writing prompts to spark their curiosity, life stories, and a range of voices. I push myself past where I'm comfortable so they might see that as valuable. I tell students, "What you write doesn't have to make sense. There is no wrong way to write a poem. Don't plan what you're going to say. Let yourself be surprised by your own ideas." While the kids are writing, I encourage the classroom teacher to as well. I sit at a desk bending over my notebook.

On this particular day, the teacher, a tall, attractive woman, came up to me while the kids were getting settled. With a bemused smile that turned down at the edges, she said, "I could never dress like you." That wasn't even a backhanded compliment. Self-consciousness overcame me and a hot blush crept from my chest to my face. How had I left the house? Ought I have taken a second look in the mirror before walking out the door, I wondered, looking down at my flowered blouse, blue slacks, and red sandals? She continued, "You're brave to wear such colors, and so many of them at once, and with that shade of lipstick!" At which point her voice faded off. I think—a little too late—she'd become embarrassed.

When had I begun arriving at schools dressed in bright, assorted colors? I remember at twenty walking into an elementary school classroom sporting a crew cut, jeans, and a pair of purple cowboy boots. Why not adorn myself and emulate nature's color range, brilliance, and excess? What we wear can reflect mood and imagination. On a sad day, I'll put on an orange blouse for its boldness. The Nuu-chah-nulth First Nations people from Vancouver Island are said to have a song that goes, "You, whose day it is, get out your rainbow colors and make it beautiful." Why should dressing be any less of a celebration than a painting? Isn't everyone a creator of his or her own look? Whether understated or outrageous, we should all feel free to express our inner colors outwardly.

A style of adornment that knocked my polka-dotted socks off can be seen in the book of photographs called *Natural Fashion: Tribal Decoration from Africa* by Hans Silvester. Young members of the Surma and Mursi tribes of East Africa's Omo Valley decorate themselves with natural elements and objects found in their home landscape. They paint their bodies using natural dyes, and craft necklaces and hats from what grows around them. Silvester's photographs show young girls and boys dressed in ways the fashion industry would never consider, but ought to. One girl has placed dry grass atop her head, and at her forehead, like bangs, are big yellow blossoms. Her face is painted in ochre with white and brown dots and circles. Another child's face is decorated white and above each ear are clusters of purple and yellow flowers. This is done without the use of a mirror—neither glass nor pond. Silvester said, "An image of oneself can only be constructed through the eyes of others." One child looks coyly at the camera; others possess serious expressions.

Some faces nearly disappear into the decoration itself. Silvester continued, "These young designers—that is what they are—are busy
at creating beauty all the time."[8] This group of people living closer
to the wealth and wisdom of nature make my socks look boring by
comparison. Their adornment is wildly inventive, resembling nothing less than nature's own elaborate flowering.

LANDSCAPE OF REDROCK AND CEDAR

The poet up before me at Language of the Soul (the San Luis Obispo
Poetry Festival), on a warm October evening, didn't rise from her
seat in the audience easily to take the microphone—arthritis, maybe,
I thought. Although not an elderly woman, she walked with a cane
and had a look of frailness about her. When she spoke, though,
Marguerite Costigan was anything but. Her words were tough and
gorgeous, something more akin to stone than language; they had a
forged quality, as if made from rocks rubbed together.

I'd never heard of her; I'll never forget her. Art gets into our
bones. Costigan's got into mine. Her poems took me outdoors but
didn't leave me entirely alone; in nature, are we ever? Costigan
worked with the earth to find authentic language and, based on the
evening's poems, the earth worked with her.

In "Resolve," Costigan writes:

> In this forever landscape
> of redrock and cedar,
> sky wide as heartbreak,
> riverbottom willows
> more golden than sun-ball,
>
> I must be something different
> than what I brought with me,

this inadequate vessel
cracked and time-checkered,
I must be made over:

I must be something bigger
to swallow such beauty –
buttes melting downslope
in pastels and pebbles,
rocks tall as battlements
riven by lightning,
ridge upon ridgeline
ranging the horizon . . .[9]

Costigan expresses the desire to be braver, stronger, and more loyal: qualities that feel more significant in the context of the land. The poet brings me to a place I've never been, giving the listener her insider's view. Not only can nature bring us to art, but art can bring us to nature.

When the artist's touch is just so, she's clearly in cahoots with the earth.

TELLING THE STORY

Through the process of telling one's story—in whatever form—the story itself transforms. This is another way art-making is reminiscent of nature; the earth, like us humans, is always in flux. Through the telling, the emphasis changes, sometimes unexpectedly. Reclaimed, an old story may become new. At times, you'll accentuate one detail and at other times another will want your attention. That which was forgotten is remembered; that which seemed insignificant gains significance. A memory that becomes art becomes more than a memory. And, of course, the story you tell may be entirely imagined.

A few years ago I wrote a one-woman play that I went on to perform. It included elements that were rooted in my life, as well as those from my imagination and spirit. The first scene of *A Woman's Life in Pieces* opens with Calla Lily sitting at a desk that has a jar crammed full of crayons and a stack of paper on it. She says, "If I take a collection of random pieces . . . cresting waves, an Egyptian bowl, questions thought but never asked—fragments—which is all we have till the end, and rearrange them, could I make a new story? Enough of the old order of things. Maybe that's the problem with my life . . . maybe that's the problem with the world—one of them. We keep telling the same story. I want a new story, one in which everybody listens to the holy mind—their own and each other's. Then kisses the ground."[10]

That's my hope—not just for me, but for the world over, and certainly for you, holding this book—to provide support in inventing and uncovering new stories, the ones most in need of telling. Through a vivid, practical relationship with the natural world we'll be able to say what we didn't know we could. We will grow our alliance with the earth.

ARE YOU DONE YET?

Some stories are never finished. Neither is nature.

Hey, I ask myself, what's wrong with that? What if the process of becoming is the point? Neither the forest nor the desert says, "You know what? I'm finished here."

Outside my living room window are a bunch of agaves. Watch out; don't trip and fall—they're spiky, dangerous plants. Last summer, overnight, the largest agave produced a stalk extending from its center, a suddenly very tall, Jack-and-the-Beanstalk type of stalk. One day it was tall as me; the next, as tall as my husband; the next, up to the roofline; and then taller than that. Out of the shaft's top, a blossoming began—the tallest bloom I have ever seen. It opened gradually, producing off-white flowers that drew the birds and the bees to it. All summer, walkers and drivers stopped to gawk at our agave. And then, the bloom finished. The agave is dying. All its parts are turning brown; the tall stalk is looking shriveled and is bending a bit. Sooner or later, we'll have to do something about it, but for now, I'm still in awe. The agave was growing in all its dangerously spiked glory for more than fifteen years before it did anything spectacular. And now it is finished. Or is it? Scattered around it are small ones working up to the next stages of their creative lives.

Which of nature's life cycles have you observed? What about your own—those connected to your creative life? Consider how you've changed through the lens of nature's metamorphoses.

I HEAR YOU KNOCKING

In a poem titled "A Box Called the Imagination," the Polish poet Zbigniew Herbert wrote:

> Knock on a wall with your knuckle—
> from the piece of oak
> a cuckoo
> will jump out.[11]

If you don't have belief in the knocking and in the cuckoo, you'll bloody your fist against the wall. Think imaginatively, and you link a known possibility to an unknown one. Do you have a proclivity for trying new things, a willingness to be wild? Join faith with curiosity while stepping out into the air, unsure of what awaits. The frame of mind that leads to song and dance is one of, "Let's see. What happens if I try this weird thing? What happens if I sing the song in this key, instead of how I've heard it sung a hundred times before?" A life of imaginative discovery in nature isn't for only a privileged few—not just for those who wear the mantle of artist, but for all of us.

The ability to imagine is also a form of resistance. You can dismantle the status quo, slay boredom, turn the ordinary into the startling, and honor what's growing at your feet. A spirited imagination will get you out of a rut and give you a way to revise anything in need of a change.

When we walk out into nature and listen to the trees, the desert wind, or a chorus of crickets, then return home to make stories of one kind or another, we'll discover that which we'd thought was undiscoverable. We'll inhabit our lives and the world most fully.

And now, back to that cuckoo, the one on the other side of the wall. Have you knocked? Now's the time. The cuckoo's waiting.

3

WHAT WE CARRY

ALL ESSENTIALS NEATLY IN PLACE, OR NOT

They carry fiddle-neck and the arrow-face foxtail,
A harmonica grinning with rust.
—Gary Soto, "Song for the Pockets"

What do we need to bring with us into nature, and what's better left at home? At first, I entered the woods empty-handed for what was usually an hour's walk. I only brought my keys and a full water bottle. Soon, I needed a slip of paper and a pen. Then, that became insufficient—holding paper against a tree's rough bark or on soft ground does not make a good writing surface. Those random slips of paper got wrinkled, lost. Next I began making booklets from gathered scrap paper that I'd embellish with collages and quotes before carrying them out into the woods with me. (I've found that making my own equipment or personalizing something store-bought is an invitation to use it.) Some of those notes became poems, some got worked into a blog that I kept for a while about the forest; all of them were the genesis of this book. The more I walked, the more things I needed, including tissues, headache medicine, a hat, a map and field guides, sunscreen, an energy bar or lunch for longer midday walks, and my father's tiny compass from the back of his junk drawer.

Personalize a store-bought notebook with quotes, images, and doodles, or make a book of your own. I find the portability of pocket-sized notebooks the best. Start bringing your notebook, plus a pen or two (or perhaps even a set of colored pencils) as you explore.

At a certain point, pockets weren't big enough and some sort of hold-all became necessary. I resorted to a practical, ugly gray fanny pack, into which I dropped an old pocketknife, because you never know. Hand wipes, too, following the time I got a bad case of poison oak and was sick in bed with it. Binoculars, I slung over my shoulder. Though shoes aren't exactly something I carry, it's difficult to hike without them. The best kind for nature walks are sturdy walking shoes. Best to leave the flip-flops and tassel loafers behind.

I hate to admit that I slipped my mobile phone into my fanny pack. If I said I brought the phone because Michael's father was ill or, later, because mine was, would you believe me? Probably not, and you'd be right. The phone came because, as someone pointed out the other day, our devices are rarely more than three feet away from most of us, most of the time. Some days I turn the ringer off when walking. Some days it doesn't matter if the volume is on high—I'm oblivious to its fake cricket chirp.

I'm never without lipstick in the woods (or anywhere). "Why would lipstick matter out there? Are the trees going to be pleased by the color of her lips?" you might ask. It's about being comfortable, that's all I can say. Not only my lips' comfort, but that of the whole of me. Though, as I've said, I love bright colors, I stick to muted tones when in the natural world. Except for my lips, I do my best to blend in.

Here's a list of useful things I've never carried along but might: a collapsible ladder to get up close and personal with the otherwise unreachable, a foldaway hammock in case a nap is suddenly needed, clippers for the poison oak when going off-trail, an insta-cold ice pack in case of a fall, a set of colored pencils in every hue and a pad of drawing paper, a wishful-thinking raincoat, and photographs of my best beloveds as company in case I got really lost. Even without a ladder and a hammock, I began to feel as though I was prepared for a walk of many days, not only with what I carried in my bag, but also with all the stuff loaded invisibly between my ears and lower down, encased in the engine of my heart.

In the children's picture book *Little Bear* by Else Holmelund Minarik, the protagonist, Little Bear, comes inside from playing out in the snow. Little Bear says to his mother, "Mother Bear, I am cold." She gives her son a hat. He goes back out into the winter day to play, quickly returning again, still cold. Even a new coat doesn't warm him. Next come snow pants, but to no avail. He's still cold. This time, Mother Bear asks her son if he'd like a fur coat. "Yes," said Little Bear, "I want a fur coat too," at which point his mother removes each article of clothing. "See," said Mother Bear, "There is the fur coat." Little Bear goes back outside to play, and he isn't cold.[1]

That's more or less the conclusion I came to. I needed everything I was carrying until it became a burden. One of my favorite authors, John Berger, made it hard to part with my pocketknife by writing these words: "One could gut a trout with it, peel a pear, cut wild sorrel, open a letter, remove a stone from a goat's cleft hoof."[2] I would be doing none of those things. The knife went back into its drawer beside the compass. The field guides and map were returned to their shelves and, temporarily, the camera too. The binoculars hang from the bedroom doorknob again, though the day I saw two bears crossing the next hillside I despaired at not having them. It's shadowy in most of the places where I walk and the brim of the hat blocks my view. Who needs it? Forget about lunch; I don't go to the woods to eat. Some days I stick the phone in the car's glove box and rush into the trees before I can change my mind. I'm down to the fanny pack that holds a water bottle, an energy bar, a notebook and pen, hand wipes and, yes, lipstick. Most of the time, I've got my phone. If you're not going farther than the park down the street, a couple of pockets may be sufficient; generally, that should be enough, even if you're going farther.

To know a natural place well, even a small one, takes time. It means being there in most seasons and weathers: in daylight and, if possible, in dark: when you're happy and when you're not. About looking at a flower, Georgia O'Keeffe said, "[T]o see takes time, like to have a friend takes time."[3] A lot of art and exploration can happen in a small city park. If that neighborhood park tickles your imagination, you've got a significant advantage—you can bring along much more than whatever fits in your pockets: a portable stage, a cello, an entire orchestra to serenade the birds.

AN INFORMAL SURVEY: WHAT OTHERS BRING

The poet Ellery Akers, who goes into the woods for about a month each summer, said, "I lug a camp chair, my daypack, binoculars, lunch, water, and books: often Rukeyser, Clifton, Whitman, Neruda and Merwin."[4] In her list of poets is Lucille Clifton, a poet I knew, though not well, but whose work I love so well, who wrote many lines I carry with me—whether or not one of her books is in my bag—like "nothing so faithful as now."[5] The artist and writer Maira Kalman dreams "to walk around the world. A smallish backpack, all essentials neatly in place. A camera. A notebook. A traveling paint set. A hat. Good shoes. A nice pleated (green?) skirt for the occasional seaside hotel afternoon dance."[6] I'd like such a skirt. I'd like the seaside dance too. But for short escapades in nature, the green pleated skirt is best left back home in the closet, especially for walks in poison oak territory where bare legs aren't a good idea.

In his book *The Last Empty Places*, Peter Stark tells of the trip he and his family of four took by canoe for a week down the St. Johns River. They shoved "twelve waterproof sacks containing sleeping bags, clothes, tent, and two large coolers crammed with food into the canoe hulls."[7] There is nothing like knowing you have most of what you need to survive on your back or stowed in your own canoe. Once, a friend and I took his canoe out onto Tomales Bay, north of San Francisco, for an afternoon. We had what we needed, though not only in the boat's hull. Above us were many flocks of low-flying birds, and we imagined that the canoe was magically tied to their feet, that they were pulling us along. We carried, too, the knowledge that another needed thing had been purposely left behind—the olallieberry pie I'd baked earlier. That's what got us back to the cabin beside the bay after the birds gave out!

I asked a number of people what they bring into nature with them. Madhu said, "My soul." Barbara brings a walking stick. Robin said she never goes out without a warm hat. My cousin Elinor always brings her dogs. Tim said, "Open eyes, open ears, open heart." Selina carries "An open mind and lots of water." From the poets, like Julia: "I bring a memory of stillness. Painted blue around the edges." Gabriella, a girl after my own heart, without knowing what's on my list, replied: "Paper and my favorite pen; lipstick, of course!" "A thimble of grace and silence" come with Kelly. Then there's Eric who, along with Robin, is a backpacker. He said, "Twenty pounds of backcountry gear, skis or snowshoes if the weather's good, and three or four of my best friends who are wacky enough to like my idea of fun."

If you're heading out for the type of excursion that Steve takes, you might follow his lead. He brings: "Gloves, a knife, and a mesh rucksack to fill with the soon-to-be-coming mushrooms. . . . Occasionally, I return with a deer or boar skull, but sometimes those once belonging to smaller varmints. Oh, yeah, and cut-off wet-suit sleeves to dissuade the poison oak." Certain things we carry for their practical uses and other things for their totemic value. It can take more than a few walks to figure out what's best to carry and what's better left at home.

Consider what to carry with you in your own variation of the ugly fanny pack. Take note of how what you need changes over time.

THE MAP IS NOT THE PLACE

In his book *The Wild Places*, Robert Macfarlane writes, "The map I was making would never attain completion, but I was happy with its partiality."[8] I carry a map in my head of Jacks Peak Park. Sometimes, walking there, I picture myself stepping along the park's paper replica. I like locating my place in relation to the rest of the park and its outlying lands. In my mind's eye I see what's behind me and off to each side. I picture what's ahead. Like Macfarlane's, my map will never be complete because I'm always adding experiences and walking on newfound trails. The map can't help but change.

Returning to New York City after ten years away, I wanted to take Michael to Astoria, Queens, to see the house that belonged to my grandparents for over fifty years. This is where my father grew up. I thought I'd forgotten the address and got on the phone with my dad, embarrassed to ask him. But just as I was about to ask, the address popped out of my mouth: "21-66 Nineteenth Street, right, Pop?" "You got it," he said. From the same forgotten place came "AS4-7784," their old phone number.

So, on a brisk March morning, going down the worn subway steps, I oriented us and pointed, "This way." We walked from Steinway to Ditmars Boulevard and turned left, strolled past the small shopping area, came to La Guli's Pastry Shop where as a child we'd stop on Sundays to get dessert—my favorite, the multilayered *sfogliatelle*, and in the summertime, tiny white cups of lemon ice. Next, we passed the Catholic church where my aunt and uncle were married and where the funeral masses for both my grandparents were held. After many years, so little had changed. Tears slammed against my eyes. Several blocks down Ditmars, the street became residential. We turned right at Nineteenth Street, went down a couple of blocks, and there was my grandparents' two-story house on the corner, just as I remembered it. The map had stayed securely in my mind; I'd carried it all these years.

During the Jazz at Lincoln Center concert in Santa Cruz, before playing "Beautiful Ugly," Thelonius Monk's only waltz, Wynton Marsalis told the packed house that he owned the original score and had tried to locate Monk's genius in its pages. "After years of studying the score," Marsalis told the audience, "I realized it wasn't there." Though the map isn't the place—not in the natural world, not in jazz—what Marsalis's band did with that score was genius, indeed.

In *The Wild Places*, Robert Macfarlane wrote: "Before it was a field science, cartography was an art. . . . We are now used to regarding cartography as an endeavour of exacting precision, whose ambition is the elimination of subjectivity from the representation of a given place."[9] I'm not hoping for a creative guide when driving a rental car through downtown Milan, but on other occasions, I prefer the subjective map. We all carry such maps of our past and our present and, in the intimate and personal sense, they're far more reliable than anything we might find printed in color on paper or on our mobile devices. The stories of what happened are maps we carry inside.

Even if you're not a visual artist, explore your own form of map making. Create the map that would take you to an outdoor place you remember well but are far from. Consider mapping your way back to the inventive thinking of childhood. Or take a look at Sara Fanelli's *My Map Book*, a colorful picture book that's good for kickstarting your map making prowess.

Sara Fanelli, *My Map Book* (New York: Harper Festival, 2001).

FLOTSAM AND JETSAM

Discussing her new novel, *Dept. of Speculation*, Jenny Offill said, "I have a magpie approach to writing. I pick up shiny things, hoping I can use them, and then eventually, with a little luck, I build a nest around them."[10] A found thing—nature or human-made—may be just what you need to spark an entire story. And if you collect objects and experiences you can use them to fill the nest of your projects.

Recently, I've been finding oak galls, those hard wooden knobs scattered with boreholes that are made when small wasps infest a tree. I love to wear them as quirky necklaces. At first, I thought finding an oak gall or a flicker feather was similar to going into a store and picking up a perfect something on sale. But no, how silly. It's nothing like that at all. Finding gems in nature is an entirely surprising experience; not one I go looking for. On the days I've gone looking, I've returned empty-handed.

For a time, the more I noticed out in the woods, the more I bent to study the forest's flotsam and jetsam—pinecones, stones, feathers. I'd pick them up, look closely, and place them back down on the ground. Until I began craving emblems of nature to take home, proof of where I'd been. First, feathers (mostly dropped when birds molt, usually in spring and fall) were token enough. Then I became like a winter-gathering squirrel: I picked up a tiny blue-white eggshell, a palm-size rock, and more, much more. Until, one day, just as I'd lightened my carrying-in load, I stopped picking things up. I gathered what I'd already brought home and gave it back to the woods. The forest was inside me; I no longer needed proof.

CARRYING THE INVISIBLE

There's the weight we carry on our backs, around our waists, or over our shoulders. That kind of carrying is physical and nicely identifiable. It's the weight of the rest of the stuff we carry that we'll take a look at now, and explore how it may influence our time in nature. We'll also consider how we may hold our time in the natural world within the scope of the rest of our lives. As I wrote this book, I devoted myself to a few of the things I love best—nature, spirit, and imagination—for many hours a day, every day. I felt the earth's presence and carried an invisible joy everywhere I went.

If you're an early-morning walker, leftover bits of dream from the night before may accompany you outside—what you're conscious of remembering, and that which is at memory's fringes. When walking later in the day, whatever has left a mark on you in the earlier hours may come too. Associations about nature from childhood experiences that have nothing to do with where we are in the moment may color present-day experiences. Long-ago memories may suddenly seem nearby. Thoughts that are easy to drown out during busy moments may vie for attention. Physical space around us provides room for the nearly forgotten to come into view. When uninvited thoughts come along, they can take up a lot of space. Some days, before I can be present, I have to acknowledge and welcome what else has come along. When I'm walking, if I give attention to and can release the distracting difficulties that sometimes join me, my imagination is able to roam more freely.

If self-doubt follows you into the woods and you carry its heavy burden, your imaginative ideas and dreams may lose their shine. Self-doubt is an aspect of an imaginative life and, to some degree, necessary. Doubtful thoughts may offer valuable insights. After a first draft or initial stab at something, it's worthwhile to step back and look at it critically. But when the evaluative mind enters into the process too early, it can stop your flow. The imagination will temporarily retreat.

Strategies that I've found to be helpful to deal with doubt include having a conversation with that disgruntled thought—aloud, on paper, or in my mind. I speak, then listen to what the doubt says, and we go back and forth like that until an understanding has been found or we arrive at a truce. I've been known to walk around carrying doubt in my arms as though it were a baby in need of love. Give your doubt a bit of nature to absorb it—a curling leaf, a misty vista, a flock of twittering finches—and watch it transform. Like the rest of you, your doubt has been captivated by something new.

If you've got something troubling you, take your thought into nature and hold it close. Let it roll around in your heart and mind, as though it were a pebble on your tongue. What does your trouble have to say in this new setting? What do you want to say to it? Jot down the experience in your carry-along notebook.

Doubt is an internal fear, one that isn't necessarily connected to what's happening in the outer world. Then there's the fear of what might actually exist externally. We'll look more closely at fear in a later chapter but because you may carry it from time to time, let's take a glimpse now. When fearless, I move unobtrusively, step as lightly as I can, talk in hushed tones. I don't sing out there—until I'm scared. When I feel the sting of fear, I always behave the same way: First I turn my wedding ring so the gem faces in. I increase the determination of my stride. If it's an approaching person I'm fearful of, I say hello. "Look him in the eye," a voice whispers in my head. I tuck the fear into some blanketed recess so I can proceed—I know I'm afraid, but I don't want a stranger knowing that too. How does that British slogan fromWorld War II go? "Keep calm and carry on."

Consider building an imaginary shield. This idea came from Somatic therapist Jodi McClean, who suggested I visualize a form of protection that I could imagine putting on when feeling fearful or overwhelmed. Closing my eyes in her office, I saw a beehive—one the bees had vacated—that I could slip over my head; it would cover my heart. To hold it in place I imagined repurposing a worn red leather belt for its straps. A shield could be made from metal, like something the knights wore into battle, or it could be formed from the bark of a fallen tree. Get out your paint box and a few sheets of paper or simply engage your imagination in designing an object that will serve as a symbol to help diminish your fear.

THE LANGUAGE OF EXTINCTION

We may also carry the loss of nature. What's lost to the earth is a loss to us as well. According to the *Scientific American*, the only way to see the national bird of Samoa, the tooth-billed pigeon, is to pick up one of the bank notes that features this bird. At the beginning of the twentieth century there were an estimated one million black rhinoceroses. 2001 is the last year a scientist sighted one in the wild. Since 2011, they've been declared extinct. The numbers of West African lions are dwindling as well; as of 2013, there were about 400 left, and of those only 250 are of breeding age.[11]

Each of those animals is or was the keeper of knowledge that no other creature has. Whenever an animal or plant is lost to the earth, we each lose something—whether it be a frog's particular voice or the teardrop shape below the Alaotra Grebe's eye and his way of moving on water. When one wildflower species is gone from the world because one too many buildings covers its environment, the knowledge that only those flowers had disappears. And when that piece of biodiversity is gone, the contribution of that flower is lost to the planet. A loss to a part is a loss to the whole. Even when we think we don't know it, somewhere in our psyches we carry that weight like a stone.

Close to my home in Pacific Grove, known affectionately as Butterfly Town, is the Monarch Butterfly Sanctuary. Each winter, the Monarchs return to this eucalyptus grove. Recently, despite community protests, the local city council erected cell phone antennas quite close to the butterfly habitat. The risk to the butterflies from the radiation emitted by antennas is basic genetics. According to Eric Chudler, a neuroscientist at the University of Washington, the blood-brain barrier can be broken down as a result of the microwave rays.[12] This can also, potentially, cause fertility and reproductive problems, learning and memory problems. The antennas may disrupt the butterflies' ability to navigate. At the meeting where the decision was made, I asked the council, "What will we call Butterfly Town if we haven't any more butterflies?" Of course, I've got a cell phone and can't quibble with their usefulness, but there were plenty of places where the towers could have been installed that wouldn't have chanced putting the Monarchs or other creatures at risk.

2013 was the driest the Central California coast has endured since 1850.[13] Typhoon Haiyan in the Philippines killed over six thousand people.[14] I could list many "natural" catastrophes, but we all know them. In part, they are the long-term result of human behavior. We may feel empathy, fear, confusion, and worst of all, powerlessness. Even when we turn away, these losses don't leave us.

If we acknowledge this and recognize the devastation, do what we can, and engage our imaginative and our pragmatic selves, we get stronger and have more to offer the natural world. If we become part of the solution, we'll find we're not as powerless as we may have felt before. When I allow myself to feel these losses, grief and empathy grow and that softening actually strengthens me.

BELIEF IN WHAT MATTERS

Ever, like me, think about the shape your imagination would have if it did have an actual physical form? I consider the following possibilities: the full moon caught up in a tree; the wing of a blackbird, complete with its fleck of red. I'd like an imagination that would have the growl of a bear to scare off anything that might get in its way. Giving our invisible imaginations a form can make them easier to conjure and help us to be more conscious of carrying them within. Could the imagination be a coyote, trickster that she is, who shows her face when least expected, appearing from behind thick undergrowth? How amazing that we carry our weightless imaginations everywhere, and they give us ideas, images, and stories, allowing us to invent entire worlds.

No matter what you bring home and what gets left behind, I hope you carry your belief in nature *into* nature, as well as faith in your imagination's possibility and a faith in mystery. My belief in art has grown, as has my belief in my ability to create art. I've increased my faith in the durability, resilience, and surprising nature of the imagination. Time in nature helps clarify what matters.

For many, many years, I asked myself, "What do you believe? Where do you place your belief?" Having been raised Catholic, my foundation in the concept of faith and its value was secure, but from the time I was a young child, my faith was not located in the church doctrine. Instead, I found it in art and stories. On my recent New York visit, I returned to the Metropolitan Museum of Art and stood in front of the Modigliani portrait of his lover Jeanne. I recalled being there as a young girl with my mesmerized father. How he looked at the painting was the way my mother looked when praying. Maybe belief has always been clear for you. If, like me, you're a seeker and you bring your seeking to the earth, your belief will be clarified and strengthened.

Joan, a former writing student, was a volunteer for the Robinson Jeffers Tor House Foundation. Jeffers, whose poem "Hands" I quoted earlier, was an early-twentieth-century American poet who in 1914 built his stone house along the cliffs at Carmel. Joan told me a story about his wife: "Do you recall the little Madonna in Jeffers's tower— in Una's sitting room? Its origin is thought to be the Carmel Mission. Each Christmas Eve, Una would bring the Madonna with her to midnight mass, placing the statue in the pew beside her." I wonder if the other churchgoers looked at Mrs. Jeffers oddly when she walked up the aisle carrying the statue. Similar to how time in nature affects me, this story rekindles my faith in the authenticity of spirit and the nonlinear imagination.

The belief I carry with me into the natural world is belief in the sacredness of the earth: in each leaf, every pine needle, all the loud-mouthed jays, the infinite directions and the wind that comes from each of them, the sheltering sky above, and the solid ground. Standing on the earth, there is no doubt, belief is carried everywhere.

THE EMPTY POCKETS

North of Sacramento and east of Clear Lake, there's a place in the hills that the American folk singer and songwriter, Kate Wolf, may have been singing about in songs such as "Here in California." She sang about there being no gold, but the hills turn golden brown in summer.[15] I've frequented that place for many years. To get there, leave the four-lane freeway behind, head into Yolo County, and drive through towns called Esparto, Capay, and Guinda. Maybe pick up a jar of local farm stand honey on your way. There it gets awfully hot and dry in summer, but in spring, fall, or winter it's as gorgeous as a place can be, if you like the feeling of being in the near-middle of nowhere—rolling hills dotted with oaks and pines, streams cutting through valleys where you can soak in the natural hotsprings. Here, you can walk as far as your feet will take you, traveling freely with the wind.

After a climb to the top of a particular hill where the meadow-larks always sing, I heard a poem enter my ears but my pockets were empty—no paper, no pen. I loved the words that were coming—this would be a take-home poem. But how to carry it? I repeated the first phrases over and over, began the long walk back, until another phrase came that I added on and said aloud. Then another and another came; the poem was building itself, phrase by spoken phrase. By the time I returned to my room in the old country hotel, I had a poem to quickly write down. Titled "Sing for Your Supper," it begins,

What if singing
were how you lived your life
day by day
year after year?[16]

This poem became what it did because of how it formed—carried in my mind and incorporating the rhythm of my steps, rather than securing it to paper right away. Some paintings can only be envisioned when we don't have our paint boxes.

Your imaginative life will be enriched the more you notice what you carry within and discover how to make it visible in the form of your chosen artistic expression. Next, we'll unfold the map you've drawn. Strapping on our carry-alongs, we'll slip into our boots and enter the places that the earth has given us.

4

THE ALIVENESS OF PLACE

A SENSE OF BELONGING

The world is a glass you drink from.
—Nadia Tuéni

For whatever we carry in our satchels, we also carry those places—
natural and human made—that have left their impressions on
us. Some take up permanent residence within our psyches; others
are momentary visitors. My friend Margaret once said, "The color
of the walls in the house where my husband and I first lived and
how the sun came into the bedroom was where we truly fell in love.
All I have to do is to remember that place to see and feel it."

How about the first time that you stood, disbelieving, overlooking the Grand Canyon or another natural wonder? Consider how we
carry those places that can't be visited: the exile's distant country that
in memory is as close as yesterday, or the forest cabin that can't be
returned to because both it and the forest are gone. Nature's places
are less infiltrated by human commerce, so the way we retain them
is unique. And non-human-dominated places live in us as they do
because of our ancestral connections to them. I believe that the rightness I feel in nature has its basis in an unforgotten sense of belonging
and a bone-deep relief in returning. Since the environments in which

we spend our time contribute to who we are, I'd rather see myself as a prairie than a parking lot.

The first time I took a long walk alone in nature wasn't till I was in my early thirties. It was a cold January day. Far away from home, I was winded when I approached the hill's crest. I stood catching my breath, overlooking the long, narrow valley below and the dense forest beyond. It began to hail but, almost unbelievably, on one side of the trail it hailed bullets and on the other side, nothing. There I stood in two weathers, in two places at once, half wet and half dry, baffled. There's nature for you. That walk marked my beginning to relate to the earth in personal and silent ways. I've returned many times and looked down on that snaking valley, but never again have I experienced that phenomenon of weather— there or anywhere else.

Within me many times and places are carried; some natural, some manmade. I was in my twenties the first time I saw the frescos in the church library at Siena—the elaborate, centuries-old stories told in color and form. Those paintings stood my world on its head and helped me develop a sense that history could be personal rather than abstract. They made me want to pull out a paintbrush and begin my own telling. Not so far back, on a late summer night, my husband and I swam in School House Pond on Cape Cod, the fire-flies twinkling like lowdown stars. I can still feel the goose bumps on my skin and the sensation of Michael's arms wrapping around me in the water, both of us buoyant in body and in soul.

In the novel *Ava*, by Carole Maso, thirty-nine-year-old Ava, the main character, is dying. The book is comprised entirely of memories that return to her during her last twenty-four hours of life—things people said to her, experiences she had, memorized quotes from books: "We took the overnight train. You kissed me everywhere. A beautiful passing landscape. Imagined in the dark."[1] Maso poignantly clarifies how place can dwell within as sense memory. It's as though these significant place memories exist within the psyche where it merges with the spiritual realm.

How we behave in one location is different from how we'll act in another. Some places stir us up; others settle us down. The quality of one place is not replicated in another, not even two of the same types of place. The way you feel standing on the soft sands of the Mojave isn't the way you'll feel standing on the sands of the Sahara. Everything that ever happened there before you arrived, mingled with your own experience, determines how you sense that place.

There are two ocean-side coves within a couple miles of each other just south of Carmel, California. Both are slung back against the rock cliff; each has a neat half-circle of beach. The smaller of the two is almost completely hidden from view and doesn't even have a name. The other, China Cove, in Point Lobos, is famous. Tourists gawk at its shifting turquoise water. China Cove is a good place for dancing on the hard sand, but I'd never dance at the unnamed cove— to do so would feel invasive. It's a quiet beach, great for writing or painting or napping. There's more of a sense of human presence at China Cove—not only from the present-day visitors but from the Costanoan Rumsen and Ohlone people who once lived at Point Lobos. There also, whalers took to the sea, returning with both the grief and bounty of their catch. Does China Cove feel like it weighs more because its history is steeped in shared human history? In the pages that follow, we will explore the presence places hold for us— the beautiful passing landscapes, what's imagined in the dark, locales named and unnamed—how they influence the imagination's welfare and how we may be called to contribute to nature's places ourselves.

STORIES OF PLACE

Upon returning to a familiar location, particularly one in nature, I'll often recall the thoughts, feelings, and conversations I had there previously. I first noticed this near the University of California at Santa Cruz campus on the Chinquapin trail. Walking there with a friend, talking about our mothers' deaths, our time was tender. When I've gone back to that trail, I return not only to the actual place, but to the grief; I find myself wondering why I'm suddenly sad before recalling what my friend and I shared along that path.

When I was a teenager, I ran into my friend Kenny downtown on a cold winter weekend afternoon. He was downcast and quiet. It wasn't till we'd walked away from town together, to the river, slipped down the embankment, and sat beside each other beneath the bridge that Kenny told me why. His sister and her husband had been murdered the day before. More than thirty years later, when I drive across that bridge, at the corner of Front and Water streets, I feel echoes of how I felt when Ken told me his awful news.

What of the stories that the places themselves hold? In a workshop I offered beside the roiling waves of the Pacific, I remember Amy Brewster writing

> Every landscape has its story
> written plainly in the expression of its features.

Plainly written, sure, but do we know how to read the stories? There's a story behind why the dunes are bare over here but dotted in long grasses over there—the composition of the soil must be different. There's a narrow path cutting through the woods that is certainly someone's regular route; the story of who travels it is unknown to me. Does that critter carry dinner home in his mouth? Is his fur black and white? What do the landscapes' long histories tell us? I'm a novice at reading the natural world. Until recently, I'd never considered there might be a reason to listen to what the wind knows in one place, and what the mockingbird singing six weeks earlier than usual imparts with his song in another place. Even if we don't have a particular experience or memory tied to a certain cove, meadow, or stretch of sand, all places have stories to tell, and we can listen.

A BEACH WITH SEA GRASS OR A CONIFEROUS FOREST

Author Paula Gunn Allen wrote, "We are the land . . . that is the fundamental idea of Native American life: the land and the people are the same."[2] This awareness is a ways away from how many of us relate to the world today. Have you ever looked from afar at a mountain range to see a human form in the shapes of the earth? You might spy the swell of a woman's hip, the dip of her waist, the rise of her shoulder. As Edward Sharpe and the Magnetic Zeros sing, "I just wanna be what I see."[3] I would like to see myself as part of the landscape—to see my shape reflected back at me in the clouds or my thoughts echoed on the wind. Might we walk and listen, write and make art inspired by the natural world to discover that we, too, are an intrinsic part of the earth?

"If you were a landscape, what landscape would you be?" I once asked via Facebook. Some, like Barbara, are drawn to the untampered sea via "a beach with sea grasses and dunes." Eric's connection is to the mountains: "An alpine meadow; deep, soft snow in winter, flowers and marmots in summer," and Kit imagines herself as a "stream bed, cradle for rainwater." Harriet writes, "I'd be a rocky desert at dawn, sun just beginning to creep into the cracks." Gabrielle envisions long-lastingness: "I'd like to be a big gray rock and watch the rabbits over centuries," and Mary says that she'd "be mostly sky, with a dazzling array of clouds." How specific, yet wide-ranging these responses were, and how telling about each person's relationship between their inner world and their outer one. Joe responds, "A redwood forest with lots of big ferns." Joe was my high school sweetheart, the first person I ever spent a whole night in the woods with—in a redwood forest, with lots of ferns. There I discovered that land could have rooms in the way houses have rooms, but instead of being divided by ceilings and plaster walls, here they were separated by trees, bushes, and nature-made rock walls.

Like Joe, if I were a place, the one that I would most like to be is a forest for its shadow and interplay of light; a place with more unseen than seen, where the ground smells loamy and the wild animals call. Author Barry Lopez writes, "Each individual . . . undertakes to order his interior landscape according to the exterior landscape."[4] I'd like mine ordered in alliance with the woods.

Lastly, there's Kevin's. His response was a poem:

> Pear orchard,
> delicate and tenacious.
> orderly, rooted in the earth,
> yielding sweetness.
>
> C. KEVIN SMITH[5]

Kevin wrote his response "from my hotel in Manhattan's Chinatown, about as far away from a pear orchard as one can get!" Through Kevin's poem, those pears were brought to my table.

If you were a place, which one would you be, and why?

PANOPLY OF PLACES

How many kinds of natural places there are! Skimming at random through *Home Ground: Language for an American Landscape*, a book that introduced me to names I'd never heard of and reintroduced me to others I'd forgotten, I find place names to trigger the imagination and challenge the tongue: aquifer, archipelago, braided stream, channeled land, chaparral, floating islands, floodplain, *marais* ("marsh" in French), marine terrace, midden, middle ground, and (my favorite) quagmire.[6]

From Robert Macfarlane's *The Wild Places*, I learned about a place called a holloway, a word that Macfarlane says has an Anglo-Saxon root, meaning 'a sunken road.' He writes, "A route that centuries of use has eroded down into the bedrock, so that it is recessed beneath the level of the surrounding landscape."[7] These were old roads that people took to market. "The oldest holloways date back to the early Iron Age . . . Over the course of centuries, the passage of cartwheels, horses, hooves, and feet wore away at the floor of these roads, grooving ruts into the exposed stone."[8] And they filled with rainwater, drained and, over time, got worn down below ground level. Some, Macfarlane tells us, are actually old pilgrims paths.

As I contemplate places, I am reminded of animal migratory routes. The day I saw two bears across the valley from me—it's likely they were walking along their migratory route from one location in the Santa Lucias to another—led me to maps of the wildebeest's migratory route in the Serengeti National Park, the migratory routes of marine animals, those that birds take above the Padre Island National Seashore, and those of Alaskan waterfowl. Migrating animals follow the same routes each year, generation to generation, the paths etched into their genetic codes.

Coming into Santa Cruz through the mountains from the north, the highway takes one tight curve after another, and drivers often take them too fast. Highway 17 is also a thoroughfare of another kind—part of the migratory route of animals. The worst curve, the one with a name—Laurel Curve—is where animals tend to cross and are often killed, in particular, mountain lions. This is where the highway crosses through their habitat; because of the road's design, the pumas can't see what they're leaping onto as they follow their route. The Santa Cruz Land Trust, a conservation group, purchased ten acres of undeveloped land along one side of the highway and is planning to build an underground tunnel to serve as a wildlife crossing. The more I learn about the earth's rich variety—from types of place to animal behavior—the more my imagination has to draw from and the sturdier and more versatile it becomes.

A NEW DEFINITION OF FRIENDSHIP

The first couple of times I explored Jacks Peak Park, a place that I now can say I know—or am at least in the process of knowing—I was on my bicycle, climbing up the steep road through the pines. Once in the parking lot, I unclipped my feet from the pedals, walked around, saw the meadow and a few picnic tables, thought there weren't any trails worth bothering with, turned around, and sped back down the hill. I wrote it off as a walking place, I think, because it was unfathomable that what's there could really be there—that so many acres of walkable nature could be close to my home.

Later, unable to ride my bicycle due to an injury, I returned to Jacks Peak Park to check out its few trails and quickly found out how wrong I'd been. Oh, the danger of assumptions, how closed off they can keep us from the beauty of the world! There are about ten miles of hiking trails—more, if you include the paths that aren't officially in the park but lead to and away from it. Some of these are on private property, not that the barbed wire fences keep anyone out who really wants to go.

After walking in this forest for many months and finding I didn't much miss my bicycle, I wondered about being friends with the park. What could that mean? My known world includes a ton of good things, but it didn't include "friending" a place—my close relationships were with humans and animals. How *does* one befriend five hundred acres? The birds didn't need me to bring lunch. No lawns required mowing. The wind didn't want the tree branches moved out of its way.

At first, I simply made sure to pick up whatever litter was on the ground. Next, I began writing about my walks, describing the new trails I found, noting various weathers. I got more serious and volunteered to open the park gates a few days a week and to inform the rangers about trees that had fallen across the trails. Just like being friends with a person, I wanted to discover the park's nuances and idiosyncrasies—what it was like there at morning compared to evening, who calls the place home. And that was good; we had something going, the park and I.

Eventually, the bar got raised to what I feared was an impossible height. Being low on revenue, the parks department decided to construct a zip line at Jacks Peak that would bring busloads of visitors to whizz above the trees. They neglected to inform the public of their plans in a timely manner. Not only is this park a quiet walking, horseback riding, and picnicking spot for many, it's one of the few places in the world where the rare Monterey pine is indigenous; the endangered Smith's blue butterfly calls it home too. Jacks Peak serves as open space in an area that's developed—other than backyards, schoolyards, and an occasional piece of leftover pasture, it is our local open space. A zip line would transform it from a tranquil slice of earth into a theme park.

Many stories about groups of citizens who try to protect a natural place have sad endings—the trees get cut down, the business "park" gets built. Not this time. A swell of support for the preservation of Jacks Peak Park formed—we held meetings and signed petitions. Fortunately, this coincided with an upcoming election, which caused a politician to come to grips with the fact that his reelection stood a greater chance if he got onboard too.

So there is no zip line at Jacks Peak Park; no hordes of people screaming as they go past the trees too fast to notice even a single leaf. My participation began with curiosity—wanting to be friends with this land—and continues as what I believe to be a mutually beneficial relationship. I courted the trees, the flickers, the wind, and hidden places, and they made me welcome.

OFFERING PROTECTION

My eight-year-old students Saul and Johnny considered the theme of protection in their poems. Saul wrote, "When I protect my house, I wear my shark tooth necklace and armor suit . . ." and Johnny wrote, "When I protect life, I wear my officer clothes. I will plant sunflowers and carrots. I will give the animals water and food. I will take care of the world as I can." Author and theologian Thomas Berry wrote, "Whatever preserves and enhances this meadow in the natural cycle of its transformation is good; whatever opposes this meadow or negates it is not good. My life orientation is that simple. It is also that pervasive."[9]

Before my local park was threatened, protecting the planet felt removed from my daily life. Not that I didn't understand the concept, agree with it, and devote my time to campaigns and do other things for the earth's benefit, but the experience didn't feel personal. When Jacks Peak Park needed protection, there went the theoretical. Like Thomas Berry, my life orientation became clear and simple. I understood the potential loss to this tree and that deer—the one who stamped his feet and lowered his antlered head at me, to these coffeeberry bushes with their bright-red berries, to the dark-eyed juncos who foraged along Pine Trail and the ones foraging along Iris Trail, as well. I, too, put on my "armor suit" to "take care of the world as I can." I joined the group, and we rolled up our sleeves and engaged our spirits and imaginations to solve the problem. We had accepted it as *our* problem. Imagining the park destroyed, we rushed in to protect the place we loved.

Just as protecting an external place requires time and effort, so does taking care of the imagination—the putting on of special clothes, metaphorically, anyway. It needs to be regarded as valuable and worthy of protection too. We deserve to be given space and time to flourish in an environment of love, leaf-shadows, and curiosity.

Consider the places nearest you to which you might offer your protection. How does this protection manifest? Why and in what ways is it important to you?

THE PLACE OF IMAGINATION AND SPIRIT

Michael's cousin Brian asked me, "So, what's the book you're writing?"

"A book about nature, spirit, and the imagination," I said.

"You mean a book about the real world and the not-real world?"

"Actually," I replied, "it's about the relationship *between* real worlds."

Like *Harry Potter*'s Professor Dumbledore sagely says to Harry, "Of course it is happening inside your head, Harry—but why on earth should that mean that it is not real?"[10]

Imagination is housed in the mind and in the brain, channeled through the spirit. As such, it is a place—the most boundless place I've known. What are the migratory routes of the imagination? What directions does it follow and through what terrain? Might the imagination hibernate like a bear in winter if sequestered in darkness? Does it emerge again, joints popping and ravenous, as soon as spring warms the air?

How does one arrive at the place of imagination? Might an ele-
vator get you there, complete with an attendant who asks, "Going
up?" and smiles, knowingly, at the affirmative response? Or might
the route require Google Maps? What's the sign that indicates your
arrival—a welcome mat at your feet? By envisioning the details of a
place that your imagination can call home, you'll have a picture in
mind that indicates *now's the time* and *here's the place*. Writer Lydia
Davis, known best for her short-short fiction, said, "Art is not in
some far-off place."[11] Imagination is one way spirit can begin to take
form.

To infuse yourself with imagination, you may find it helpful to
envision its environment—complete with weather and natural
features. When I soften my vision, let it unfocus, I can see it:
the ground is colored with fallen leaves. At night, the mists are
slung low. What does your place look like?

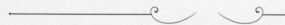

Ask a group of young children, "How big is your imagination?"
and their answers will range from "It's as big as my desk!" and "No
bigger than this classroom," to "Mine is as big as my house," and one
grinning kid with his arms stretched impossibly wide will say, "Bigger than the whole, entire universe." There's always one who'll shrug
and say something like, "My imagination's like a black crawling ant."
Just because an imagination appears small or ordinary doesn't make
it any less important.

The student who looks at me glumly and says, "I haven't got
one," is the child who worries me. Such kids have been cut off from
their creative essence before they've had a chance to even begin. But

if coaxed, over time, the imagination will find a way to engage and dazzle. That's its nature.

How do you preserve and protect your own imaginative self? How might you serve it most truly?

A WRITER'S PLACE

The nine-foot-long desk in my office that Michael built me is covered, prow to stern. If it actually were a boat, it would have sunk by now. I don't work at that desk; it holds the scraps of my life that I believe to be important until I go through them and find that most are not. When I clean it off, that desk is something to behold. I'll walk by it several times a day just to touch its smooth, white surface. It may look like a pristine field of snow, but the tidiness must not set well with me. After a few days, that desk is completely covered again.

These days I don't even write in that room. I've set up camp in the living room in front of the fire. Michael's quite understanding about my piles of papers and books. Out the window is our front yard. The street is just past the yard, but I pretend it isn't. Since it's a quiet street, that's not hard to do. But I don't often look out the window. In the mornings, it's too dark to see anything and by afternoon, I've pretty much forgotten that anything exists besides my work.

Joyce Carol Oates, most prolific of writers, however, is quite aware of what's outside her second-story window. It faces her backyard that slopes down to a creek. She writes, "There is surely some subtle connection between the vistas we face and the writing we accomplish, as a dream takes its mood and imagery from our waking life."[12] This echoes and reaffirms the impact that the woods have on my writing. Though they're not the physical environment I face when doing most of my work, they have become so much a part of me—no wonder I want to respond to what happens there. Oates concludes by saying, "I love my study and am unhappy to leave it for long. Yet I think I most envy writers who look upon the sea or rivers."[13] My dream is to live in a cabin in a meadow with a pond surrounded by thick forest like the place Yeats wrote of:

> I will arise and go now, and go to Innisfree,
> And a small cabin build there, of clay and wattles made.

I like to think that what I'd write in such a cabin would be my best work, but I don't completely believe that to be true. Place is important, yes, but we imbue it with value—the pictures that face us from the walls, the art supplies waiting in their drawers, the living that occurs and all the imagining that goes on. Maya Angelou's writing place needed to be devoid of personality; she rented nondescript hotel rooms to work in. The blank walls gave her freedom.[14]

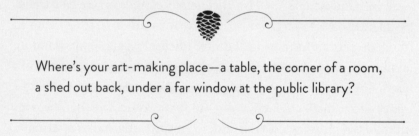

Where's your art-making place—a table, the corner of a room, a shed out back, under a far window at the public library?

THE EMBROIDERED WORLD

One winter when I was a young girl living in Hyde Park, Chicago, a huge snowstorm dumped more snow than had come down in a single storm for many years—snow that made our old world new. As the poet D. A. Powell tweeted: "Snow is a lesson in the beauty of erasure and later—when it melts—the wonder of the most ordinary things."[15]

The snow stopped everything. Most importantly, school! People retreated to warm places. But after a couple of days inside, we children got awfully restless and our parents gladly let us outside. From one end of our short block to the other, the neighborhood kids made a snow tunnel big enough to crawl through. Curiosity and energy were in abundance, hungry as we were for the alive feeling that is possible only outdoors and that is heightened by cold and snowy weather. The new world gave everyone a sense of awe, but children felt it most—we wanted our hands, tongues, and whole bodies in it. Back and forth we went through the tunnel, delighted to have made something ourselves from the suddenness of snow.

My best friend Alexandra lived in that neighborhood; we crawled through that snow tunnel together. She played the cello. Alexandra and her mother, a university professor and single mom, got along well together—there was something conspiratorial about them that I envied. Alexandra's mother reinforced the possibility that there might be an artist within me.

After my family moved away, Alexandra and I stayed in touch occasionally, as children will, and then we didn't, though I continued to remember my old friend. Recently, we reconnected and I went for a visit to her rural north coast home. She met me where the road turned to dirt. While waiting, she had sat in her car, embroidering. After a greeting-hug, it was her stitch-work that linked us. The intricate, multicolored, many-textured world that she was creating was a story told in fabric, and reminiscent of my own such stitching, except that her artistry far outdid mine. Her stitches were as tiny as an insect's step. In the middle of the country, not another house within view, her artwork, along with the same smile she'd had in fourth grade, dropped the years away and brought us back to a shared place once more. On silk and velvet were flowers and leaves; intertwining vines in brilliant orange, yellow, green grew in gardens small enough to hold in my hands. Alexandra had stitched her spirit and imagination onto fabric.

A WATERFALL APPEARED

The painter Norma Bhaskar is a clear-eyed woman in her late eighties who walks the steep climb up to Jacks Peak Park almost daily. She dresses in bright clothes—often paint splattered—so the cars can't miss her. When I told Norma I'd like to interview her for this book, she said, "Oh, yes, but I don't really paint nature."

I thought I'd seen nature images in some of her work. My interest in chatting with Norma was less about what she painted and more about how frequenting this natural place has influenced her work.

"What about your abstracts?" I asked.

She thought a moment. "Oh, yes, yes!" was her enthusiastic reply. "Once," she said, with the hint of a smile, "a waterfall appeared, and I don't know where it came from."[16]

That painting was featured in her last solo show, so I had seen it, a thick swath of indigo pouring down the canvas. The painting wasn't called "Waterfall;" she titles her pieces with numbers. I've seen other natural forms—skies and trees, bodies of water, falling rain—in her bold, color-rich abstract oils.

This is the way in which place works on us; it enters us. Even when we don't plan for it, nature is there: in holloways, animal migratory routes, tunnels made from snow. Your imagination is a natural place.

5

TO WANDER AND WONDER

ROVE, MEANDER, STRAY

Traveler, there is no path;
the path is made by walking.
—Antonio Machado

Amble. Meander. Roam. Out in the air, your eyes touch on one thing, your feet on another. Tree branches brush your sides as you go. Are you taken by green clustering leaves defined against the sky above? The air feeds those leaves and you, and the leaves feed the air you breathe. Your body knows the way. Straggle. Rove. Stray.

Returning to our ancestral home, we're reminded, step-by-step, of the rightness of doing so. An innate awareness links us to the earth. Walk along the path, feel the long-lastingness of nature, an ancient familiarity. Know that sense of your broader existence, a connection to leaf and shadow, starlight and snow, river and rocks—all of it studded with a new vibrancy. You'll feel your own life infused with both a greater effortlessness and intensity. The ground you stand on is firm. Saunter. Stroll. Drift.

When did you last leave your home and let your feet find the way? No hurry. No order. Whistling, perhaps? The Sunday drive is pretty much a thing of the past, for very good environmental reasons, but I remember the pleasure I felt as a little girl when my father would say, "Let's go for a drive and see where we end up." I'd quickly have my shoelaces tied. Perhaps you'd care to balter with me along the sand? Having only just learned that word, I've rarely done it, intentionally anyway, but from now on I will: "dance artlessly, without particular grace or skill but usually with enjoyment." Ah, such permission!

If you stop in the woods and wait and barely breathe and move no more than your smallest muscles, your heart will gentle itself. The deer that startled you—to be fair, you probably startled her first— will stop running away through the oak trees and look slowly over her shoulder right at you so that your eyes lock for an instant. You may hear and then see her companion who is watching you too. The deer may allow you to witness their world, offering you momentary grace, whoever you are.

The more you wander, the more such scenes will present themselves. Under the guise of productivity (does that come from economic necessity or an outlandish lust for all things tangible?), we've lost our way to wandering, to the joy and solace that may be found while moving through the wild world. Have we become fearful of the unknown quality, the unpredictability of it? If you wander for a little while, a sense of wonder will take hold.

WHAT DO YOU WONDER?

Childhood's fiber is constructed out of wonder. Young synapses fire with possibility because the entire world is new. Children are natural inventors, making up things all the time. A discovery of nature can revive this ability once we are grown. Searching for peace, in an effort to recover from his awful World War I experiences, writer Henry Beston spent a year alone in a cottage on a remote Cape Cod beach. There he discovered that nature pours herself into life.[1]

Maybe it's nature's pouring out of herself that's awakened my wonder too. As we grow, we begin pinning things down. As much as we want our questions to be attached to answers, sometimes it's beneficial to let the question drift for a while. Looking at something up close that I'd previously not given a first, let alone second, glance increases my wonder, and the world comes nearer. Kahlil Gibran captures it this way: "Forget not that the earth delights to feel your bare feet and the winds long to play with your hair."[2]

Wonder can be found in the most pedestrian of places. The rubber tree that grows tall and free in my bedroom, leaning over our bed, needing little water, taking its sustenance mostly from the air. Almost every day we have a little chat, that plant and I. Michael thinks some night it may reach out and grab one of us, but I don't worry. It grows so beautifully I can't help but think it takes pleasure in its location. I love that plant. Does it love me too? There's a close link between wonder and love. One definition for wonder is "to be filled with admiration." Through admiring and wondering at the world around me, even in the smallest of ways, I grow to love it more and more.

What in the natural world do you wonder about? How about in an imaginative one? Mull it over under the stars.

WHERE WILL YOU WANDER?

Briar? Thicket? Ice field? Indeed, there's value in variety. New places can stimulate imagination, but I spend much of my walking time— sometimes five to six days a week—wandering through Jacks Peak Park. Depending on its size and how often you frequent it, your neighborhood park—if that's where you're heading for your nature infusions—may after a while lose its sense of adventure, though it is lovely as ever. Borders are comforting until they're not. You may find your creative self bouncing off those edges and crave places that are slightly larger and less familiar.

The American poet E. E. Cummings put it this way: "i will wade out . . . And set my teeth on the silver of the moon."[3] The silver of the moon has wildness in it, and restores our ancient wildness to us. That's part of the pull to explore places that we can't easily see the edges of. And yet, friends have wondered about the frequency of my walking in the same place, asking, "Really? Don't you get bored?" After six years, I haven't yet. I once heard someone say, "Live your life like someone left the gate open," perfectly summing up the idea of wandering. Whatever world that gate opens onto: meadow, beach, forest, lane.

IN PLAIN SIGHT

Downtown in the nondescript parking lot near the copy shop, I noticed a tree I'd never seen before, no taller than me, tucked against the stucco building, hidden in plain sight. The tree was dressed for a coronation. Orange and pink, red and yellow heart-shaped leaves fluttered in the breeze, as if announcing autumn's return to the central coast of California. A crowd ought to have gathered, swooning. Someone should have been delicately tapping a tambourine and I ought to have gotten out of my car and danced. Alas, there was only me.

Often, the hidden things are right behind what's obvious, ready to spur us on. The poet Marianne Moore, who suggested that solitude is the antidote to loneliness, wrote that "the power of the visible is the invisible."[4] If we perk up our senses, might we see the seemingly unseeable and find the unfindable? The as-of-yet unwritten poem is the poet's favorite. The color still absent from the canvas is what keeps the painter up all night. What note is missing from this tune, wonders the composer? The imagination goes wild over the thing whispering just out of reach and so do the feet! To find what you don't know you're looking for, wander into wonder.

Recall a time you've been surprised by what was right in front of you.

THE ART-MAKING WANDER

Making art can be a process much like ambling along through an untamed physical place. To begin, you need only a sense of an idea— a quiver at the edge of consciousness. What gets you to the page or the stage is usually one of two things: either you've scheduled this time to create, or you're compelled by a feeling of inquiry and have a sense that something is brewing. Best to catch it while you can. The path to what you may make or say has only to be a narrow parting of the grass, barely wide enough to enter. Begin with that first whispered thought; the next will come, and the next, thought following thought like raindrops chasing each other down from the sky.

While writing a poem, notebook on my lap, an odd pairing of words or a recent experience nudges me, so I put the image down where the paper holds it securely in ink. Why one word is chosen over another, a certain phrasing over a different option, I don't know—nor do I need to know. The idea—if it's even developed enough to call it that—won't have to run through my head over and over now that the paper has it. Once held in place, another phrase or sentence can come forward, my mind having relinquished its hold on the previous thought.

There's a common misconception about art-making—that we must have a clear idea of what we wish to accomplish at the outset. Lots of artists do not have a clear idea of where they're going. I frequently don't, and this gives me great joy. For me, it's true in writing poems and in constructing collage—the process of making art is a form of wandering. It's one of curiosity, the outcome unknown. You may be a bit off-balance, walking on unsteady ground, into a new place. A willingness to be surprised will lead you to what you'll create, given time, space, patience, and curiosity. Focusing on the outcome is for later. Bring in thoughts about an end product too soon and the untamed imagination may slink behind the curtain.

Think of imagination and play as siblings who do well when left alone together. Drift. Dream. And pretend. Nietzsche said, "In any person lies a child who wants to play." It's pretty nice to have a little unstructured time in which to ponder, to wonder, and to wander. When you arrive at a completed—or nearly completed—piece, there's often a sense of recognition—"So this is where I was headed"—the feeling akin to closing a door behind you.

This book began as a glimpse out of the corner of my eye. Through wandering in the woods, I came up with a flexible outline, having a sense of the job each chapter would need to do, but not knowing how. If I had had an entire plan constructed from the get-go, with no room for variation and previously unconsidered possibilities, I would not have been inclined to start writing each morning.

Writing is such a delightfully baffling experience. I'm typing a phrase and beginning to feel nervous—my heart's picking up speed because I don't know where I'm going, and just before I get concerned, the next words appear from their hiding place, as if quietly laughing. When they don't, I wander—reread what's newly written, stir the fire, take a few deep breaths, pet the cat, stretch my back, curse a few times for emphasis—and then return to the page. There's the next sentence, ready.

If you need to refresh yourself, revive your wonder by taking that thing that's stuck—hunch, idea, or project—outdoors for a walk. Carry a notebook to record what pops up. While walking, let yourself alternatively play with your idea and forget about it, turning your attention to the waves or the desert walls. By the time you return to your work, your relationship to it will have changed.

An afternoon nap is another way to rejuvenate your thinking and to see things from a fresh angle. If you're ever feeling like your path to wonder is blocked, doze for an hour or so in the afternoon. When you wake, ask yourself how you feel. Did you dream? If so, about what? What's different now than it was before?

THE WANDERING STORYTELLER

The best storyteller I've ever known was my mother. She had two kissing stories; one about her Uncle Tom being kissed by the cow. But I loved most the one about when she got kissed by a boy who innocently pulled a loose thread of her dress—she'd made it in home economics class—and at his slight tug the entire garment began unraveling, so she had to run home holding tight to what was left of the stitched seams.

My mother's stories were never short, and she went off on tangents, but she always returned to the main theme, eventually. Her stories didn't require patience because she told them so well.

If my father were present, however, even when I was little, I'd listen to her while watching him to see how far into the story she could get. It usually wasn't long before he'd turn red in the face, jump in, and stammer loudly, "Get to the point goddamnit, Peggy, would you?" He'd do this at a crowded dinner table, where everyone but my father was rapt. What he failed to see was that the meandering details were all part and parcel of the story's whole. I always felt safe in the hands of my mother's stories. There's the fact of story and then there's the truth, the essence, which goes deeper than face value and may diverge unpredictably but never unimportantly. Imagination, spirit, and storytelling intersect in this way. Imagination has a mind of its own that will take you along for the ride if you let it—both as teller and listener—sweeping you up in its wonder.

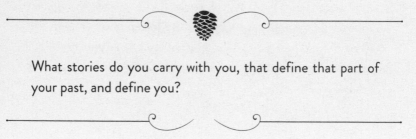

What stories do you carry with you, that define that part of your past, and define you?

GEORGIA O'KEEFFE GOES TO NEW MEXICO

For many years, Georgia O'Keeffe traveled from the east coast to spend the summer in New Mexico. In the desert, she gathered rocks, bones, fallen tree limbs, and flowers for her paintings. At night, she might climb a ladder to the roof so she could be closer to the stars. A loner, O'Keeffe often walked out into the desert. "Such a beautiful, untouched, lonely-feeling place, such a fine part of what I call the 'Faraway.' It is a place I have painted before . . . even now I must do it again."[5]

In 1940, O'Keeffe went to Abiquiú, New Mexico, for the first time and quickly decided to move there, purchasing a house at Ghost Ranch. Even as a child, O'Keeffe had loved nature, but this nature—the land of New Mexico—is where her intimacy with the place crystallized into a lifetime engagement. Looking out at the Painted Desert, O'Keeffe noted, "[The] cliffs over there are almost painted for you—you think—until you try to paint them."[6]

That which is far away allures us with its inaccessibility, bringing to mind all that's longed for. In writing about New Mexico, the photographer Ansel Adams said, "The skies and land are so enormous, and the detail so precise and exquisite that wherever you are you are isolated in a glowing world between the macro and the micro."[7] Through interacting with the earth, we find that these spots aren't necessarily far away. Shortly after O'Keeffe's move to Abiquiú, she began to receive wide acclaim. In 1946, she was the first woman artist to have a retrospective show at the Museum of Modern Art in New York.

The land of away, over those hills and beyond those valleys, awakens the dreamer, the visionary, and the wanderer in us.

Is there a nearby location that you've overlooked, or one you haven't visited in a while that might draw you in?

GUIDES FOR THE WANDERING

Once upon a time, we didn't need to open the door to nature. There was no door! People had no illusion that they were separate from the earth. We were in and of it, at no remove, unequivocally from birth to death. The floor of your home was packed dirt; water was carried from the creek or the well; travel was on trails, by foot or on horseback. Your work likely took place out in the open air. Most of us are far from that now. When I think of the many children I know who go outside only to travel from home to car to school to gymnastics to car to home again, and then do the same tomorrow, I know we're missing out on something essential.

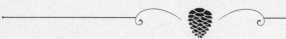

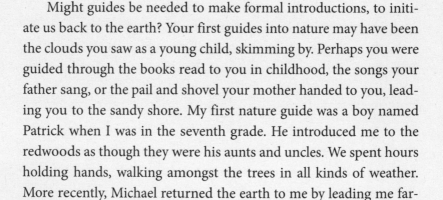

Write about a place you dream of returning to. Why do you wish to return? What would you do there if you could?

Might guides be needed to make formal introductions, to initiate us back to the earth? Your first guides into nature may have been the clouds you saw as a young child, skimming by. Perhaps you were guided through the books read to you in childhood, the songs your father sang, or the pail and shovel your mother handed to you, leading you to the sandy shore. My first nature guide was a boy named Patrick when I was in the seventh grade. He introduced me to the redwoods as though they were his aunts and uncles. We spent hours holding hands, walking amongst the trees in all kinds of weather. More recently, Michael returned the earth to me by leading me farther out—into the Sierra where we walked on granite, slept above the tree line, and plunged into the icy lakes.

Michael's father, Roy, introduced him to the untamed world, beginning his lifelong love of nature. Some Sundays, instead of going to church (Roy was not a firm Catholic), he'd insist, much to my mother-in-law Barbara's chagrin, that the family celebrate

Mass outside in the backyard. He'd usher everyone outdoors and say, "God? Well, God's here in these trees. And see that squirrel in the bushes? There too." Michael was a supplicant. Now, my goddaughter Kyle and her husband take their son to Nature Church. On Saturdays, Kyle posts an invitation on Facebook, inviting friends to join them at a park not far from their home. She provides directions to whichever location they'll explore that day. By Sunday evening, there are photos up for those of us who couldn't make it—children climbing trees, families wandering down paths, fancy fungi, leaves as large as faces.

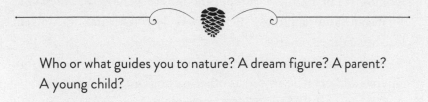

Who or what guides you to nature? A dream figure? A parent? A young child?

"SO I CAN GO"

My father had a friend from when he was young, a guy from the neighborhood—Astoria, Queens—who worked with him at the filling station. Ray became my friend, too, when I was a teenager. More than that, though. Better than that. He was a guide—he recognized and cherished me. Ray often told me that I was bright in the way starlight is. Nobody else had ever paid me a compliment that sounded like a poem.

A Clio-winning advertising man and a photographer, Ray took black and whites of me when I was little. Every summer, beginning in high school, when I started returning to New York by myself for extended visits, Ray and I always saw each other. I'd arrive from my grandmother's at his sixth floor, Fifty-Ninth Street Manhattan apartment with a view of the Queensboro Bridge and he'd have the strongest coffee ready, serving it with thick whole cream and toasted Thomas's corn muffins. We'd sit on his red leather couch and talk, and I'd read him my new poems. My first volume of Lorca's poetry was a gift from Ray. Each summer, Ray and I spent at least one morning together, and, because of his belief in me, I always felt him steadily nearby, no matter my location.

The last time I called Ray, illness quieted his voice. He invited me over. We breakfasted sitting on the couch in front of the big window. He told me he'd been in the hospital and was instructed to quit smoking. He lit another cigarette, and out we went to see an exhibit of Tibetan sand paintings. His gait was slow. As usual, we walked close beside each other.

In sand paintings, the artists pour colored sands made from minerals and crystals as well as other natural or synthetic dyes onto a flat, horizontal surface. From pencil-thin lines to solid swaths, the paintings are elaborate and brilliantly colored. The Tibetan ones are of mandalas that mirror rays extending from the center of the sun. They can take days or weeks to complete. Shortly after the paintings are finished, they're destroyed—the sand is swept away and the picture is transformed into memory.

After a little time at the show, Ray's energy began to flag and we walked the few blocks to Fifth Avenue—I was heading downtown. We hugged goodbye. The weight of that parting was like a sinking stone. I wanted him to tell me again about starlight and my brightness, so, despite the crowded sidewalk, I walked backwards, blowing kisses, hoping Ray couldn't see my tears, until he called out down the avenue: "Go now. So I can go." I turned and walked to the Village. That was the last time we saw each other. About a year later, a mass card with no note or return address arrived in the mail—a laminated picture of the Virgin Mary on the front and on the back the dates of my friend's life and the name of the funeral parlor.

Years later, his words "Go now. So I can go," linger. There began my journey into the world of everyday without him. On the journey toward imagination, as in many of life's journeys, absence may be necessary in order for fulfillment to come, a kind of preparation. You may get pushed out, feeling raw and unready and like a part of you is missing—because it is. Perhaps you may totter a while, like I did walking down Fifth and after, feeling my guide's departure.

Over time, the absence loses its potency; if the presence was important to you, that is what remains. When someone stands beside you, without an iota of hesitation or disbelief, that person stands in for more than himself. He becomes emblematic of the essential faith necessary in the development of self-confidence and in the trusting of one's imagination, a faith in spirit. For me, that trusting—in life and imagination—has not been easy to arrive at. Ray is long gone, though I do retain the starlight he gave me. I look up to it when doubt and disbelief cloud my creative process. And others too—Michael stands tall for me, my students do, and more than a couple of friends. Odd as it may sound, so do the trees. Not one has turned its back on me or shuddered unless touched by the wind, no matter what I write or say in the presence of the forest.

Beyond that, if you are going to embark on a life fused with imagination, you have to stand for yourself, even waveringly. Imagination has been my constant guide, and has saved me over and over again. It's never far from my pen for long, and it always takes me to places I'd arrive at no other way. The spirit of imagination is as reliable as rain on a heavily clouded day.

6

THIS WAY, PEGGY

LOSING AND FINDING OUR WAY

"Not until we are lost do we begin to find ourselves."
—**Henry David Thoreau**

As though being pulled by my feet from a dream, a strange sound woke me in the night. Something was just outside the window, but I had to swim through layers of dream consciousness to get to it. Awake, listening, seconds moved into more seconds. Still, I was at a loss. What was it? "I know this," I thought. Suddenly, the obvious: a raucous downpour. I woke Michael, and we listened hard together, relearning the sound of long-absent rain.

The loss of familiar seasonal weather makes for not only a lack of recognition, but an underlying, significant discomfort. The plants know the loss of it. The animals do. Even we, sheltered away in our beds, know the necessity of rain. We feel it, try as we might to shove the truth of drought and man-made disturbances to the earth to the backs of our minds. I once heard a little girl say to her grandmother, "I love the voice of the rain." She knew. That voice—how could I have forgotten my way to its ordinary sound?

E. E. Cummings writes, "For whatever we lose (like a you or a me)/ it's always ourselves we find in the sea."[1] Ahead, we'll look at lost things—a you or a me, our way to rain, and more. Might there be value in getting lost in both the natural world as well as in the imaginative one?

THIS WAY, PEGGY

Preparing to perform my play, *A Woman's Life in Pieces*, I walked in the woods with the script, memorizing the lines. The birds didn't mind me talking to myself. Out there, gesticulating to the trees, I met a couple, clearly lost. The guy seemed to want to conceal the fact, busy looking up at the sky. The woman had no such reservations.

"Hello, hello!" she cried. "How do we get back to the parking lot? Do you know the way?"

"Continue along this path," I said, pointing straight ahead, glad I could answer her, "till you come to a *T*. Turn left at the yellow fire hydrant and head up the hill. You'll come to the parking area in less than a mile."

Eyebrows raised, she looked at me dubiously, asked, "Will there be a flashing sign that says, 'This way, Peggy'?"

My jaw dropped. A sign from my mother? That's how I took it. For five years before her death, my mother hadn't wanted me in her life, but a few days before dying, she welcomed me back. The odd encounter in the woods sweetly brought us back together for a moment, as though from afar she was voicing her approval of my endeavor. Credit goes to my mother and her messenger—*A Woman's Life in Pieces* went off without a hitch.

Michael's spent a lot of time backpacking in the Sierra where, if you walk a short distance off the trail, it's easy to lose your way. One tree isn't the same as another, but they are related. Ditto for slabs of granite and small bushes. If there isn't a clear marker—a mountain peak to your right, a trail-blaze, a café with a welcome sign outside—it's easy to get confused. Although my mother would have said, "You're splitting hairs . . . ," there is a difference between not knowing where you are and being lost. I love not knowing where I am—it's the ultimate in wandering, the making of new associations, the inability to rely on previous experiences, and, best of all, the absence of fear. When I don't know where I am and I'm scared, that's when I know I'm lost.

Being good at getting lost in nature is a particularly bad thing when it's combined with a fear of being lost. The sensation of the ground slipping out from under me that I get at those times turns my pulse into a rabbit's and I sweat like a marathoner. But the more I walk in the woods, the better my sense of direction and the less I worry about getting lost. "Paying" attention gives one purchasing power: in my case, and maybe yours, it's the power of paying attention to where I am before I think about where I'm going.

Traveling with Michael in Italy a few times, I'd ask a stranger, "Dov´è . . . ?" and not understand a word of the reply except that we needed to turn left . . . somewhere. That rarely concerns Michael—knowing he'll find his way eventually, he's happy to wander and to be lost. If you have the ability to get lost, usually you have the ability to get found. Not always though, making a compass and a map useful carry alongs. My friend Diane once said: "I love getting and feeling lost. Recently, I got lost in the maze-like Moroccan market in Fez. I kept thinking I'd recognize something, but soon realized that so much looked alike, I couldn't count on anything. I had forgotten to bring the business card from our small hotel, just a block away from the market. Unable to speak with any of the shopkeepers or shoppers, I continued to meander until, finally, I recognized an exit." Michael and Diane have a comfort in being lost and a confidence in being found that not everyone has. In his poem "Lost," David Wagoner wisely wrote, "Wherever you are is called Here," reminding us that the forest knows where we are and, if we stay still, the forest will find us.[2]

LOST IN ART-MAKING

Like the writer he's not and like the husband he is, the other day when I got overwhelmed with writing—when I'd lost my way and felt unmoored, Michael said, "But, babe, getting lost is part of the deal. It goes with this. You can trust your process. You've been here before and you know what you're doing." He kind of sounded like me trying to talk to myself, only better—because it was him. Getting lost in art-making is a part of the process that can be hard to accept. For many of us, getting lost doesn't feel good—not in a car, not on foot, and not with a pen or a blank music score in hand. Instead of stomping my feet and wringing my hands, I reach for acceptance and understanding. I practice sitting with the pen in the air, uncertain of its words; outdoors, I stand with my foot in the air, uncertain of its trail. And that makes the whole thing less painful. "I'm only lost again," I tell myself. "I'm not dying. Being lost won't kill me."

The English artist best known for his photorealist work, Malcolm Morley, said, "The idea is to have no idea. Get lost. Get lost in the landscape."[3] Because of the uncertainty that occurs when we're lost in imaginative process, we become less attached to what we know and more receptive to what we think we don't. When I feel lost, I'll explore anywhere if I think it might lead me to getting found. I stumble upon ideas I would otherwise shy away from, ones I'd consider paltry or silly. I try to remember that the sense of being found is never far away, and that it will return.

Recall a time you've felt lost in the making of something— writing a poem, telling a bedtime story, preparing a new dish without a recipe. What got you found?

THE LOST AND FOUND POEM

Turn your head to the left and there's a song, painting, or the promise of a one-act play. If you hadn't turned your head, you wouldn't have found it. Possibilities abound all the time. If you don't write your poem, it becomes as lost as the kiss you turned your head away from and, years later, wish you hadn't. That is why when the barest of whispers, the merest rustle in the grass of an imaginative possibility comes to you, it's worth stopping for. Your life will give you art because you ask for it, because you stop and notice the baby who's giggling; the gnarled old apple tree in bloom.

You could ask, as I have, "What if I look away? What if that poem gets lost? What if it is never found, never written?" It's a fair question. I've lost plenty of 'em. Bet you have too. Art, however—this mystery of linking one phrase to another, of putting one swath of color next to another bit of color—is a startling, not-to-be-missed experience. The imagination fuses with the material and something new gets made—something new with your name on it. You hand the poem to a friend and she has a moment of intimacy with not just your imagination but with her own spirit. The distance between you shortens. And we are found—writer and reader—because the world is made of stories. When we share them, the world gets smaller. And then it expands, because now we know something we didn't know before. Our lost-ness diminishes. We find ourselves linked together in abundant mystery.

IF THE OCEAN LOST ITS COLOR

On a California visit from their home in the Midwest, I took my niece and nephew to see Richard Diebenkorn's exhibit, *The Berkeley Years*, at the de Young Museum in San Francisco. Although already I'd seen the show two times, once again his "greeting" painting on a wall by itself made me weep. The painting had large lakes and fields of brilliant color and more intricate, detailed shapes that pulled me in. Something lost within me, which I still can't name, got found when I stood in front of that picture. Laurel and Garrett were nice about it; they didn't walk away or show any sign of embarrassment, but stood looking at the painting with me. "Aunt Patrice," said Garrett, "it's okay," his hand reassuringly on my shoulder. And then we moved into the rest of the show.

Between 1953 and 1966, when *The Berkeley Years* (abstract and representational works) were painted, Diebenkorn was living in the Bay Area and painting his place—the abundant natural world, the interior one, and the intersection between them. A number of the abstracts feature the ocean and an ocean-side wall, a large field and its fence. These paintings find the light and boldly hold it. As *Huffington Post* writer Priscilla Frank said of the de Young Show, "Capturing the ethereal glow of the Bay Area is no easy feat."[4]

Diebenkorn had some guidelines for painting that he called "Notes to Myself on Beginning a Painting," including my favorites: "1. Attempt what is not certain. Certainty may or may not come later. It may then be a valuable delusion." *Certainty? What certainty?* I ask myself. What I take from this point is to stay open and not fall back on the too-comfortable familiar. "3. Do search. But in order to find other than what is searched for." And, toward the end of his list: "9. Tolerate chaos."[5] Chaos is another way of being lost. When things in art or life are chaotic we may not know where we are. That off-balance experience is fuel for the artist's fire.

About Diebenkorn's work, artist and curator Kyle Morris said, "This type of painting does not start with nature and arrive at paint, but on the contrary, starts with paint and arrives at nature . . ."[6] Laurel stood contemplating a painting with a curious frown on her face, her head inclined toward the picture. "If the ocean lost its color, it would be here," she said.

RECOGNITION: ROACH CANYON

When my old friend Beekeeper Jim, a man as big in body as he was in spirit, and I used to go out walking in the woods, we only went far enough to forage food for supper. Jim knew what to look for and what do with it once we got home. Can't say our meal was always delicious but, with a lot of added garlic, more than edible. Out walking, Jim would point at telephone poles; broken-down tractors; and dumped, rusted-out car parts, and say, "Keep an eye on the manmade things you see. They're the best things to use as markers, should you get lost on the way back." That advice has helped me more than once. But if you mostly walk in places where the only human evidence other than the trails themselves is the occasional trail sign and old falling fences, relying on human design isn't going to help. You've got to rely on nature and on yourself.

One day, heading out from Jacks Peak Park, I took a circuitous trail a long way down through dense forest. Trees stood knotted close together; the poison oak at trailside was abundant. When I finally arrived on flat ground, I stood looking out onto an unforgettable narrow tract of openness bordered by canyon walls. An animated chorus of scrub jays, finches, and grasshoppers sang—before which I took a seat, happy for a ticket to the show. This was a place I'd heard about, the one with the unlovely name—Roach Canyon. Not a roach anywhere. The only insects I saw that day were a few spiders and a parade of ants.

Weeks later on a visit to the home studio of Carmel artist Paola Berthoin, my eyes locked onto a small oil painting, and I gasped—I'd been there! That was Roach Canyon, only this time without the long walk down and the steep, sweaty climb back up. I left without purchasing the painting, but months later, it wouldn't leave me alone. I wrote Paola to ask if it was still available. Now, Roach Canyon exists not only on the earth—an homage to it is on my office wall. It's like a window, looking out.

Have you ever recognized something in a form other than its original one, similar to my Roach Canyon experience? Consider that sense of recognition. How does it play out in your imaginative life?

FOUND AGAIN

This morning, a red-shafted northern flicker darted through the air in front of me. I had been missing this bird. The red-orange underside of the bird's wings was plainly and beautifully visible. It had been too long, even during molting times, since I'd found a flicker feather on the path. God may be in the sky for some, but for me, more so in each bird, leaf, branch, stone, and pebble. A mystical sensibility infuses my relationship with nature and with imagination. There's more out there than meets the eye. The earth's wisdom can't be experienced with a closed hand, a closed heart, or a closed mind. A belief in the *more than*, in the *way down below*, and the *far above* joins me on the land. When my belief in all I don't understand goes missing, a flicker can bring it back. My spirit finds its wings again. Am I a magical thinker? You bet I am.

And the right or wrong of it is of little use to me. I don't doubt my experience; life has shown me too much. I take proof of depth and mystery where I find them, as in the messages from the flicker bird. Yesterday was a difficult day, in the way that days with family can be at times. It had caused me to toss and turn all night. But when that flicker darted close, I lost the weight that had held me down. That's a kind of losing that I'll take.

Once, people knew where they were based on their relation to all that was around them. What methods let you know where you are? How does that help when you've lost your way?

BIRD MESSENGERS AND THE LOST FRIEND

On the ten nights following the sudden death of my longtime friend Diana, I slept fitfully, and was woken in the thick middle of each night by a pair of owls calling back and forth. This was the conversation I wept to, remembering my friend. Diana had been an ally, an anchor, and an advocate. Being ten years older than me, she offered me guidance and direction, sometimes when I was quite lost. At nearly every book reading I gave in Santa Cruz, she was sitting in the front row, to be sure I could see her.

In the last hours of Diana's life, when I stood beside her hospital bed, she squeezed my hand tightly. I sang lullaby after lullaby as the doctors continuously adjusted the machines they'd hooked her up to. When her body was brought home from the hospital, a few of us gathered to bathe, dress, and adorn her with flowers for an informal wake. Many people came to bid her farewell.

Over the course of the next several weeks, her friends and I chatted often, in person or on the phone. Jean, in Los Angeles, told me of a mockingbird who, following Diana's death, had, as never before, begun sitting on a tree branch right outside her kitchen window. Each evening as Jean did dinner dishes, the little visitor sang for her. The day of Diana's memorial, Bhavananda, who gave the eulogy, told me that beforehand she'd been unsure of her ability to speak. That morning a small bird had appeared on her deck. When he opened his mouth, no song came out. Over and over the bird's mouth opened, but only silence. Bhavananda said, "Just that—contraction and expansion, contraction and expansion. Finally he flew off. All day, I was aware of the bird's presence and felt his longing for song."

For ages, birds have been considered symbols of freedom. Perhaps Diana had come to let us know that she wasn't lost. Maybe she was trying to say that she'd achieved her final liberty, that the weight of the world and the sadness she'd carried over the recent loss of her husband were now gone from her. To the ancient Egyptians, birds represented the power of the soul leaving the body. Did the soundless bird that Bhavananda watched represent Diana's reluctance to leave us?

When we are sorrowful and our hearts are open, we're more able to perceive life's otherworldliness, and we may become available to that which our rational minds exclude us from at easier times. That softening is one of the gifts of grief. The loss of my dear friend continues to make me sad. I'm fortunate that she hasn't entirely left me, though her body has gone.

The off-balance vulnerability we experience when we're unsure of which way to go can incline us toward art as a positive outlet. Art may be the only way into certain lost places within. When we begin to notice how we're affected personally—emotionally, spiritually, artistically—when life or the natural world doesn't behave in familiar ways, the primacy of our link to nature and each other and our empathy for the earth may be restored.

I felt grateful for the birds' presence those nights. They kept my sorrow company. After the tenth night, they were gone.

7

A RACING HEART

FEAR AND THE UNKNOWN

Life shrinks or expands in proportion to one's courage.
—Anaïs Nin

Once upon a long time ago, I used to think: "If I'm not worried, there's something I've forgotten." Okay, not such a long time ago. I can worry about my usefulness to the world, my life's value, if I've got enough money or enough love, and a whole bunch of other things. And worry, of course, is just nasty fear-fuel. This is not an advisable way to live. I hope that you have not suffered similarly. Although there's usually *something* to be worried about, if I let it, my fear for the well-being of the earth and her inhabitants can overwhelm me—easily and deeply. But I can't function from that position, nor am I of much use to anyone or any place. Worry and fear constrict us, limiting our mobility. Breath becomes shallow, gets stuck at neck level. Not enough oxygen gets to the brain. There's no freedom there; to think imaginatively, we need to feel free. In this chapter, we'll consider fear's limitations, its benefits, and the loveliness of liberation from it.

A BEAR, A LION, AND THE KNOWN WORLD

My orientation toward fear has its origin from years ago and far away. I'm sure that's true for most of us. The children's song goes: "The bear climbed over the mountain. The bear climbed over the mountain. The bear climbed over the mountain to see what he could see. . . ." The melody is sweet and easy, but when I was in preschool, and the class began that song, I'd flee the circle, rush to hide underneath a table, and curl up into a tight ball, certain that when the bear peered over the mountain to see what he could see, it would be us, and we would be his dinner! My reaction was the same every time the class sang that song. That the bear was never conjured in physical form did nothing to diminish my certainty that next time he'd show up, for sure.

An overactive imagination? A gullible child? Yes, on both counts. Had I ever seen a bear? At the Bronx Zoo maybe. But the idea of "bear" as frightening had been imprinted by the time I was three. Fear can leave its stamp on us early. I'm glad for my imagination's strength but wish I'd been as open-minded about the bear as the other children appeared to be, happily sitting on the floor with their hands in their laps, singing their little hearts out. By the time I began regularly walking in the woods, alone or together, most any unexpected sound—no matter how inconsequential—would make me jump. A beginner in nature, I'd stop, listen, wonder, "Is that a bear I hear?" It took a lot of walking before my hair trigger began to relax.

On the first day I decided to go it alone at Jacks Peak Park, I pulled into the parking lot, opened my car door, and was about to get out when a man came bounding toward me.

"I just saw a mountain lion!" he exclaimed. My heart began to hammer.

He continued, "I've walked in the Sierra for years, and other places, too, and never have I seen one. Until now. It was resting right beside the trail as I walked by."

Oddly, he seemed happy about this. "What happened next?" I asked, timidly.

"The lion looked at me, slowly got up, stretched, and walked away."

"Uh, where were you?" I inquired, trying to sound calm and mildly disinterested.

The man pointed behind me, in the direction of Pine Trail and Lower Ridge Road. I wished him a good day and took off in the opposite direction of his lion. Not that the puma would have still been in the vicinity. But you never know. What I wanted to do was get back in my car and head home to the safety of four walls, one ceiling, and a wood floor. But I knew that if I did, I'd never venture into any natural spot alone, and that would have been giving in to my fear; it would have deprived me of expanding my known world. I would have lost the possibility of a small modicum of self-reliance in the woods.

For the first six months of my walks, fear was my near-constant companion. If I turned left, fear did too. When I sat down on a bench to catch my breath, it sat beside me and stared me down with its beady eyes. It said, "Look out!" and "Over there!" After taking the bait so many times, terror clamping my throat shut, only to see a squirrel jumping from one branch to another, I'd had enough. I didn't want to hold hands with fear anymore.

There were really only two things that scared me when walking alone: mountain lions and crazy men. Not necessarily in that order. Mountain lion attacks on humans are rare. Statistically, the odds are against being eaten by a bear or a mountain lion. There's more chance of being attacked by a neighbor's dog. But our culture has demonized the wild, and in particular, wild animals. Truly, "There's a higher chance of being killed in a car accident," my friend Margaret once reminded me, "and many of us drive every day."

As a woman, I was raised to be conscious of my physical vulnerability. I know that I'm not as physically strong as most men, but I don't feel kindly toward how fear can dominate my life. When Michael walks in the woods, a sense of fear is much further off in his consciousness than it is in mine. My friend Robin, who frequently walks alone in the wilderness near her eastern Sierra mountain home and occasionally backpacks solo in winter snow, said, "I often don't know the difference between fear and intuition." I know what she means. When our ears prick up, we can mistake fear for awareness. They're similar but they're not the same thing. It's important to become proficient at knowing the difference between fear and intuition. Intuition is an ally; it's a sensibility reliant on inner ways of knowing that are beyond the most obviously evident. Fear may be an enemy. It can override the reality of experience.

If you have fear about being in nature, alone or otherwise, what scares you?

FEAR AND THE DEAD DOVE

It's not my habit to walk alone at Jacks Peak toward the end of day. Morning is best. In Monterey, fog rolls in most late summer afternoons. It can mask what I think of as the actual day and transform it quickly, as in Wallace Stevens's poem, "Thirteen Ways of Looking at a Blackbird": "It was evening all afternoon."[1] When I arrived a bit after five, evening's approach was in the air. The sky was low to the ground, fog billowing in big wisps from the ocean. Uneasiness settled in my belly.

On a recent walk with Michael, he'd said, "You must know these trails quite well by now."

STEP INTO NATURE   97

"In a sense," I replied. "A certain few paths have become my familiars, like Skyline Trail, Iris, and Rhus. I know the ups and downs, twists and turns of those routes. I know some of what's growing where."

Though I may take the same trails day after day, I'll never wholly know this place. The park is not a freeze-frame. Since it always changes and is always new, what appeared familiar one day may look very different the next. I change too. The day of that late-afternoon hike, with the eeriness of low-hanging fog, discomfort tinged everything I saw, especially on a switchback section where I came upon a freshly killed dove. Some of the bird's pale gray feathers were scattered around his body. A deep hole had been bored in the belly's center. The contrast of colors between the gray feathers and the bright red blood was a sad and beautiful thing. Its little face had been ground into the dirt.

Looking at that bloodied dove, another emotion came over me that distracted me from the fear. Using the only standard for dignity I have and feeling a bit like I'd recently swallowed too many empathy pills, I gently nudged the dove off the path, dug up some dirt to cover it, and said a prayer before continuing along. Where does empathy for animals come from? Who has it and who doesn't, and why? My friend Margaret told me this: "Last spring my mother and I were driving and a bird flew precariously close to the windshield. 'Slow down,' said my mother, 'it's spring. The hatchlings are learning how to fly!'" Then again, maybe my form of dignity isn't so human, really. One day, outside watering some seedlings, my neighbor told me her pet rabbit had died and that my cat, who was friendly with him, came over and sat for a long while on top of the spot where the rabbit had been buried.

The fog and the dead dove continued to haunt me after I'd buried the bird and continued on my way, but I kept walking. The experience reminds me of the proverb of unknown origin of two wolves.

A wise person has two wolves, one named Love and the other, Fear. A child asks which one is bigger and the wise person answers, "The one I feed." Sometimes I'm good at knowing which one to feed; other times, not so good. Where empathy is concerned, however—that particular love—I'd always like to keep that wolf well fed.

Consider empathy—your own, others', and that evidenced in the animal world. How does the experience of empathy enter into the art you make and want to make? What about a lack of empathy, perhaps toward yourself? How do you experience that lack, and how does it influence your creative process?

FEAR AND IMAGINATIVE PROCESS

Pablo Picasso said, "The artist is a receptacle for emotions that come from all over the place: from the sky, from the earth, from a scrap of paper, from a passing shape, from a spider's web."[2] Artistic and other imaginative people tend to be highly sensitive. Engaged in writing a poem, a poet is like a house with all doors and windows open—what pours in is what pours in. There may be a bit of wind from the south carrying smoke and with it the associated fear of fire; or a bit of wind from the east coming in with the scent of artichokes growing in the fields. Arriving from the west come the sea breezes. From the north, perhaps snow recently fallen on the distant mountains. The artist doesn't know in advance what will arrive until it's there on her doorstep. Art-making is a process of engaging with uncertainty and the unknown, and thus can be like standing at a cliff's edge.

When I feel uncertain about what I'm doing with my artistic life, fear often follows. It happens when I'm on the verge of growing, pushing my boundaries. It's as though the cells of our being have to rearrange themselves and find another order so that we can get to this new awareness—it's an unrefined process. If I'm writing something that is, or feels, just beyond my knowledge or what I believe to be my ability to articulate, fear may show up, or when I'm just about to say something I'd been told long ago I should never say. When feeling deeply, fear may make itself known too. Novelist Michael Cunningham, author of *The Hours*, used this metaphor, "A writer should always feel like he's in over his head."[3]

The English poet John Keats wrote, "The poetry of earth is ceasing never." I frequently repeat that line to myself in an effort to achieve calm when it's missing. In December 1817, Keats wrote a letter to his brother about the ability to accept life's instability, its lack of predictability, and to nonetheless live contentedly. Keats wrote, "Negative Capability, that is when man is capable of being in uncertainties, Mysteries, doubts, without any irritable reaching after fact and reason."[4] Oh, my irritable reach! And this wisdom from a poet who lived in artistic obscurity, impoverished; in love but away from his beloved, and who died when he was twenty-five. Much as there is wildness and wilderness in nature, so there is in everyday artistic practice. When we make art, we enter our own wilderness. We may try to tame it, but the unconscious has elements of the wild that are untamable. Uncomfortable as it can be at times, it's necessary in the making of art.

How do you live with uncertainty in your art-making life?

FEAR AND THE AGE OF ANXIETY

The moment your brain thinks there's an oncoming threat, the fight-or-flight response kicks in. Your brain does this for all threats, real and imagined. Its response causes a release of chemicals that, should you really need to run, will give you the energy to move fast and get the hell on out of there, or to put up your dukes and take it to the mat. However, for many of us these days, the fear wires get crossed from time to time. Most of us are not born feral in the least, yet our fight-or-flight response is hypervigilant. Our brains don't know that all the stressful little things on a regular basis don't require this degree of reaction, so our systems are glutted by a chemical release; and that's not good for the body or mind. Every-day stress can drain us—our central nervous system, endocrine, and immune systems.

Out in nature, where we may be by ourselves and in a less than familiar environment (and because we're not multitasking and aren't inundated by competing demands), some of us may be more suscep-tible to underlying fear. The anxiety that we carry with us at other times may become more obvious because there's space around it. The New York City poet Frank O'Hara, in his poem "Meditations in an Emergency," expressed his discomfort in open space with this: "I can't even enjoy a blade of grass unless there's a subway handy or a record store or some sign of people that do not totally *regret* life."[5]

Psychotherapist Mary McKenna discusses reasons for this. "We are each affected in multiple ways by the context within which we reside," says McKenna. "Today that larger context includes, but is not limited to, economic strife here and abroad, the breakdown of political discourse, stalemate in governance, wars going on around the globe, dwindling resources, and in a major way, the emergency situation regarding the health of our planet. Layer onto that the additional personal stressors of work, relationships, health, financial issues, and whatever else; and we have a cauldron of anxiety, depression, fear, overwhelm, and sometimes, hopelessness and despair. Since our emotions are being 'triggered' by these many elements throughout the day, it is very difficult to determine exactly what the root cause of our anxiety is."[6]

Much as I resisted meditation for years, I've found it to be (along with walks in nature), what helps the most in relaxing that overzealous trigger. If you haven't yet, consider incorporating a few moments' meditation into your day.

Notice wild animals in nature and their fight-or-flight response. They're alert, especially the most vulnerable ones—birds, squirrels, and deer. They know how to turn their hair trigger on when it's required, and when to turn it off. My cats are like this, as well: Ace will be curled up, sound asleep in front of the fire; she'll hear an unexpected sound, prick up her ears, lift her head, look around with a bit of wild in her eyes. After a moment, if there's no further interruption, she'll place her furry head down and fall back to sleep. Ace is an especially vigilant cat because she was born feral. She knows to be prepared for unexpected danger. My very domesticated cat, Stella, on the other hand, requires more commotion to respond; the house might fall down around her before she'd be roused.

If we lose our ability to relate to many of the earth's workings and no longer are seemingly much affected by its basic functions: light and dark, weathers and seasons, don't we lose our intrinsic selves, and might that not be an unconscious part of our fear? In German, there's the word I can write but not pronounce: *verfremdung*: to make strange that which is familiar. This is what's happened to many of us. The earth has become *verfremdung* and that's another reason we may be fearful when alone. But this is something to reconsider. Is the fear response warranted? If so, why? Might we learn to live with and even benefit from this fear?

RESPONDING TO FEAR

When we are afraid, the tendency is to retreat, either actually or emotionally. Retreating from fear physically can keep us ensconced in the comfortable familiar. You might, instead, bring your fear along with you, like you might welcome a less-than-favorite relative who wants to join you for a walk. When the fear receives attention, it tends to shrink.

Take your fear out for a walk. Talk to it. Ask it questions. Have a conversation. What happens when you do?

In one of my favorite novels, *Extremely Loud and Incredibly Close*, Jonathan Safran Foer's hero, nine-year-old Oskar Schell, says he's got "heavy boots" when he's afraid.[7] When I'm scared, my boots get heavy too. Maybe we could invent a special device to carry along—boot-lighteners. It would work like a can opener; you attach it to the heel of the boot and crank the heaviness of fear out.

My friend Robin suggests I bring an emblem of fearlessness into the woods with me, "How about a frosting piping bag?" Silly, clever, or both? Alternatively, how about one of these: an ink-flush pen to write the fear out, a laser flashlight to burn it away, a friend to share your fears with as you venture out, or a favorite song that immediately inflates like a cocoon of comfort when you sing it, lifting you into the air to float, cloud-like, above the fear?

In trade for a writing workshop, Santa Cruz artist Jan McGeorge gave me a pastel of a seaside landscape in which the fog is on the move—it's drifting in or drifting out, depending. A couple of years ago, Jan's son died tragically and awfully young, and this loss moved her to want to do something she'd never done before, to take herself out of the familiar, alone. She filled her backpack and went to Ecuador. Her first posts on Facebook made me afraid—she was afraid. I wanted her to come home. I wanted her to stay. From her travels, Jan wrote,

> I have been experiencing tons of fear—fear that I don't know what I am doing or where I am going. Fear of being robbed. Fear of being alone. I think this is probably why I came. It just has to happen, and I have to feel it and just keep reaching past it. Next week, I leave the city and head to the jungle for five days. I think it will be a relief to be scared of snakes, caimans, piranhas, and scorpions instead of human robbers.[8]

She did stay, and said that later, she lost her fear. How? As she reached through her fear, joy took its place.

After many months of walking, I changed my strategy toward fear. I stopped believing it. Finally, fear packed its banged-up bag and slunk away. I didn't watch it go, because I wasn't conscious of its going. One day I went for a walk and noticed that I wasn't afraid. By walking alone over and over and over again and having, mostly, nothing bad happen, my fear got disproved. I'm sure it will return from time to time—I'd be worried if it didn't. The artist Louise Bourgeois said, "I pushed away the fear by studying the sky. . ." But in the woods I didn't push anything away; the fear accompanied me until it didn't.[9]

A DISPERSAL OF FEAR

At nearly ninety-two, my father is becoming the artist he's always dreamed of being. As a young man, at Queens College, he took a few art classes. His father was a metal craftsman who helped build the doors to Rockefeller Center and the gates to Columbia University, but he didn't see himself as an artist. Nor did my grandmother, though she drew fashion designs in a now-tattered sketchbook and made elaborate feather decorations for hats to support her family during the Depression.

My father's childhood was centered on hard work and a traditional Italian ethic with family at the center. After the army, art turned my father upside down. My guess is his infatuation with art had begun before that. Many times, he and his father went to Manhattan and got standing-room tickets to the opera and Italian dramas. Or the girl down the street would have tickets to Toscanini concerts and would invite my dad to go along. As a young man, he frequented the Museum of Modern Art. When he was ready, art gave my father a way to express the complexity of himself—a smart, renegade, first-generation Italian-American from New York City, the black sheep of his family.

Life did not lead my dad down art's path—the truth is, my father let go of art because he didn't believe in his own possibility. Afraid of failure, he failed to pursue his dreams early in life. Despite doing his best to pass on that same lack of self-belief to me, he failed there, too, because he had succeeded so well in passing on to me a cellular-level love and reverence for art. We spent hours and hours together at art museums when I was a girl. Try as he might, he was never able to abolish my childlike joy in play and the wonder that comes through making art—in both written and visual forms. And though the act of creating may frighten me, joy always eventually wins out.

Age has reawakened my father's suppressed artistic sensibilities; and no longer working for a living, he's got time to devote himself to art. He now lives in the mountains above Santa Cruz, a couple miles from the Pacific, and last summer, he decided to repaint a bird-bath that had fallen into disrepair. Setting up an art studio on the back deck, he began to work. Three months later, the birdbath was still not finished. He fell in love with his labor and the process of watching something that had lost its beauty return to beauty again; he was in no hurry to complete the project. Not only did he give the birdbath coat after coat of paint, he added embellishments, both two and three dimensional—from a delicately painted bee, head leaning toward a flower, to a regal raven perched bath-side, ready to watch his live brethren drink. Lastly, he added bits of shell and sea glass. The flower-like bowl he repainted in a striped mix of milky purple and chartreuse, reminding me of the wild paisley shirts he often wears and the hats often atop his head. Then there were the naps he took waiting for a coat of paint to dry. He relished sleeping in the sun and waking to his project. All summer he worked outdoors beside the redwoods, accompanied by the family's many dogs and cats.

My father wandered through the summer of his ninety-first year. His imagination was lit by sunlight and paint and possibility. Should that be his last summer—and there's no indication it will be—ah, what a summer he'll have had. To finally linger, unrestrained, in his imagination and to choose to paint as he did; to let go of an old fear that, finally, he decided was no longer his. Could it be called the summer of his liberation? Perhaps I was wrong and my father didn't fail at an artist's life; he was fortunate to have the time he needed to get there.

There used to be a popular bumper sticker that said "No fear." I'd see it on the backs of cars and wonder, really, does anybody live by that code all the time, fist pumping at the air and full of bravado? Fear, in the right situation, is a most healthy response. But if mak-ing art is something you want to do, and fear or its stepsister doubt is holding you back, or you're afraid when you set your feet on the trail, reach for whatever fear-busting implement you've got handy. Remember the value of uncertainty—in nature and in art-making—and the surprising places it can lead. Your imagination, too, will be lit by sunlight and your spirit revived by flower-scented air. You'll find that possibility is yours whether you're repainting an old birdbath, singing a just-composed aria for an audience of trees, or uncovering your hidden artistic nature at long last.

8

FROM FEATHERS TO STARS

FINDING YOUR FORMS

The order that rules music, the same controls the placing
of the stars and the feathers in a bird's wing.
—Louis Zukofsky

In Fresno, California, there's a place called the Underground Gardens. They were built by Baldassare Forestiere, a Sicilian man who came to the United States in 1901 to get away from his difficult father. As the second-born son, Forestiere wasn't entitled to his father's wealth; he asked for and was denied a share of the family land. It was all given to his older brother. So Forestiere departed for New York City where he worked, briefly, helping to build the new subway system before leaving for California.

Fresno can be stiflingly hot in the summer and cold in the winter; its hardpan topsoil is like concrete. Ever resourceful, Forestiere built his home and his unusual garden underground by hand, using picks and shovels. Not a trained architect, he put no plans to paper, but having a vigorous imagination, he built his maze-like structures after the ancient Sicilian catacombs, complete with patios, grottos, and passageways, and dominated by Roman arches. For forty years, during his spare time, Forestiere continued to build and plant—there are over ten acres with fruit trees, mostly sct below grade where the temperatures were many degrees cooler, but open to the sky. By planting as he did, Forestiere was able to grow trees that would otherwise have withered in the summer heat and been daunted by the winter cold. At the time of his death in 1946, he'd built over fifty subterranean rooms that were connected by tunnels. Apparently, as an artist can be, he was a bit compulsive. In an interview, Forestiere, a devoted Roman Catholic who incorporated symbols from the church into his buildings, said that at times he was overwhelmed by the visions he had.

Fresno was a quiet place in Forestiere's day, but now his work is an oasis in the middle of that large city. His gardens attract thousands of visitors each year. Many of Forestiere's trees and vines, nearly one hundred years old, continue to produce fruit. Forestiere found his imaginative expression in most unusual forms, but inspiration and expression can manifest in a seemingly endless kaleidoscope of ways. In this chapter, we'll look at various kinds of imaginative expression—from poetry to painting in snow—with an eye for uncovering your true forms, whatever they may be.[1]

YOUR FIRST FORMS

Expressing ourselves is what we humans do from the moment we're born. In a sense, poetry is our first language, to-the-heart-of-the-matter utterances, not tied to the rigors of grammar, that begin with early baby talk of "aaaah" and "oooh" and "goo-goo-gaa-gaa." The American poet Donald Hall put it this way: "His small tongue curls around the sounds, the way his tongue warms with the tiny thread of milk that he pulls from his mother. This is Milktongue, and in poetry it is the deep and primitive pleasure of vowels in the mouth . . . His whole body throbs and thrills with pleasure. . . . The mouth-pleasure, the muscle-pleasure . . ."[2] Watch a baby move his hands as he coos and you see how the body and the mind are engaged in interplay of sound, movement, and meaning, out of which art may later come.

A story goes that someone once asked the poet William Stafford at what point he became a poet. He allegedly responded by asking when everyone else stopped—all children make things up, and some of us *don't* stop. That essential thing we're bound to say may spring from our earliest moments. As a kid, did you sing freely and without need for the contrivance of someone else's tune? Or tunnel into the dirt, build sculptures in the air and sand and mud? Have you always been inclined to beat out the rhythm you hear in your head?

When we follow our innate, imaginative inclinations, we can dip into not only our personal mystery, but that of the collective unconscious and the earth's magnificence. Great energy can be found there. The artist in all of us searches to find form for what is, ultimately, beyond form. What might be uncovered drives us further. The motor of seeking furthers the artist, moving ever nearer through all the layers to our essence, definition—*raison d'être*. The sculptor Henry Moore said, "The secret of life is to have a task, something you devote your entire life to, something you bring everything to, every minute of the day for your whole life. And the most important thing is—it must be something you cannot possibly do!"[3] I keep tapping at the keys, getting closer, closer . . .

The dancer and choreographer, Pina Bausch said: ". . . [Y]ou have to believe that dance is something other than technique. We forget where the movements come from. They are born from life."[4] From dancing beside a waterfall to playing flute in an orchestra, your need for imaginative expression may be met through any number of modes. Whatever you choose, whatever forms you're chosen by, what you create through them will be the result of what calls to you.

IDÉE FIXE

I once had a poetry student named Billy who went to school in Salinas, California. From the time he was six until he was twelve, I came to his school as the traveling poet for ten weeks each year. Billy was part of a group of kids who came to the school library, where we wrote poems together. Hard to settle down, Billy was often fidgety. His smile, when it came, inched reluctantly across his lips unless he was thinking or writing about his grandfather, and then his smile was easy. There were a number of children in Billy's conflicted family; this tender, sandy-headed boy got lost amongst them. His parents drank too much and fought too hard—the target of their fists was sometimes Billy. The school was unsuccessful, at least when I knew him, in doing much to help. All I could do was to offer this child the chance to express what he needed to—to give voice to his grandfather—and to listen closely, to put my arms around him when he leaned in.

Make a list of the forms that draw you in—either as a creator or a viewer—and allow yourself outlandishness in your attractions. Though I doubt at this point in my life I'll ever be an oil painter, I do dream of a studio with tall walls and the smell of turpentine.

All those years, Billy never, not once, veered from his chosen subject. Or had his subject chosen him? The group might be writing about what's lodged in the heart and Billy's poem would be about his grandfather because that's who resided there. If I gave the children time-traveling; or if you could be any animal, what animal would that be; or if I asked them to imagine how the world began, the focus of Billy's poem was always the same. Once his poems were on paper, Billy relaxed. He stood proudly in front of the class, happy to read to the other children what he'd written. The day I came to school and our subject was trecs, Billy wrote about his grandfather, sitting up in a tree's highest limbs. That's how I learned his grandfather had died. Billy's life got more difficult after that.

From Billy, I witnessed the concept of *idée fixe* at work. Literally a "fixed idea," it's a desire or obsession that claims one's focus. In the early 1800s, composer Hector Berlioz coined the term, using it to indicate a recurring theme in his Symphonie Fantastique, a piece about the life of an artist.[5] Are themes and obsessions more recurrent in artists' lives or (due to our sensitivity and attentiveness), are we just more likely to notice and comment on them? Are artists more obsessed than others by the things in life that repeat themselves, more plagued by patterns? Matisse said, "You have only one idea. You are born with it, and all your life you develop your *idée fixe*, you make it breathe."[6]

Sometimes an *idée fixe* sneaks up on you—it certainly did for me or my awareness of it did anyway. As many poems as I've written to Michael or the natural world, the amount of material inspired by—written to and about—my mother exceeds them. Alive as well as dead, she's my muse.

Italian author Italo Calvino said, "Everything can change, but not the language that we carry inside us, like a world more exclusive and final than one's mother's womb."[7] If we consider that the language we carry inside—our mother tongue—comes to us through our initial observations, experiences, and the resultant need to identify, clarify, interpret, and respond, we see how an *idée fixe* may be its result. This is especially true for those inclined to look deeply for meaning, to make art out of that mélange. There may be one thing in your life that you need most to say; you may say it in a thousand ways for all your years, in any number of forms, each time getting closer to its essence or veering away, only to return again the next time.

Do you have an *idée fixe*? Over the course of your life, has there been a theme or subject that's repeatedly pulled you in? Or are you drawn in a number of directions?

FINDING YOUR FORM(S)

Perhaps like Baldassare Forestiere, your forms—the way you manifest what you need to say—may come to you spurred on by a challenge. An imaginative determination can come from that. And you, as well, may find a form unlike anything anyone's imagined before. You might be inclined to explore one form of expression for a period of time and later, another. Each allows access to new ways of seeing. For example, perhaps ceramics has always been your go-to, but now, it's the portability and immediacy of charcoal on paper that claims you. The author John Fowles said, "What is irreplaceable in any object of art is never, in the final analysis, its technique or craft, but the personality of the artist, the expression of his or her unique and individual feeling." Our forms are how we give our imagination shape.[8]

I've drawn and painted since I was very young. Not a day went by that didn't include a crayon, paintbrush, or pencil and paper. But because the visual arts were my father's domain and our relationship was fraught, I turned to writing poems. Writing them was the one time I felt still; doing so gave me a sense of control over my life. I kept what I wrote to myself; no one could tell me I was wrong or attempt to steer me in an opposing direction.

For a long time, writing was my only form until the visual arts returned—quietly at first. There was something that needed saying that couldn't be reached through words. That's how a new form may come to you—through necessity. If your favorite form becomes limiting rather than expansive, consider experimenting with a new one. If, like me, you're not inspired by or skilled at drawing but are good with a pair of scissors and not too bad with color, collage is a great choice. Collage often leads to poems that I would not have written otherwise. Carefully made and quickly stuffed away, this fledgling form of mine eventually found its way out of the drawer, into frames and onto walls, and into a show here and there. Some became the covers of book jackets. Both forms are a part of my life: collage, because of its lack of linearity, is where I feel most free and playful, and the literary arts, with their layers of unveiling, are how I uncover the deepest truths. Neither form offers what the other does; they complement each other.

The play I wrote began as a novel that I stuck in the same drawer as those collages, until a local theater director asked if I had written anything on women and aging. I gave her a copy, and the director surprised me by selecting her favorite parts and encouraging me to perform it myself. From that material, I developed a one-woman play that I performed. I loved the entire experience—going (far) past my comfort zone, embarking on something I'd never considered exploring, having small-pond success, and even making a few bucks—a most pleasant surprise. A form I'll take on again? Unlikely.

Jasper Johns said, "Take an object. Do something with it. Do something else with it."[9] That's certainly what nature does. A rock worn away by the ocean slowly becomes sand on a beach. Water in a river evaporates and then condenses into clouds. Birds gather bits of what we consider trash to build themselves nests. Trying out the forms that you're least familiar and comfortable with is a great way to get lost and found in art and startled awake, pushed beyond your expectations. Stretch these boundaries, see where you end up—it might be a new beginning.

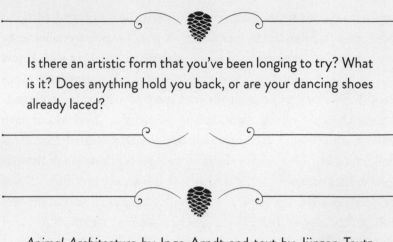

Is there an artistic form that you've been longing to try? What is it? Does anything hold you back, or are your dancing shoes already laced?

Animal Architecture by Ingo Arndt and text by Jürgen Tautz presents photos of weaver ants' nests. These are elaborate woven wooden structures made by insect larva, the paper-thin multilayered nests of wasps. Tautz's photos are so close up, it's as though we could walk inside. Could we take up such forms as places for our art to nest in?

Ingo Arndt and Jürgen Tautz, *Animal Architecture* (New York: Abrams, 2013).

THE FORMS OF NATURE AND THE NATURE OF FORM

In his book *Survival of the Beautiful: Art, Science, and Evolution*, David Rothenberg writes about forms in this way, "Why is it, then, instead of being so distinct from one another, that the forms of life often take the same forms of the natural world beyond the limits of the living? Spirals, lattices, tessellations, undulations, waves, and crystalline forms are all found in living cells, both creatures and plants, but also in clouds, sand dunes, storms, rocks, even the arrangements of planets and stars."[10] Our bodies have forms that demonstrate how much a part of nature we are: the little spirals in our ears resemble conch shells, the whorls of our fingerprints, ripples across a dune; the patterns of our irises, the hearts of distant galaxies. The poet Gary Snyder noted that our imaginative work "could be seen as the swoop of a hawk, the intricate galleries of burrowing and tunneling done by western pine bark beetles, the lurking-at-the-bottom of a big old trout, the kamikaze sting of a yellow jacket."[11] What might the line of a poem, swooping downward like that hawk in the air, say?

What part of the natural world is your art most aligned with? Does it resemble the flight of a hawk or the smooth roundness of a river stone?

The English artist Simon Beck makes art out of snow. He "draws" in the snow itself, on flat areas, and some of his pieces are as large as three football fields. Many of his designs are geometric in nature; they look like images you might see through a kaleidoscope or a tiled mosaic, but completely white. Beck spends hours simply measuring the area he's designing. He goes out into the cold landscape with his earbuds in place; listening to Beethoven, he says, gives him the tenacity to work for ten hours at a time. Having finished a snow painting, he'll go to bed, but often wakes up in the morning to find that the wind and snow have disappeared his creations. That his work is so quickly undone doesn't bother the artist a bit. Seeing that only the barest outline of his recent work remains, Beck says, "So it looks like it's a clean sheet to make a new one." Once finished with a picture, he goes to a local internet café near his home in Switzerland and posts his new work on Facebook. Beck says, "The mountains improve the artwork. And the artwork improves the mountains."[12]

Unlike the glow of the sunrise or the exquisite glimmer of fire-flies at dusk, the electric brightness of neon has never invited me in. As a medium, it strikes me as cold. The only exception is the time I was lost in North Beach, in San Francisco. Young, afraid, and new to the city, I was unsure where left or right would lead me. Eventually, I spied the red lights of stripper Carol Doda's pert nipples, flashing in the darkness on the large Condor Club sign like a compass—true north! I found my way back to my new apartment off Union Street, and that night I was mighty glad for neon.

The newspaper photograph announcing a Tracey Emin art show at the Museum of Contemporary Art in Miami made me see neon as more than a means of getting home. Though at first glance it appeared glib, at second glance it was revelatory. The top line of pink neon text was crossed out, making it difficult to read the words "Love not a flower;" below that was "Sorry" on a line by itself; and below that "Flowers die."[13] What Emin's work did for me was, without a flower in sight, make me not only see the blooms themselves, but contemplate their inevitable decline and return to the earth, like all living things—and to think about what it means to love when all life eventually ends. In this way, one form disclosed to me what another form couldn't. Reappropriating a form, such as neon, was enlivening; something usually taken for granted no longer was.

WHAT IF: UNLEASHED POSSIBILITY

One thing I know for certain about the imagination is that it doesn't like a leash, not even one made of the softest leather. Don't offer it a diamond-studded collar, either; it'll just squirm out. The imagination isn't a dog who'll obediently sit when you tell it to, nor politely wag its tail. This dog drools, does things in public you never would. Your imagination will never be free from the flea's bite. Sometimes you'll be able to scratch it, while other times your reach won't be nearly long enough. If you were to tame your imagination, it would curl up on the floor and not even chase the cat in its dream. It would lose both its bark and bite, no longer surprising you with its antics.

Art generates from the question "what if?" When we question basic assumptions, imaginative thinking and art can flourish. Let yourself gnaw on the bone of unrestrained possibility. If we quickly rush to this or that conclusion; limit ourselves with preconceived notions; or try to make art nice and tidy, predictable or formulaic, the imagination will retreat from the process and the finished product will end up flat, lifeless, and uninspired. "Don't hurry me," says the imagination, and "don't pin a name on me too quickly." If we try to tame this nascent impulse, we diminish our own possibility. Authenticity lets in contradiction because life is contradictory. If we welcome that, we're often led to new connections.

I find the rallying cry that declares art must be in service of any particular cause to be barking up the wrong tree. Make art and see what happens, that's my rallying cry! Though it may get co-opted by various causes, ultimately, as I see it, art is always for art's free-roaming, unleashed, curiosity-at-the-helm sake, and it's enough for art to stand thusly. Our best work will come without having a rigid agenda. It will come through curiosity and exploration. Let the work come to you. When you let your creative nature hold sway, the imagination can roam freely and thrive. This way, through the art you make you may be, as the Polish poet Anna Swir said, "Happy/ as a dog's tail."[14]

"A RIDDLE, WRAPPED IN A MYSTERY"

Many artists have chosen to spend their entire lives working in obscurity, because for them the making of art is a satisfying end in itself, to give form to what had been formless. But far more have been unable, for one reason or another, to succeed in bringing their work into the larger world. I'm often introduced, either in person or through my reading, to enormously talented artists—jazz musicians, nature photographers, a nineteenth-century French painter, and a glass artist, to recall a few—whose work demonstrates no less skill, beauty, and originality than artists we're all familiar with.

I'm reminded of Vivian Maier, a career nanny and photographer whose work was left in a forgotten storage locker for years. The locker holdings were put up for auction and then purchased by John Maloof, who only knew that there were a lot of photographs and negatives in the cache. In fact, the locker contained close to 100,000 pictures, the work of an entirely unknown photographer. Maier picked up her first camera when she was in her early twenties and showed her brilliant work documenting urban life in the second half of the twentieth century to nearly no one.

Long before selfies, there were Maier's self-portraits—mostly taken in shadow, looking in mirrors, or through windows. Did she see herself only by way of reflection? How much did her life's circumstances, taking care of other people's children and living in the families' homes, contribute to her choice or need to keep her photography cloistered away? By living as she did, was she deprived of fully having her own life? We often forget, when we consider external artistic success, all that goes into it. If you don't at first, or ever, make a financial living from your art, how do you live a life centered on it? It's one thing to make the art, it's another thing entirely to get it into the world. The website that features her work calls Vivian Maier "A riddle, wrapped in a mystery, inside an enigma."[15]

Where is the success in all this? Does a lack of fame represent failure? These questions remind me of the line from a Bonnie Raitt song, "What is success? Is it doing your own thing or to join the rest?"[16] What if the work you do brings fruition to your life in ways other than recognition? For some artists, it's a matter of growth and development, naming and witnessing their worlds, of saying, "This is what I love." Might your life itself, the form it's taking, be your greatest imaginative act? Does nature fail because some of her trees come down? Because you haven't, till picking up this book, known my name and my work, does that make me less of a success, though I, for many years, have written seriously and passionately, grown my soul, and worked at my art forms to my best ability?

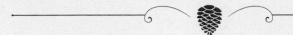

Consider what the word "success" means to you regarding the art you make. Might you have your own new and brilliant definition?

Kurt Vonnegut said, "Practicing an art, no matter how well or badly, is a way to make your soul grow."[17] Much of the value in artistic creation isn't contingent on what happens with that work when we get up from the desk. It's about what gets us to sit down in the first place and what happens while we're there. Whatever forms are yours, if you practice them, the unfamiliar will become less so; what's far will come near. The thing you may have considered peculiar will lose its oddness; your empathy will grow, encompassing what you turned away from before. You may cry more easily and hesitate less to do so; you may stand tall for that which you believe in without a doubt; notice the hidden small things that others might consider inconsequential. Your consciousness will deepen and expand; your relationship with the world around you will, as well. What will float the boat of your art and let you set sail? What form will your imaginative life take?

9

OWL-EYE WINGS AND SHADE-MAKING CACTUS

FOLLOWING NATURE'S LEAD

Life creates conditions conducive to life.
—Janine Benyus

Butterflies keep clean without the use of soap; both thorny devil lizards and camels, as well as many plants, store water without plastic bottles; not only do paper wasps chew up wood and mix it with saliva to build their waterproof nests, but just like humans, they recognize each other's faces; woodpeckers who bang their heads daily never suffer from concussions, thanks to their built-in shock absorbers; saguaro cactuses have ridges along their lengths that protect them from the sun by producing ribbons of shade; the loose skin around the honey badger's neck gives her the flexibility to turn her head nearly all the way around to quickly bite predators sneaking up from behind.

You have to look carefully to see the orange tip butterly *Antho-charis cardamines* if he's on a blossoming mustard flower, because he blends in so well. (Never having been the most highly skilled at blending in, I find this trait particularly compelling.) Then there's nature's ability to transform herself—showcased so strikingly in the owl butterfly. His fearsome "eyes" in the middle of his wings would scare off any predator. The earth can leaf-out and later shrivel; she can glitter and soar. One being can stand on her head quite effortlessly, while another, like me, can't. The closer I look at the huge variety of what nature does, the more enamored and inspired I become.

Thinking about what nature does that we do and don't, I look out my suburban living room window early on the first day of the new year. My young cat was oddly eager to go outside this chilly morning. Why? A flock of turkeys was slowly ambling down the street. Stella's learned to watch out for them since the day she got too close; en masse, they quickly came after her. Now she likes to hide safely underneath my car and watch them walk by, angrily beating her tail against the ground. Those birds carry a hefty load on two spindly legs with no apparent trouble.

I scratch my head; does art ever balance a lot atop a little? Yes, indeed, in many ways. Sculpturally, for sure, and in dance, definitely—think of the ballerina, up on a single toe shoe, though, of course, a dancer is far slighter than a turkey! Consider the popular poetic form from Japan—the haiku—a seventeen-syllable poem that can deliver more than its actual word-weight in merely three lines. Take this one, written by Eleanor Carolan, my writing student who's practiced the form of haiku for many years:

> In spite of the cold
> I walk barefoot into
> the moonlit garden[1]

Three short lines provide a whole constellation of experience. I see the moonlight shining down on her chilled bare feet, and I feel her reluctance to go inside despite the cold. We'll spend this chapter looking at what nature does, how she might inspire us to follow her lead and we'll consider all that art does too.

FROM THE BOTTOM TO THE TOP

What the artist does has its genesis in nature. Humans are emulators, plus—that's how we enhance our skills and extend our reach. Since the beginning of our species, nature has been our primary teacher. The science writer and innovation consultant, Janine Benyus, originator of the term biomimicry, said, "In the natural world, life builds from the bottom up, and it builds in resilience and multiple uses."[2]

Consider the enormous number of shared actions of the world around and within us. There's falling, often without getting hurt—rain, leaves, and birds. Waves curl and so do armadillos. Rivers and gazelles are both great runners. Nature surprises—the owl that swoops down a mere few feet in front of you or the sudden rain squall. Patterns get made and patterns get broken—take "woven" tree limbs, waves on sand, and my cats—both the patterns of their fur and their patterns of behavior. Nature pounces—a lion attacking its prey—and it pounds—a herd of elephants and a single runner's nimble feet. Nature sings—birds, humans, whales, insects, and even gibbons sing.

And there's dancing. Honeybees do the "waggle" dance. Small enough to fit on your fingertip, a peacock spider does an elaborate ritual mating dance, lifting his peacock-colored back into the air and raising his feelers up to shake them, even making music with the vibration from that movement. Put my husband on the dance floor and he'll shake more than a leg. Rattlesnakes slither. When I try getting into a too-tight dress, I slither too. Who knew that having eye-like markings on your wings could make you appear to be someone you are not? Nature fakes it, and I do that too—offered something unappetizing at a dinner party, I pretend to love it. To top it off, nature whoops and hollers, sways. Simply put, nature dazzles us with her moves.

FROM VELCRO TO HOUSE PAINT

In recent years, many industries have begun following nature's lead. Velcro was invented after a hunting trip when a Swiss engineer had to pull a lot of burrs from his dog's fur. He looked at the burrs under a microscope, and children's shoes have never been the same. To reduce the noise on Japanese high-speed trains that was causing passengers awful headaches, a bird-watching engineer redesigned the shape of the train's nose to resemble that of the kingfisher, a bird who is silent upon entering the water when fishing for dinner. From the lotus flower, a German company learned how to make a better paint. Their paint repels dirt naturally with tiny nail-like bumps that mimic the structure of the flower petals' surface.

In his book, *The Shark's Paintbrush: Biomimicry and How Nature Is Inspiring Innovation*, author Jay Harman reminds us that the Aboriginal Australians copied birds' wings for the design of boomerangs. Polynesians looked to floating seedpods as inspiration for their canoes. Might we do the same?[3] Could we employ the sloth's slowness or learn to change as quickly as the chameleon transforms to blend in with her surroundings? Consider some of the other enviable qualities nature possesses that we might incorporate into the art we make—its brilliant sunset colors, the interweaving tapestry of leafless tree limbs, and the precise edges of jutting mountain peaks against the sky. We can copy how the heavy dampness of fog makes a familiar place new again; how a flower bud can look like clasped hands, and a day later transform into splayed rays with a scent that calls from across the room.

ART'S BUILDING BLOCKS

What are the fundamentals of art, its principles, and its building blocks? Like the natural world, art often makes and breaks patterns. It cuts and splits, folds and unfolds, can be symmetrical and asymmetrical. It offers gradations and contours, casts shadows, blends and separates, and creates texture and shape. In art, we see the use of space, unity and a lack of it, emphasis and de-emphasis, and all directions—up, down, left, right, backward, forward. In all the arts, in one way or another, the value of dark, light, intensity, and hue play a part.

Art moves in many ways. Consider how a line of people on a stage or a line on a page—written or drawn—takes you from here to there, often in an instant. There's meter, repetition, rhythm, and the breaking of them. Events may occur in intervals, segments— paragraphs and chapters, lines and stanzas. Art offers us imagery, denotation, and connotation. There are all kinds of relationships in art, just like in a thriving ecosystem—some push us to the very edge of the canvas.

Art conveys emotion, brings us close and turns us away. What pitch is it in, from low to high? Is there harmony in the composition—soft to loud, sequence, tempo—speed, variation, vibration, octave—separation of sound, beat—regular pulse, crescendo and decrescendo, modulation, cadence, phrase, alliteration, tone and mood, structure and style? Whew! Art steals; it sings, clambers up and slides down. It resists and triumphs. Art does; artists do.

And of course, art tells stories—from the most straightforward narratives to the least linear ones. Take the same essence, the same nugget of story, and express it through various forms and the story will transform in as many ways. Stanley Kunitz, who was named US Poet Laureate when he was ninety-five, said, "Poetry, I have insisted, is ultimately mythology, the telling of stories of the soul."[4] Many of the stories of our soul are comprised in large part by the earth, where our lives happen. When Walt Whitman wrote, "Read these leaves in the open air," did he mean his sheets of paper filled with poems, the actual tree leaves, or both? Nature tells stories, too, and since we are nature, our stories are a part of those the earth tells.

WIND THROUGH THE PINES AND
· SEEDS UNDERFOOT

Naturalist and geologist Paul McFarland avidly listens to the wind:

> I've had this notion for some time that you can identify what
> trees you are around by the different sounds they make as
> the wind passes through them . . . I live in the Eastern Sierra
> where the desert rolls up to meet the mountains on the western
> edge of the Great Basin. We are blessed over here with a nice
> diversity of conifers—Jeffrey, lodgepole, limber, whitebark,
> bristlecone, piñon, western white, three kinds of junipers,
> along with two firs and the mountain hemlock. Each has its
> own needle style—differing in number, length, stiffness, and
> relative placement and abundance on their individual branch-
> ing patterns.[5]

The idea that wind's sound might be affected by the kind of
trees it blows through came to McFarland after "too many moments
huddled in a copse of whitebark while alpine winds blasted over the
Sierra crest." Brrr! If I'd been the huddling me, I doubt I'd have been
such a careful listener.

> You can tell the type of pine forest you are in by the pitch of the
> windsong—the individual hum, buzz, hiss, or *shwoosh* made as
> the wind blows through the conifer foliage. In general, the lon-
> ger the needle, the lower pitch the song; the shorter the needle,
> the higher pitch the song. Stopping to listen to what the trees
> have to say and being able to differentiate their voices is just
> another way of talking with the land, of being not just in place
> but part of a place. Encouraging folks to be outside, listening
> to what the land has to say and talking with it, is something we
> need now more than ever.[6]

Through his relationship to the trees, McFarland has shown us that nature creates her own symphony if only we prick up our ears.

In a scene from the movie *American Beauty*, a lonely high school student, a young filmmaker, shows his newest work to a friend. As though sitting beside them, we watch his brief film of wind filling and tossing a white plastic bag along a stretch of gray concrete; red autumn leaves are blown by the wind too. The young man finds beauty and story in nature and even in an object we'd rather not see blowing in the wind—a plastic bag. He says,

> One of those days when it's a minute away from snowing. There's electricity in the air; you can almost hear it. This bag was just dancing with me like a little kid . . . That's the day I realized there was this entire life behind things, this incredibly benevolent force that wanted me to know there was no reason to be afraid . . . Sometimes there is so much beauty in the world.[7]

FORAGE, SALVAGE, SAVE

When the winter holidays come around, the card I look most forward to is the one Bernice sends. She includes a handwritten letter on handmade paper that tells me about her year and all I've missed. Her envelopes are always full of surprises too. Once, she sent an old family letter, written in flourished script on onionskin paper. Usually, there's a small collection of postage stamps—old ones, from far away. This year there was a slip of green-and-white crocheted lace. All of what she sends, sooner or later, gets worked into a collage because her gifts inspire me.

Occasionally, I've come across seedpods in the woods—about an inch and a half long and about an inch around, oval-shaped. They're hard and have irregular ridges. Shake one and you've got a tiny marimba. Their silver-gray-green color was my favorite part until I opened one up. Cutting carefully around the circumference of the pod, I splayed it open. Inside was another pod—brown and hairy, difficult to remove from its mother pod. Cutting that inner pod open, an insect-like thing fell onto the table. Oval-shaped, also, but far more intricately designed than either of its bigger pieces. This brown-black bit looked as if it had wings pressed close to its body. A bunch of tiny black seeds fell onto the table. I don't know what, given a chance, they'd grow into. Perhaps I'll plant some and see what happens. These seedpods are small wonders—one of many I encounter almost daily. Some days, it's the sound of wind or the possibility of a found seedpod that gets me out the door.

Humans and squirrels aren't the only ones who forage, salvage, and save. Ravens, magpies, raccoons, and ferrets fancy shiny objects—even rats do. I've heard that ravens gather materials to decorate their nests. Most famously, male Australian Bowerbirds gather objects, particularly blue ones, to create structures designed to attract mates. The most elaborate, ornate constructions get the girl.

The odds and ends that nature provides as fodder for our imaginations are not always things we pick up and carry with us, in the physical sense. One morning, the Brazilian artist Jarbas Agnelli, who communicates his ideas through film, photography, and music, saw a flock of birds sitting on the electric wires outside his window. Agnelli says, "I was just curious to hear what melody the birds were creating."[8] He took a picture of them and, using the birds' location on the wire as notes, he wrote the music. The result was a sweet melody that sounds a bit like Gamelan music.

If you haven't yet begun to gather objects for inspiration, give it a try. If your dwelling place is a small one, no worries. Just take a notebook out with you wherever you go and write down or sketch what you see—from nature or a city street—that strikes your fancy, the things you'd take home, if you could. These will lead you to the next place your imagination's gearing up to take you.

Challenge yourself to gather one or two inspirational items—physical or otherwise—from your surroundings each day. A pretty stone on the beach, the distinctive call of a bird, a leaf found on your favorite trail; whatever speaks to you.

What if we wrote a story *with* the trees? Or painted a picture using berries for paint? Might we translate the wind into words, dance, or song? Explore the different ways in which you might directly engage with nature to create your art.

NATURE, TIME, AND DORMANCY

If you've been away from art-making lately, for whatever reason, and are feeling poorly about it, think of the queen bee. She finds herself a private, dark, and quiet spot to spend an entire six to eight months in hibernation. Or consider the cicadas, who live underground for nineteen years. After the ground reaches sixty-four degrees, they emerge, only to live above the earth for a few weeks. Outside, so much unseen work takes place underground when there's no evidence above; the same holds true for us.

The roses in my mother-in-law's garden are spectacular—abundant in summer and so fragrant, but they're not always in bloom, and the apricots on her tree—the ones the squirrels don't get to first—are delicious, but only come in spring. Constant output is impossible. If your creative impulse has gone temporarily dormant, that's a good time for editing and revising, cataloging, considering future projects, or just being out in the natural world to take it all in and to devote yourself to supporting that world. There's the business side of an imaginative life to deal with too—have you got enough paper? Are your pencils sharp? Is there a book you've been longing to read?

A mother bird will nudge her nestling toward flight, as we may need to nudge ourselves every now and then. Part of living a life of imagination is recognizing the difference between a brief mulling over, a fallow period, and pure, unfettered procrastination. They may all look the same from the outside, but dig down and you'll find there's quite a difference. The act of engaging your imagination is often just the thing after you realize you've held off for long enough.

Take a little idea—the color lemon yellow, a spiraling seashell—and dangle it in front of yourself. Bait your imagination and then hold on. What emerges?

The natural world can change our perception of time. Nature's not in a rush; time moves in its own time in the natural world. The determining factors aren't ours—there are no minute and second hands, more like leaf and sand hands. The subdued light of the forest alters my experience of time—morning or afternoon? The famous English author, John Fowles, wrote a book about nature and art, *The*

Tree. There he said, ". . . trees warp time, or rather create a variety of times: here dense and abrupt, there calm and sinuous—never plodding, mechanical, inescapably monotonous."[9] This viewpoint helps me to not hurry or feel impatient. In the awareness of the eons, how nicely, how slowly, I am put in my place.

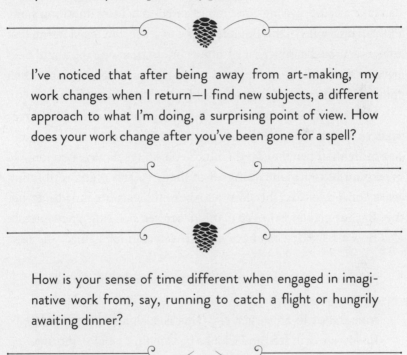

I've noticed that after being away from art-making, my work changes when I return—I find new subjects, a different approach to what I'm doing, a surprising point of view. How does your work change after you've been gone for a spell?

How is your sense of time different when engaged in imaginative work from, say, running to catch a flight or hungrily awaiting dinner?

THE TIME IT TAKES: UNCOVERING THE NATURE OF YOUR IMAGINATIVE PROCESS

Making art can take a long time. For me, there's the first draft—that blush of here's-what-I've-got-to-say-and-here's-how-I'll-say-it—but after getting the initial words down, I often realize I've not quite said what I set out to. The flush of inspiration causes the artist to race to her materials. There's no better feeling! What follows, of course, is the reality of the entirety of the imaginative process. A single poem may take hours; it may take days, weeks, or years. I might write a poem, put it away to ferment, take it out days later, and realize it's in need of this and that and, after tending to it, put it back undercover again. The goal is always for my writing to become itself, and that can take a lot of revising. I'm embarrassed to tell you how long some of the paragraphs in this book took me to write; but considering that to make a sixteen ounce jar of honey, more than one thousand bees have to travel over one hundred thousand miles to visit more than four million flowers, I'm comforted by the slowness of things.

Master painting conservator Gu Xiang-mei works for the Freer Gallery, which is part of the Smithsonian Museum of Asian Art and has more than two thousand Chinese paintings in its collection. Gu is responsible for maintaining all of them.[10] After doing restoration work for forty years, she says that she's still learning how to do her job. Big Sur painter Erin Lee Gafill described painting a new picture and how art-making can have its own determining nature. She says,

> Art-making is asking, not telling, and it's a thrilling question. Sometimes a painting just wants to get a little nostalgic and time travels to an earlier era. This is such a painting, and I finally gave it its lead and let it go back in time—old California, East of Ventana, near Big Sur. I really wrestled with it, even painting it over completely at one point so that I could begin again without attachment to its roots or waywardness. But the painting immediately went back to where it had gone before. And so I tipped my hat to it and let it go.[11]

The picture she's referring to is a landscape, "a nostalgic light, the colors of hills in drought, a waiting sky."[12] The hills are dotted with trees and the sky looks tumultuous—perhaps a storm is on its way? Those hills, those trees, that particular tumultuous sky—they had their own agenda, and Gafill let that agenda speak through her as she created, freeing the painting's story with her brushes.

Often, I'm writing or making a collage and suddenly it's as if a cloud lifts, allowing me to see what I'm doing and where I'm going. In those moments, I get a bit of valuable distance from my process that helps me know where to go next. Other times, I start out with a pretty clear sense of what I want to do, but the work takes over and directs me, as Gafill described. At times, I experience a conflict between where I want to go and where the piece wants to go. I've found that under those circumstances it is best to let go of my tight grip of the reins and allow myself to be swept away by my imagination itself, like a leaf on a sudden breeze—a heady experience. This is the true nature of art-making, and when the call comes, I feel lucky and want to answer, expressing my imagination and spirit through my chosen forms. Why resist such goodness?

10

KNOWING THE WORLD
AND OURSELVES

OUR FIVE-PLUS SENSES

Put your ear down close to your soul and listen hard.
—Anne Sexton

We live in our senses. That's our first knowing of the world. What we experience through one sense can be entirely different from what we discover through another. What your ears know is not what your eyes know, and your eyes perceive uniquely from how your hands do, which is not the same as what your nose tells you, which is close to, but not quite the awareness that comes through your tongue. Your fingers experience a dried leaf as rough and brittle; your eyes know it as curled and brown. What your ears tell you beachside—that the waves are raucous and a storm is coming in—isn't what your feet appreciate about the sand—that it's warm and soothing and you never want to wear shoes again. Our senses work in concert with each other, bringing us ever closer to the world around and within us.

Five senses—that's the number I was taught, but some claim we have many more: knowing where you are with your eyes closed, a sense of balance, that oh-so-impossible-to-forget sense of time. Thirst and hunger are senses, too, as is the ability to feel pain (nociception), and the awareness of where all the parts of our bodies are (proprioception).

Just as we know the world through our senses, so the earth knows the world through hers. When I walk through dry leaves along the forest path, the birds, hearing my footsteps, skitter away. Owls will call back and forth as I'm walking until I stop; then they do too. I know there's at least one mountain lion living around Jacks Peak Park. She can hear me long before I'll ever hear her, and, more than likely, will disappear before I can catch a glimpse. The sights, sounds, textures, smells, and tastes of the natural world tell us much about ourselves. Do we learn tenacity and endurance from the trees' ability to weather rough wind?

The first word Helen Keller learned when she was a young girl was *water*. Her teacher, Annie Sullivan, placed Keller's hand beneath the well spout. Keller wrote,

> As the cool stream gushed over one hand, she spelled into the other the word water, first slowly, then rapidly. I stood still, my whole attention fixed upon the motions of her fingers. Suddenly I felt a misty consciousness as of something forgotten—a thrill of returning thought; and somehow the mystery of language was revealed to me.[1]

Though Keller could neither see nor hear, she could feel, and she made the connection. Sullivan opened a door into Keller's life and from there, the world.

"The things we see, hear, smell, and touch affect us long before we believe anything at all," wrote the author Flannery O'Connor.[2] Each sense—seeing, tasting, smelling, hearing, and touching—can be awakened and developed, and by doing so, brought into the service of the imagination. From the sound of your mother's voice to the look in her eye, from the clank and hiss of an approaching train to the scent of your father's cologne, from ice clinking in a glass to the soft stillness of flannel against your baby cheek, and from the feel of wind's rush to the scent of pine stirred by that wind: all this wends its way into who we are and how we perceive the world.

The natural world educates us in being attentive to our senses. When I walk in a new place, I notice how much more alert I am than in familiar locales—the newness perks up my senses. Ahead, we'll look at our senses' nuanced beauty and the seamless link they provide to our imaginations.

THE SCENT OF LILIES

Early one morning, I padded into the dark living room, and before I could reach for the light switch, I felt myself slip back in time, returning to the New York City apartment where my family lived when I was a child. Without at first understanding why, I was suddenly inside the red brick building on Bennett Avenue. This wasn't a dream carried into waking. It was the tall green vase brimming with slender-stemmed lilies that, until this morning, had been fist-tight and now were opening, to fill the room with their distinctive scent. I don't remember my mother ever placing lilies in our living room. But when I put my face near these flowers, memory was awakened. I see myself standing in my black patent leather shoes; there's the touch of my father's hand on my shoulder and the sound of my mother singing.

I wish I could lift the bouquet from the vase and reach across the page so you could smell them. The appearance of the flowers isn't difficult to describe—five yellow-white, oval, pointed petals on each bloom; each one is larger than my open hand; the upright stamens extend from the middle. These lilies stand over a foot tall; their leaves are long and pointy. About fifteen blooms—some open and others waiting their turn.

How to describe a flower's scent? We humans don't have as developed a sense of smell as other animals do. Bears are the land animals who are best at this—they're able to catch a scent from eighteen miles away. Polar bears can smell something that's three feet underwater. Through their sense of smell, elephants can find water that's twelve miles away, and then remember its location for the next time they're thirsty. We can distinguish many scent differences—sharp, tangy, sweet, rich. There's a great difference between citrus and antiseptic scents. Just the word "gaseous" written down may make your stomach turn. There aren't a whole lot of words to describe scent very specifically, though. Some scents aren't simple, but present our noses with various "hues" simultaneously. Oftentimes, the way we can best describe scent is through comparison. "The lilies smell like my childhood." This, too, is narrow—my childhood flowers may not smell like those from yours. Though we may lack the ability to capture a scent in words, one thing is clear: the smell of something can bring back a rush of memory faster than most anything else, and from that rush of memory often comes the inspiration to record, however imperfectly. According to Annie Paul Murphy in "Your Brain on Fiction" from *The New York Times*, scientists have discovered that stories affect many parts of our brains they had not before known were affected, "suggesting why the experience of reading can feel so alive. Words like 'lavender,' 'cinnamon,' and 'soap,' for example, elicit a response not only from the language-processing areas of our brains, but also those devoted to dealing with smells."[3]

Since I can't reach across the page and the miles and the days to give you these lilies, what words might do the trick? They're not as powdery smelling as a rose; spicy like a carnation, they have an uplifting odor. Their sweetness is heavy but not enough to make one want to walk away. They give off a tart greenness. Can something smell green? It is akin to a bright newness, especially when they've just opened. After a while, the green scent will be gone. Then they'll smell like the third day of my grandfather's wake. Just the thought of it and I'm back, grieving, a young woman standing next to my father in a dark room beside an open casket in Queens, New York, during a humid summer.

WHAT IS MY SONG?

In northern Namibia along the banks of the Kunene River live the semi-nomadic Himba tribe, one of the few groups of people who count a child's birthday, not as the day they were born, nor from the day of their conception but from the first day the child was thought of by her mother.

According to *uMthwakazi Review*, a Zimbabwean periodical, when a woman decides to conceive, she goes off by herself and sits under a tree, where "she listens until she can hear the song of the child that wants to come."[4] Then she sings the song to the man who will be the father, teaching it to him. When they make love, they invite the child into their lives by singing the song. Once she's pregnant, she teaches it to the midwives who will welcome the baby into the community by singing the song when the child is born. The entire village learns the song over time so that "If the child falls, or hurts its knee, someone picks it up and sings its song to it. Or perhaps the child does something wonderful, or goes through the rites of puberty. Then, as a way of honoring this person, the people of the village sing his or her song."[5]

If this person grows up and commits a crime,

> . . . the individual is called to the center of the village and the people in the community form a circle around them. Then they sing their song to them. The tribe recognizes that the correction for antisocial behavior is not punishment; it is love and the remembrance of identity. When you recognize your own

song, you have no desire or need to do anything that would hurt another.[6]

Much like the concept of *idée fixe* that we talked about earlier, certain songs sing to each of us. A lullaby, a jazz riff, a blues melody, the sound of your mother's voice, or the crashing of the waves at your favorite beach—we're all listening for something.

SIGHT, MEMORY, AND IMAGINATION: WHAT WE'RE BLIND TO AND WHAT WE SEE

Objects in the mirror are closer than they appear—the text on our cars' side-view mirrors leads me to think about human blind spots—we're all blind to something. Everyone has actual blind spots in their eyes; the other eye will compensate for what one can't see. Something can be only inches away from me, but I don't see it at all until it's pointed out. This is literally as well as metaphorically true.

Seeing is a process, not a state we're born into. Author Rosemary Mahoney, in an interview about her new book, *For the Benefit of Those Who See: Dispatches from the World of the Blind*, put it this way:

> We are not born with effective vision. The human infant has to learn how to see . . . We learn how to see in a way that's very similar to the way we learn how to speak. It takes a couple of years. If the brain is deprived of this visual information at a very young age, it can never learn how to see again."[7]

There are also those larger blind spots we all experience in life, when we get taken by surprise by what we never thought would happen. Time and distance mutate perspective, and these alterations can infiltrate our imaginative work. Through making art, we may find what we thought was empty space is actually full of vibrancy and possibility.

My student Kathleen Blount had no memory of the day her beloved brother suddenly died. Understandably, this distressed her. Close to tears, wanting to write about her loss, she kept coming up empty: "I don't remember any of it. That entire day is gone to me, and so is my brother."

It was painful to see her trying so hard to live with both her brother's death and her inability to remember its details. Our minds can shield us that way, which is helpful, up to a point. Once the emotional trauma is no longer acute, art-making can be a way to complete one's healing.

"Write, 'I don't remember,'" I suggested to Kathleen.

She looked at me, perplexed. "What do you mean? I just don't remember. You want me to write that?"

What I suggested, I'm sure, seemed ridiculous. But I persisted. "Yes, start with those exact words, 'I don't remember' and write what you've forgotten, such as 'I don't remember what time of day it was,' and 'I don't remember where I was when I got the call.' Just keep writing everything you don't remember, and you will remember. You will remember all you're ready to know."

I could only suggest this to Kathleen because of my experience as both a writer and teacher. She took my suggestion and emailed me a few days later. "I remember," Kathleen wrote, "I remember it all!" Not only did the details of that day return to her, she also wrote a lovely tribute poem to the brother she so missed. Whether writing's the form that you're drawn to or not, writing down what has been forgotten may enhance your art.

Here's an excerpt from Kathleen's poem, "A Shattering":

> I don't remember picking blueberries
> Or that the August day warmed us,

Or laughing with Amanda . . .

I don't remember her saying my name
I do remember her voice faraway
Down the echo of a tunnel,
"Hugh died this morning."[8]

THE SCENT OF A WOMAN

Scent is the first sense to develop *in utero*. According to Dr. Alan Greene, a clinical professor at Stanford University, "By the end of the first trimester, baby can smell foods that Mom is eating. It's the predominant sense, very early on, because smells cross the amniotic fluid."[9] Through scent, newborns can even distinguish the difference between their own mother's milk and that of another woman.

Is part of the job of our senses to help us identify what's ours, to whom and what we belong? Scent is a major component in the formation of relationships; we're attracted to those whose scents are partially immunologically dissimilar to ours but with whom we have some genes in common. Typically, our noses steer us in the right direction when it comes to picking a reproductively compatible partner.[10] I remember when Michael and I first got close that I thought he smelled good. Years later, I still love putting my nose against his skin.

Shortly before she died, my mother was hospitalized. When she was conscious, we shared songs and memories—glimpses of happiness. Just before her death, I went to her house to pick something up. From the bottom of her dresser drawer I pulled out a sweater— one with decorative stitching down the front. She'd bought it before she'd been married, back when she was able to spend her money on beautiful clothes; she'd not worn it for years. I brought the sweater home and slipped it under my pillow. Every night after a long day at her bedside, I climbed into bed and breathed in the scent of my mother until, many weeks after her death, that familiar smell—a mix of Chanel No. 5 and garlic with a hint of smoke and a whiff of cheap sherry—was gone. But the memory remains.

THE SOUND OF IT: LATE AFTERNOON, TWENTY-THREE SOUNDS

How many sounds does a day have? Shortly before beginning a recent forest walk, I heard myself say out loud: "There, there." I tend to speak my mind without thinking, but this was not exactly that; more like a parent trying to calm a hurt child. Once my feet found the trail, I calmed. There, each thing has its place; each sound has ample space around it. That late afternoon, over the course of a brief hour, I counted twenty-three sounds: scrub jays in the bushes; mourning doves at a distance; something like a cricket, only not a cricket; two birds in the brush sounding like little girls in the corner of a room sharing a secret—with a rushing rise and fall of their voices, shared excitement over the thing that cannot wait to be said; yet another bird sounded like blowing bubbles through a straw at the bottom of a near-empty glass; wind late to get to its next appointment; one bird's voice is a blown kiss; traffic on some road I'd already forgotten existed; a small someone hopping in the bramble; a woodpecker knocking against a tree; my own footsteps; an airplane taking off—oh, poor travelers, moving at such unnatural speeds, desiring another location; twigs falling; a pinecone rolling downhill; a high-pitched cry, but I don't know whose; more wind rushing through the Monterey pines; a loud chorus of jays when I unexpectedly interrupted them; my car door opening, shutting, a responsive engine; tires on gravel; the sound of me reluctantly going home but happy. My own song: sighing appreciatively for having heard these twenty-three sounds.

BARE FEET AND FALLING WATER

"[W]e had worn our bare feet/ bare..." writes Anne Sexton in her summertime love poem, "I Remember."[11] All the places their feet must have touched! A gentle hand on the shoulder of someone who's sad can make the tears come harder. In addition to cooing, isn't touch the way to soothe a troubled baby? From bare feet on wild grass to your body skimming along the icy sidewalls of caves, how many ways there are to touch and be touched in nature, and how differently feet know the grass from how the cheek does.

In Robert Macfarlane's book *The Wild Places*, he reminds us of the value of the real, not second- or thirdhand, but firsthand experience. In some cities, where the lights are always on, children may never see the stars, or catch only a few bright ones now and again. Macfarlane writes, "We have in many ways forgotten what the world feels like."[12]

Just what does it feel like? If we were to touch a hundred things today (and we might), and record those sensations, how might we increase our sense of connectivity to the planet—literally and spiritually?

THE DEPARTMENT OF NOISE ABATEMENT

Tucked away from view at the San Francisco Airport is the Noise Abatement Office. Because of my neighbor, with his Harley Davidson motorcycle and his cadre of friends with their loud bikes and their propensity to go inside to visit while leaving their bike motors running and to then come back outside and rev their engines for each other's pleasure, which is, need I say, not my pleasure, I wish I had a Noise Abatement Department in my front yard that came with a neon sign signaling "Keep it Down, Please!" Instead, I fume and feel frustrated. Maybe if I went over with a dish of chocolate chip cookies and said, "Please," that would be better than a Noise Abatement Department, except my cookies aren't that good.

Not every airport has such a department; only the busiest and noisiest ones do. Because of San Francisco's cool fog, which makes sound travel quickly and farther, this department at SFO is busy. Additionally, to make the airport less of an ear-sore to neighbors, $136 million was spent to insulate the nearby homes.

Many artists listen to music when they work; others keep the television on, because the background noise supports their process. The poet Philip Levine writes into the night, listening to jazz. Others go to a café to work, surrounded by coffee-guzzling humans, and find inspiration in that cacophony. In *Annie Hall*, Woody Allen's character said that he couldn't have sex in the country because it was too quiet there. But could he write? Some of us are more sensitive to noise than others. Usually, when I'm writing, anything louder than my purring cats is unwelcome noise—it's plenty loud enough in my head. Some days, there's a crowd in there. Oddly, writing this book, I could be at a busy railway station and I don't think I'd be too bothered. I've ignored plenty that's gone on around me over these many months and continued writing happily, even those damn motorcycles.

EATING THE EARTH

On a September holiday in Umbria, Italy—during truffle season—Michael and I decided to try them. We chose the black ones, as their flavor is stronger than the more delicate white ones—I don't always trust myself with subtlety. Anytime I eat something expensive, I'm determined to like it. The first time I tasted caviar was during a Paris winter, when I was young. My girlfriend and I went for lunch to her just-widowed mother's apartment. After dishing out small dollops of caviar to my sweetheart and me, the widow dragged the tub of caviar close to her and, spoonful-by-tiny-spoonful, inhaled it all.

The Umbrian truffles came shaved on top of a bed of fettuccini. With my taste buds on alert, I picked up the truffle flakes. The feeling in my mouth was gritty, unpleasant on my tongue and against my teeth; it felt like dirt, and the taste was nothing much. Because it was a delicacy, I couldn't write off what I was eating, so I gave it more attention than I would have eating the tried and true. And there was something oddly appealing about the sense of eating the earth.

There's a word for this: "geophagy." I've known pregnant women who've taken to bringing a spoon with them into the garden to eat bits of soil, as doing so satisfies a nutritional need, and perhaps an elemental one as well. Of course, children eat dirt too. Geophagy has roots in both health and culture; people around the world eat clay and dirt. In some places, it's a part of religious ceremonies, and in others, it's a remedy for illness. The clay eaten in places in Africa contains such minerals as magnesium, phosphorus, and potassium. The Pomo people of northern California added soil to ground acorns to neutralize the acorns' acidity. Despite our nature to turn up our noses at what we don't understand, the imagination says: Don't turn away. Take another bite. What's to be found on the other side of revulsion?

SENSE MEMORY

My hands were happy in the hot, sudsy dishwater when I heard an unseen bird in the backyard call out. She was shouting, "Do it now! Do it now!" Whatever that bird was instructing me to do, I doubt it was the dishes.

On a rainy day, another bird—one I've heard many times—called out to me. Like a banana slug, he favored being out in the weather, and his chirp sounded just like the scrunched-up newspaper squeak on glass when washing windows. That thought sparked a memory of how my mother and I washed windows together when I was a child— she was on one side and I on the other. She'd point at a spot I'd missed or I would, and we'd scrub until there was nothing but the hard illusion of separation between us. A singing bird on a wet morning took me back in time. You'd probably hear something else in that bird's sharp squeaky sound, based on your experience. Is it the sound of knives being sharpened or the squeal of a car's braking tires on a wet road? Our senses have an amazing ability to reconnect us to our pasts.

If one sense is lost to us, another one fills the gap. A big old lab walked right up to me on Lower Ridge Trail one day, putting her muzzle into my open, waiting hand. I noticed her eyes were milky. Along came two other dogs, followed by their person, an elderly man, who said, "That's Molly; she's totally blind. But she's got a great memory! She remembers just where there are logs blocking the trail and jumps right over them."

"She certainly knows this trail; she walks with confidence. I'd never have guessed she couldn't see," I said.

"Not just this trail," he said proudly. "We walk in lots of places; Molly remembers them all."

As reported on NPR, in a recent study, scientists from Johns Hopkins University and the University of Maryland found that mice who were kept in the dark, deprived of visual stimulus, had an increase in their ability to hear.[13] If people with hearing problems were placed in dark rooms for periods of time, their hearing might improve as well—even those who'd not had success with cochlear implants could benefit from this treatment. Evidence demonstrates that people who are blind from birth hear exceptionally well; much better than those of us with sight. When we block one or more sense, whether by choice or by circumstance, the others often rally to make up the difference, like Molly and her exceptional knowledge of the paths she walks. Someday, I'm going to stay up all night and write in the darkness. Deprivation can strengthen our longing for what's missing. There's grist for the artistic mill in that.

Take a look at *Nocturne: A Journey in Search of Moonlight*, by James Attlee. He goes searching for places dark enough to truly see the night sky. If you have access to such places where you live or within traveling distance, seek them out and find what you discover there.

James Attlee, *Nocturne: A Journey in Search of Moonlight* (Chicago: University of Chicago Press, 2011).

"O, TASTE AND SEE!"

That's what poet Denise Levertov said: "O, taste and see!" And don't we?[14] One sense will carry another in its arms. In this passage from his travel writing on Italy, D. H. Lawrence describes a visual scene, but what comes along are smell and taste. "And in the marketplace they were selling chestnuts wholesale, great heaps of bright, brown chestnuts, and sacks, and peasants very eager selling and buying."[15] Reading that excerpt, I can smell them roasting and taste the warm earthiness of their Christmas flavor.

Some people have synesthesia, the transfering between senses, when one sense activates another. Letters and numbers can be associated with color. Scents can be seen. Sounds can have taste. There's a sommelier named Jaime Smith who sees the colors of the wines that cross his palate. He described a particular white wine as "beautiful aquamarine. . ."[16] Nabokov had this ability. He said that the long sound of the letter *A* in English "has for me the tint of weathered wood, a French *A* evokes polished ebony."[17] Composer George Gershwin saw musical notes in color. So did Franz Liszt, who asked musicians, "a little bluer, if you please."[18] A woman I know woke up with synesthesia one day and it wasn't a happy occurrence. In addition to hearing the garbage truck, she could suddenly taste the garbage!

When creating a piece of art, experiment with your senses. Bring in one you don't usually consider. What's the scent of a trumpet? If the night sky had a taste, what would it be? What sound does the color orange make?

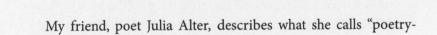

My friend, poet Julia Alter, describes what she calls "poetry-induced synesthesia":

To me, feelings are always colors . . . The feeling actually becomes the color. And nature, most of the time, is song, or a type of music. The leaves in wind are an orchestra of violins. The red of the rose is a hallelujah gospel choir. My children's raucous laughter bathes the room in lemony light. When I slip into that deep well of writing, where I have no edges and am squinting the world away because I am in the swim of the verse, this is how I experience the world.[19]

Synesthetes are not the only people who can experience the world through unusual relationships to the senses. Because most of us see, feel, smell, taste, and hear the world in the usual human ways (unlike say, birds, who can see ultraviolet light, or snakes who, at night, can see heat, or rats whose eyes see independently of each other), bringing imaginative thinking into the picture makes our mindsets more expansive. When I get stuck in what I'm doing, I try to take some advice from Sylvia Plath and ". . . wait and live harder, eyes, ears, and heart open, and when the productive time comes, it is that much richer."[20] Taking time to experience the world anew through all of our senses can bring our imaginations back from wherever they go when they hide from us.

I OBTAINED THE MELODY OF THE PAST WITH MY HAND

As a grown man the French author and artist Jean Cocteau returned to the village he'd grown up in, where as a boy he'd walked along familiar streets, trailing his finger against the walls of the buildings on familiar streets. But upon his return, it wasn't till he bent his knees and touched the walls at a height closer to that which he'd reached as a boy that his childhood memories returned:

"Just as the needle picks up the melody from the record, I obtained the melody of the past with my hand. I found everything: my cape, the leather of my satchel, the names of my friends and of my teachers, certain expressions I had used, the sound of my grandfather's voice, the smell of his beard, the smell of my sister's dresses and of my mother's gown."[21]

Connecting to our senses can return our lives to us, enhancing our imaginations and deepening our creative expression.

In order to balance the important and not-so-important external duties and details of life, we'll benefit from employing all we have at hand to achieve artistic and spiritual equilibrium. Just noticing and developing our senses—including our inner sense of knowing—

will give our creative lives ballast. We'll be inspired by the feel of
moss beneath our feet, the sound of rolling rocks, the scent of pine
in view of the trees. Consider Ed, an elderly, retired forest ranger in
Snohomish County, Washington, who had a wish before dying—to
be among nature. Area firefighters wheeled him along a forest trail
in his hospital bed on a final sojourn and, rubbing their hands on the
pine fronds, brought their hands close, returning Ed's beloved trees
to him one last time.[22]

11

A STRANGE FRENZY IN MY HEAD

INSPIRATION AND INTUITION

There's a strange frenzy in my head of birds flying.
—Rumi

That strange frenzy in my head—a rush and whir—Rumi's birds of inspiration have flown in!

It's said that the ancient Celtic poets would lie down with a blanket over themselves, and when inspiration struck, they'd throw the covers off, and jump up, shouting, "There's a fire in my head!" I know that feeling. The word 'inspire' comes from Latin, meaning "to breathe upon or into something." What, just moments ago, appeared ordinary has become startling and new. We wonder, "How could I not have noticed that before?" An inspired thought arrives as if from nowhere, or so it seems—there is no conscious progression that leads us to it. Inspiration sends a bucket down into the well of buried possibilities. We'll spend this chapter discovering the authentic link between listening to your intuition and being inspired.

When we feel inspired, we're actually experiencing intuition at work—gaining access to a level of awareness that lets us make connections we otherwise wouldn't. Inspiration is intuition in action. The ability to channel intuition into inspiration and then onward into creative output of all kinds occurs when we're willing to suspend disbelief,[1] as the nineteenth-century poet Samuel Taylor Coleridge put it. Nature can put us in this receptive state of mind, allowing us access to this elevated awareness. Away from our familiar territory, we may be more receptive to that which is beyond explanation. About inspiration, Joyce Carol Oates said, "Yes, it exists. Somehow."[2] In remembering Philip Seymour Hoffman, John le Carré said that Hoffman's "intuition was luminous from the instant you met him."[3]

My favorite thing about art-making may be the often subjectless impulse that says: sing, make, speak, dance. Your subject is there, it's just hidden in some tunnel of the self where it joins the world. If you lean in, senses open and intuition unblocks, so what's next can follow. Given the chance, what wants or needs to be said will be. To go there, you don't need to know how to go, because the making of art is a process of wandering toward and around, backing away from, and sidling up to that which is there for your saying. Poet Donald Hall refers to poetry as "The Unsayable Said," and this applies to all art forms.[4] Art is often created out of a composite of feelings, experiences, observations, and intuitions. You include a dash from over there and a hint from over here. It cannot be gotten to through a prescriptive plan; it needs to be encountered, to be happened upon.

If we stop ourselves or censor our inspired possibilities, we experience a contraction that doesn't just put the brakes on one thought, but on a whole slew of imaginative thinking. Rather, consider the word "play" in relation to the chain reaction of intuition, inspiration, and creativity. In *Dinner with Lenny* by Jonathan Cott, Leonard Bernstein says, "Play is a very big word. Because we use the word play for music—we play the piano, we play Tchaikovsky's Sixth Symphony. We go to see a Shakespeare play. . ."[5] Art-making is the grown-up's way to engage in play, to follow inspiration's lead, freely taking chances as children at play do, without concern over where you'll end up.

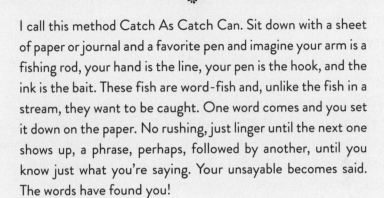

I call this method Catch As Catch Can. Sit down with a sheet of paper or journal and a favorite pen and imagine your arm is a fishing rod, your hand is the line, your pen is the hook, and the ink is the bait. These fish are word-fish and, unlike the fish in a stream, they want to be caught. One word comes and you set it down on the paper. No rushing, just linger until the next one shows up, a phrase, perhaps, followed by another, until you know just what you're saying. Your unsayable becomes said. The words have found you!

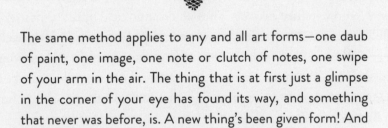

The same method applies to any and all art forms—one daub of paint, one image, one note or clutch of notes, one swipe of your arm in the air. The thing that is at first just a glimpse in the corner of your eye has found its way, and something that never was before, is. A new thing's been given form! And you've arrived at it not by beating yourself over the head, but through play and trusting your imagination.

FIRST INSPIRATIONS

Mr. Thorp, my fifth grade teacher, was a dour man with fat lips that protruded like a frog's. That's not nice of me; but I didn't care for him, nor did he care for me. He wore sandals with no socks every day, even in winter. One Friday, the only worthwhile day of the school week because it always had art in it, we were given a homework assignment to look out a window of our house and draw what we saw.

Outside the big, living room picture window across our small city street was the big, brown-roofed house where an old couple, who rarely came out, lived. I chose a thin piece of charcoal to draw the house, but was unhappy with the inaccuracy of black against white. So I went outside, sat down in our yard, and picked up bits of dirt, rubbed them into the roof. I got excited about how the picture began to take shape, and drew some trees next to the house, not that there were any, but the color was perfect for tree bark too. This was inspiration at work, though I knew neither the word nor the concept.

Proud of my resourcefulness, I handed in my picture on Monday morning, daring to tell Mr. Thorp how I'd done it. He merely raised an eyebrow, looked askance. Though disappointed by his response, it didn't matter. This was the first time I sought approval I didn't really need. The value of what I'd done, the inventiveness of it, was what mattered, and I knew the truth without anyone's help. It would be a long time before I racked up many more such experiences, but it was a first step.

Several years later, seventeen years old and eager to flee my mother's house, I moved north to a land of cold winters. One morning, sitting alone by the fire with the bright February sun flooding in, I felt a distinct sense of inspiration—a mandate to sit down. I grabbed a piece of paper, listened for the rush of words I could barely catch. I didn't have a name for the feeling then, nor did I the many times inspiration arrived like an unexpected visitor bearing gifts over the following years. I'm still discovering my relationship to inspiration today, even though I now call it by its name.

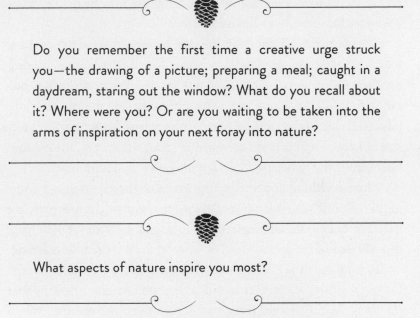

Do you remember the first time a creative urge struck you—the drawing of a picture; preparing a meal; caught in a daydream, staring out the window? What do you recall about it? Where were you? Or are you waiting to be taken into the arms of inspiration on your next foray into nature?

What aspects of nature inspire you most?

ANATOMY OF INSPIRATION

The experience of art-making is quite different from most daily things, which concern themselves with life's outer appearances. Feeling inspired is certainly unlike fretting about a love affair or racing down the freeway to pick something up only to realize the pocket for your wallet's empty. It's a lot like the swooning quality of falling in love. Inspiration is a way of coming up close to something untamed. Every time I think I may have caught inspiration by its powdery wings and begin to feel a bit smug about it, I open my hands to find nothing's there. When I stop clutching at it, inspiration may, like a brilliant butterfly, slip in through a barely opened window. It's not mysterious in that way only; an impulse to create, to express ourselves through this form or that, may come to us from dreams, while preparing dinner, or coping with ill health. We may be led to follow a long tradition or strike out on our own.

The elements of my daily life that inspiration and art-making most resemble are dreams and prayer—even daydreams, staring out the window into the rain, lost in a reverie. When dreaming, our rational minds tune out and we're unrestrained, able to let more possibility in. I love waking from a dream and knowing I've been somewhere else and that the world is greater than my linear mind has ever led me to believe. So it is with letting inspiration in.

Though writing a poem may argue a point, the experience is nothing like arguing with your spouse. A song may arrive late, hair escaping from her once-tidy bun, making no apologies whatsoever. And you, dear servant of the melody, will be grateful for her breathless arrival.

In how much of life, outside of making art, do we long for the just-right word, this perfect sound, or that precise hue, knowing that the route we take to get there may outwit even the creator? When else do we turn a word slowly over again and again in our mouth like an ice cube on a hot summer day? We welcome the unbidden flit of the perfect phrase like a cat's tail whipping around a corner. We leave saucers of milk out at night in hopes of its return. We allow ourselves to freely embrace contradiction, strangeness, uncertainty.

Inspiration can transform a mountain in the distance into an enormous wing or the spine of a giant beast; when you say this vision out loud, you nod your head in recognition. What other moments does life offer to bask in silence, celebrate illogic, delight in the unknown, and feel struck by lightning—without any of the actual fire and little of the burn?

A FOREST OF SIGNS

Art happens at the confluence of intuition, inspiration, intention, and attention. The inspired thought is one that's taken its cue from

intuition; making art proves intuition's veracity. Intuition—a knowing we can't explain—a pure and spontaneous awareness, whose
genesis can't be wholly umderstood. That's part of it, but both
intuition and inspiration are also the result of attentive observa-
tion. When we engage the ways we have of knowing, including our
senses, we're more able to notice subtlety—the feel of something,
its quiet sensibility. The past comes quietly forward; and the future
doesn't hesitate to show its hand, while the present loses some
of its priority. The intuitive mind doesn't question sacred ways of
knowing. We hold the reins on our linear minds with an easier
grip, connecting to our deepest selves and the world. What we get
is nothing counterfeit, only the real thing—golden autumn leaves
swirling at our feet. The surrealist André Breton said that the world
"is a forest of signs."[6] When inspired and following our intuition,
we recognize them.

Some years ago, Michael and I took a holiday to Kona, the big
island of Hawaii. It was our second visit to the quiet neighborhood of
Pahoa. We rented the same small cottage we'd stayed in before, with a
natural swimming pool that filled only when the tide was high. During the last hour of the hours-long drive, with the windows open,
excited to recognize familiar things—like the trees we don't have
at home that form a tunnel of the road and tropical birds calling
out loudly, oddly, we both felt uneasy. Michael wouldn't call himself
intuitive (though I see him that way), but he would acknowledge that
he's observant. The closer we got to the bungalow, the worse we felt:
on edge, jittery, butterflies in the belly, you know.

Pulling into the driveway, I was shaky for no reason. I put the
key in the front door and pushed it open to find the room too full
of flowers. On the kitchen counter was a note saying that homes in
the area had recently been broken into during the night but "Don't
worry, no one has been hurt. They just want your computers, cell
phones, and wallets."

Needless to say, we found other accommodations—not nearly as nice but far more hospitable. That's the only time in my life I experienced such a strong sense of shared intuition. It increased my confidence in that mysterious way of knowing. If we trust we can perceive and experience our lives in ways that make logical sense as well as in ways we don't understand, and that both ways of knowing are true and valid, we pave a way for art to come more freely. In this way, we don't discount intuition; we accept reality as being vastly more interesting, varied, and surprising than we may have previously believed.

Is your intuition something you trust and rely upon, or something you're unconnected to? What are your experiences with ways of knowing that are beyond the rational?

EVERYWHERE AND ALL THE TIME

After my book *Writing and the Spiritual Life: Finding Your Voice by Looking Within* came out, I found the book's best sentence—not necessarily the most well-written sentence, but the most important one. Actually I didn't find it, readers did. When writing that book, it hadn't occurred to me that there could be such a sentence. But there it was on the page, dressed in black against white, just like all the others. The sentence reads, "If you put your faith in doubt, it can turn your belief around so that your conviction lies in your weakness rather than your strengths, your soul, your curiosity."[7]

Writing this book, I've been on the lookout for "that" sentence. In the middle of a page, surrounded by other thoughts and observations, might there be a sentence (or two) that this book could hang its hat on? Though I don't think a hidden morsel like this can be found ahead of time (if it exists at all), I can't stop myself from looking.

If I were to pick one, it might be this: *Inspiration is everywhere and all the time.* That short sentence isn't the result of pondering for hours. Nor did it come through copious reading, though I certainly did that in researching this book. The idea that inspiration is everywhere and all the time came through my experience. Although sometimes I wish I'd known it sooner—my creative life over the years would have been less fraught, I'd have been easier to live with, and wouldn't have needed to resort to midday caramel breaks quite as often—I also realize that this truth would not have come to me if I hadn't lived through the creative troubles and missteps that brought me to where I am today, inspired by nearly everything, a whole lot of the time.

Kafka put it this way: "The world will freely offer itself to you to be unmasked. It has no choice. It will roll on the ground at your feet."[8] One afternoon, out on a beachside walk in winter sunlight, each bit of the natural world I saw led me to a constellation of images, thoughts, revelations, reveries, and artistic possibilities. How one thing is attached to another was at once obvious, as it never had been before: Waves caught by the sun appeared to be birthday hats from childhood parties. The stones rolling in and rolling out reminded me of music I'd heard performed once in a village, thousands of miles away. Each time the wind came up and tossed the sand, I pictured women dancing in flared skirts. Possibilities for poems and books and collages were on each stretch of that beach, in every corner of the sky. I wasn't finding solutions to global warming or world hunger. My inspired thoughts have never pointed to The Next Big Thing, but they are vigorous, surprising, and meaningful. And that day it became clear that the inspiration I so often seek, long for, and at times declare missing, abounds everywhere.

JUST BEING THERE

My friend and chiropractor, Ed Jarvis, writes his poems at the end of a long workweek—that's when he has time. He said, "I was worn out, not a thought in my head, but still I sat down with an open notebook because that's what I do." The materials and practice of an art form can themselves be inspiring—the scent of oil paint and turpentine, playing scales on a piano. Ed continued, "A memory came, something I'd not thought of in many years. I was about five years old." With a young friend, Ed walked through an empty drainage ditch, going farther away from home without an adult than he had before. The young boys came to a place where the walls of the ditch were covered in "golden flakes," making the boys think they'd struck gold. With this invitation, Ed's inspiration returned unexpectedly and gave him a new poem.[9]

In "Fool's Gold," he writes,

> Nearing the end of our fifth year
> my friend and I entered the ditch
> which bisected the north
> side of our small valley town, its
> banks well above our heads and began
> following it eastward . . .[10]

Contrary to what you might think, inspiration isn't necessary to begin imaginative work. Some of us begin first and the inspiration follows. William Stafford, who advised writers to lower their standards when they got stuck, used to get up very early in the morning to write. He'd make himself a cup of instant coffee and a piece of toast and lie back on the couch with his notebook. Watching the sunrise outside the window, he'd begin to write. If you take what comes, give up the pursuit of the next big idea, and trust your imagination, one thought will lead you to another. In his poem, "Just Thinking," Stafford wrote, "No one stirring, no plans. Just being there."[11] If you're "just being there," not pushing, not feeling impatient and restless, not wishing you were elsewhere, and not rehearsing the day ahead, the imagination engages with spirit, and ideas come. They come because inspiration is everywhere and all the time. Walt Whitman said, "We convince by our presence."[12] It's like inspiration gets persuaded because it "knows" we're available; we have set up the conditions for its arrival.

If you feel dull and thoughtless, devoid of inspiration, dry and disheartened, go out to where all the somebodies and the somethings sing, whisper, and dance their names. Inspiration comes most freely there. Wait. Watch. Listen.

Susan Sontag said, "Do stuff. Be clenched, curious. Not waiting for inspiration's shove or society's kiss on your forehead. Pay attention. It's all about paying attention. Attention is vitality. It connects you with others. It makes you eager. Stay eager."[13] Compare that with Jack London's advice: "Don't loaf and invite inspiration; light out after it with a club."[14] Everyone has a different approach to accessing inspiration. Some sit back and wait for it to come to them, and some take a more active stance—club or no. You'll discover your own best approaches to access inspiration as you delve in.

In an interview with Terry Gross on *Fresh Air*, film director Paul Thomas Anderson, who directed Joaquin Phoenix in the movie *The Master*, said that Phoenix began to move in the way he thought his character would, keeping his shoulder bent in a particular way. Anderson said, ". . . these movements that were so incredible . . .

I just didn't want to jinx anything and say, what are you doing, or what's going on? You know, it's kind of—you're in the middle of make-believe. You don't want to break the spell."[15] When we make believe, we act as though we do believe, and through this, belief often comes. When I feel a lack of inspiration or I am encumbered by doubt, that's what I do. I make believe I feel inspired and pretend I'm free of doubt. That helps me to not take myself too seriously, allows me to be more lighthearted. When I was young and someone asked, "What kind of work do you do?" depending on the moment and my degree of confidence, either I'd say, "I teach poetry to children" or "I'm a writer." If the second answer was the one I'd leapt into, I'd hold my breath, waiting for the follow-up question. "What have you published?" "Nothing yet, but I will," was the answer I gave on a good day. Over time, I imagined my way into becoming the person I wanted to be, the person I knew all along I was.

WAYS OF LOOKING

Wallace Stevens wrote a poem about thirteen different ways of looking at a blackbird. He believed that reality was a product of the imagination, not the other way around. And so, he looked. Stevens said, "The imagination loses vitality as it ceases to adhere to what is real. When it adheres to the unreal and intensifies what is unreal, while its first effect may be extraordinary, that effect is the maximum effect that it will ever have."[16] I think that's partly why nature works on us as it does—it's absolutely real and provides a location for inspiration to adhere to. In his blackbird poem, Stevens notes that the river is running; thusly, "The blackbird must be flying."[17] One thing leads to another; everything is connected to something else. When inspired, these connections stand out and become clear. Making art helps us identify, clarify, and expand our vision, and even alter our point of view. If we observe something from this side and that, from

above and below, inside and out, we gain a wider footing from which
to know, respond to, and love the world.

Sometimes I can't see from any perspective—my inner life and
the outer world appear clouded—I'm tired, or bored with what I'm
doing, or lost in it. A woman who took a collage workshop with me
emailed afterward to say, "Isn't art amazing? I don't know what I
would do without it. Yesterday I was running into myself all over
the place. And not in a good way! I've been feeling very constricted,
which I think is a response to feeling out of control. And it shows
in my art. So I plan to remake my collage with that in mind." The
piece she'd made that day had a small door in it. Maybe when she
makes it anew, inspiration will walk her through that door. When I
feel constricted, if I can turn what I'm doing upside down and look
at it in ways that may seem ridiculous, change comes. Could I see
as the blackbird does, from his perch? Looking at things anew happens without us trying when we're inspired, giving the artist a fresh
vantage point.

The poet Mary Szybist said, "Sometimes when I find myself in a
dark place, I lose all taste for poetry. But the 'miracle,' is how much
it can do . . . how much it does do."[18] And my friend, the poet Elliot
Ruchowitz Roberts, writes about such a time this way: "I've been
going through one of those up and down periods where I just try to
stay focused on what is right in front of me, and much of the time
it's the birds, the waves, the light on the grasses, the vastness of the
ocean, the bobcat, the deer, one flowering poppy. . ."[19]

When we give our attention to the real world, we make a place
for reverie, an aspect of inspiration that can transform difficulty. No
matter what depths of trouble we may delve into, through observing
and making art we say, "Here's what happened, here's the truth." And
an honoring of truth can be a form of reverie. Honoring what is real
for us, we hold it up to the light. Your intuitive self will show you the
world and yourself and deepen your sense of reverie.

What do you praise? How do you experience reverie? Is this experience always a joyful one, or do sad and difficult things enter in?

ENLIVENED AT ART'S EDGE

For all about art that is beautiful and joyful and that can make us swoon, another important aspect is inspiration's edge. Art works on us as it does because of the edge that the artist stands at, peers over, backs away from, returns to, and sometimes catapults over. It's part of the process of creating, communicating with the edge that we're pulled in by and sometimes push away from. When we engage in art-making, we are not only standing at an edge, we're blindfolded! To fully respond to the imagination and be alert to your inspired intuition, you're going to approach and maybe go over that edge. There might be some bruising but nothing that a bit of time won't heal.

The edge of inspiration is made up of questions like: "Can I say it?" "Do I have it in me to do this thing that feels infinitely bigger than I am?" "Will I fail?" "What if I don't measure up?" Obviously, this isn't comfortable; it's, well, edgy. You may experience vertigo. Your stomach may lurch. Sleep may evade you. It can be difficult to carry on in-depth conversations. The other day, Michael said, "You're not very lighthearted these days." I didn't argue. I'm with him, but I'm also consumed elsewhere, engaged in an endeavor that's not always easy. I can only make art when I allow myself to shimmy up to the edge, lean over it, skitter back, and return again the next morning. I'm led to that edge by inspiration.

In her book *The Old Way: A Story of the First People*, about the Kalahari Bushmen she lived with as a researcher, Elizabeth Marshall Thomas writes that the people viewed the land where they lived

> as a series of small, very distinct messages—a freshly broken twig, flattened grass without dew where an animal was resting, the footprints of a certain kind of beetle that begins to move about after the day has reached a certain temperature, each tiny item an important clue as to what has taken place in the vicinity.[20]

I remind myself of this, that all the parts of what I'm writing are distinct messages, clues about the entire vicinity of my subjects. The clues are there; I don't have to strive, just soften my focus and notice what's there. The I trust my intuition and have faith that I'm being led where I need to go, where I *can* go, and that I can say what I feel called to, the less overwhelming my experience of the edge is.

If you were to follow "a series of small, very distinct messages" from nature or from your creative nature, what would you follow? What have you followed in the past? What do you follow now?

Some days, I rip off the blindfold, back away from the edge, take a bath, eat a few caramels, and go back to bed to collect each and every atom of myself. Or I go outside and take a gentle walk, leaving my notebook behind. I talk to nature's surrounding world, "Hello, little-close-to-the-ground bird. Your wings remind me of hands clapping.

Hello great tree. You remind me of my Irish grandmother. Thank you for the comfort of the lap of shade." There I go, communing with the tangible. Might that bird be applauding the day? After a day of writing, I give thanks for what's come and even for what's remained hidden. I am grateful for intuitive knowing, joyful at having been touched by the mystery of inspiration, and ready to do it again tomorrow.

12

DIGGING IN THE DIRT

IT'S ELEMENTAL, AFTER ALL

"You are made of star stuff scattered into space long ago."
—Michael Seeds

Predawn, car lights flicker starlike through the darkness. Travelers on their way to work zoom along past either side of dancer Storyboard P., who arrived at the Manhattan side of the Brooklyn Bridge to dance the day in. Yogis do the Sun Salutation. Elemental Storyboard P. greets the day by popping, twirling, lifting, and curling his long, lithe self along the near-empty walking midportion of the bridge. The look in his eyes: fire; his ability to move through space: water; the lightness of his feet: air; the foundation that connects him: earth, plus an essential force that you see every now and then in an artist or someone wise that inexplicably lifts them beyond the ordinary. In his movements there's something of a bird and something of a knife. Storyboard P. stretches his bird-feather arms and prepares to take flight.

In an interview with *The New Yorker*, Storyboard P. said,

Your soul is hundreds of layers. You cannot really fully convey the layers to live by, but what you can do is give people a summary of it, and I just put it into some dance forms, some

169

steps, a couple fours and eights . . . What I'm trying to do is get deeper and deeper until the music vibrates, so the beat is, like, coming to life . . .[1]

As with our senses, what we discover through one element will be different from what the others offer. Air travels invisibly, effortlessly most everywhere, especially in a dancer like Storyboard P.; the earth is mostly steadfast—its solidness the thing we rely on; water always finds a way, and, undeterred, it goes over, around, or under; and fire doesn't take no for an answer. The way of spirit, that divinity, is the unifying force.

The way that fire stimulates and ignites creativity is quite unlike the effect of water. Sit me before a calm lake and my imagination floats; I'm lulled by the placidness of water. In front of a hot, contained fire, my doubt and hesitation get consumed. Here, we'll delve into the natural world elementally to see how earth, water, fire, air, and spirit can each offer our artistic lives their riches, guiding us ever deeper into our imaginations' infinite layers. We'll explore how an awareness of our connection to them links us to the earth.

THE WAY OF EARTH

Wherever we stand—high as the forty-third floor of a high-rise in the middle of a city, or low as a musty cellar in a small-town neighborhood—the earth has us. Even rising on a swing at the playground, gravity keeps us from a quick departure. Out on the ocean, beneath the turbulent water, the seaweed and fishes, there's the earth—the bowl the water fills. Take an airplane ride swiftly traversing continents until your feet find land again, sure and secure.

In his book *The Sacred Universe*, Thomas Berry wrote, ". . . [t]he Earth acts in all that acts upon the Earth. The Earth is acting in us whenever we act."[2] It's at work in the dancer popping on the bridge, in the man memorizing his part for a play during his coffee break, and, just as surely, in the prisoner who carries a small notebook in her pants pocket and the stub of a pencil to write the novel that is her only freedom, as well as in the sailor out at sea composing love songs to the longed-for beloved back on shore.

Not only that; we *are* the earth, made from earth's essence—calcium, potassium, sulfur, and sodium. My friend and student, Rachel McKay, who actively advocates for the earth's care, uncovered another aspect of her own connection to the natural world through writing. She said, "My loss is a gain to myself. Had I been rich, I should have been an idle. I have no gold, I must dig in myself for iron."[3]

The mountain goats of Colorado climb up the nearly sheer rock face, finding places to stand where there appear to be none, as our imaginations do. A black widow spider made herself at home in a room of Michael's house before it was my home, too, and that was fine by him; there she was, busy in her web, when I moved in. Shortly thereafter, other accommodations were found, but work on me, she did. I watched her up close—the movement of her delicate legs, the shiny black orb of her body, how clear her intention, how focused her action. Out in the yard, the earthworms are happily composting. Earth: our reliable foothold that daily accepts our steps. This very earth that has been worked upon in ways it ought not, whose nature is daily denied. The weight of our neglect of the earth works upon us too—imaginatively and otherwise.

What aspects of the actual earth—the ground, the hills, the green summer grass—call you? Are deserts your home place, or a forest of scrub oak?

THE WAY OF WATER

The NASA satellite photograph looking down on California in January 2014 as compared to the picture from 2013 is frightening.[4] We're in the midst of a drought, and if we don't get rain soon, it's going to be a very bad one. It's been unseasonally warm. Mid-January in Central Coastal California doesn't generally include this many warm days. In fact, the first six months of 2014 were the warmest ever on record.[5] It's disconcerting. Unsettled by the heat, I reach for wool sweaters. What makes me feel off isn't just the lack of rain, it's my concern for why we're without rain. I think about the very human factor in that why, and how during a drought—the worst since records have been kept—hydraulic fracturing can still go on in the Central Valley. I feel guilty—how have I knowingly and unknowingly contributed to the mistreatment of our planet, and how does that work on my imaginative thinking? The imaginative soul doesn't function at its best in an atmosphere of lies—in the water, or out of it.

American spiritual philosopher and self-named "practical mystic" David Spangler recently wrote a prayer that he posted on Facebook, "Prayer Request from the Water of the World." It reads, in part: "When you use water, please send loving, healing, and uplifting energy (Light) to the kingdom of the water spirits, for many of our kind are suffering and are under siege from the continuing and increasing pollution of water by humanity."[6] Wherever you stand in terms of spiritual belief and whether or not you "listen" to the messages of water, Spangler is saying something important about our regard for water.

For the life of each and every one of our cells, water is essential. Janine Benyus said, "Water is at the center of every chemical reaction, and therefore should be the earth's most precious gift."[7] According to the *Journal of Biological Chemistry*, 73 percent of the brain and heart are made from water, about 83 percent of the lungs are water. We have watery skin (64 percent) and, even, watery bones (31 percent).[8]

Think about water in terms of creative process: consider a flow of ideas, or a flood of them. I like the idea of the imagination being a near-cresting river, chock-full of salmon rushing to the sea.

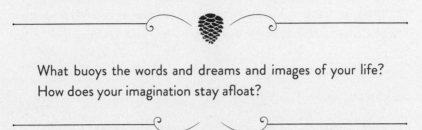

What buoys the words and dreams and images of your life? How does your imagination stay afloat?

THE WAY OF FIRE

To be perfectly authentic, I'd dedicate this book to my house, where I build my morning fires in the living room's brick fireplace, using the fuels of paper, wood, and imagination; I'd dedicate this book to the fire itself that heats my mornings and shares its life-giving light with me. Ezra Pound wrote, "What thou lovest well remains, / The rest is *dross* . . ."[9] What these daily fires do for my imagination is what remains; the dross is what they burn away.

How often I've taken collages and writing that's no longer serving me and fed them to the fire, along with letters I needed to write but would never send. To make fuel out of what the fire will transform into heat, ah, that's elemental. We have it wrong when we think that everything the artist touches, everything the writer writes, is brilliant. If I spend a week of evenings reading a novel, I try to remember it was made possible by an author's many hours, days and weeks, months and years of work. I want to remember there was, likely, a lot they fed to the fire as I do. Fire itself is indiscriminate; it'll eat anything—the artist gets to choose. I find it helpful to keep everything until I'm sure (or sure enough) about what carries the flare of promise and surprise with it. My dry and bony words, the fire recycles.

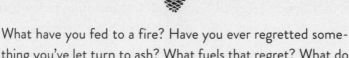

What have you fed to a fire? Have you ever regretted something you've let turn to ash? What fuels that regret? What do
you wish to burn away?

THE WAY OF AIR, SPIRIT, AND IMAGINATION

Just because I can't see it, doesn't mean it's not real. And despite knowing what I do about flight and birds and gravity, I am often struck by
the sight of raptors coasting on the wind, the sheer, seeming absur-
dity of it. Out in the woods, the air is infused with something better,
a spellbinding manna—ether. Long considered the fifth element,
"aether" or "ether" originated with the Homeric Greeks. It originally
meant fresh air or clear sky. To the ancient Greeks, it was more—ether
was what the gods breathed, as opposed to the regular air mortals did.
It's also aligned with translucence, that which shines. We might think
of ether as rarified air, which exists in natural places that are not infiltrated by noise and pollution. We could also see it as quintessence,
which is how the medieval alchemists looked at the fifth element: the
pure, distilled substance, and the essence of something. Might this, in
part, be the essence out of which imagination comes?

The moon's there this morning, floating low, when I open the
door for my cat. It's bright enough to read by. Does the moon mark
my progress? Does she see how far into this project I am? Does my
endeavor please her? What of the stars, those jewels? These shining witnesses in the sky remind me there's more at work than what I
myself bring to this book. Artists have been talking about this forever.
Dare we welcome the ethereal, the invisible ether, that which, once
we begin, may feel as basic as breath itself, into our imaginative lives?

According to Thomas Berry, "The word *hsin* is written as a pictograph of the human heart . . . It could be translated by saying that the human is the 'understanding heart of Heaven and Earth.'"[10] This is another aspect of imagination—let's not underestimate the role that love plays. And there's an inventory of more, waiting to be discovered as only you can. See something out of the corner of your eye that no one else does? When it comes to imagination, that's elemental.

What elements comprise your imagination? Are you firmly rooted to the earth or floating up above it all in the air, or perhaps your imagination is a hearth fire, always burning?

THE ELEMENT OF TRUTH

Robert Battle, Artistic Director of the Alvin Ailey Dancers, said, "I look for dancers who have a necessity to speak through their bodies to tell some truth about themselves, and about the work, every time they go onstage. That's why people relate to the dancers, because they feel that impatient urgency to say something through movement."[11] Art gives us a way to speak our essential truths. A traditional song of the Crow people, called "Song of the Bald Eagle," goes like this: "we want what is real/ we want what is real/ don't deceive us!"[12] The Crow were known for their openness to others, particularly to children, and for their songs and dances that celebrated the Great Spirit. They had plenty of reason to sing about deception—their kindness toward the white settlers was repaid with broken treaties.

Irish author Edna O'Brien, in her memoir, *Country Girl*, writes about an experience with her husband:

When Ernest discovered the draft of the story I was writing, which many years later would come to be called "Small Town Lovers," an argument flared up. The opening line was "It was a country road and tarred very blue and in the summer, we used to walk there." He erupted, saying there was no such thing as a blue road, but I knew that there was. I had seen them. I had walked on one, the hot tar smearing the white canvas of my new shoes. Roads were every color, blue, gray, gold, sandstone, and carmine. He was categorical about it. It was as if by saying it, I had defied some inalienable truth.[13]

Oh, what fundamental vitality may be found in pushing against preconceived ideas presented as fact.

One artist who doesn't accept the status quo and won't turn a blind eye to the truths he is called to tell is Daniel Horowitz, a young New York artist. Horowitz said:

My work often critiques human callousness in its overt exploitation of natural resources. In fact, I confess, I am a member of the only species of whom I am truly embarrassed, whose varying myths of sky gods and afterlives has caused a profound disconnect from the here and now. I remember reading that in some native traditions, no decision would be made without consideration of its effect on seven future generations . . . In a recent series of works, I painted with a petroleum-derived enamel on glass, depicting figures sitting on discarded furniture completely drenched in poured petroleum. In my work, the ubiquitous television set serves as an orifice for waste and pollution. I certainly have my opinions on the matter.[14]

I read this to my friend Margaret, who kept repeating, "Seven generations."

I said, "We're not even thinking of one."

Margaret raised her eyebrow, looked at me, and said, "We're just thinking third-quarter profits!"

If we are deceived and told we're incorrect for questioning the deception, but know in our bones, minds, and hearts that we're correct, what happens—psychically, spiritually, emotionally, and imaginatively—to us? If we give up our own truths for the sake of another's, where does our belief in ourselves go, and what about trust in our leaders? What happens to our actual knowing? We may lose faith in our own perceptions. Then a very basic human truth-seeking essence goes underground.

Psychotherapist Mary McKenna writes,

The soul knows. The wisdom of the ages and sages resides in each of us, if we have ears to hear. When we do our work of clearing away the admonitions, untruths, and get to the truth of who we really are, then and only then can we access this greater wisdom. That process of becoming is greatly enhanced and advanced by surrounding ourselves by the natural world.[15]

Through imaginative work, we can restore and secure the authenticity of our elemental truths. By developing artistic practices, we can maintain and develop the validity and strength of our own voices.

THE RITUAL OF RAIN

Humans aren't the only ones who partake in ceremony. Nature has her own rituals that are absolutely elemental. Consider rain—first, a few drops, and then comes the downpour. The clouds deposit their wealth of water, and then the rain stops slowly, much as it began. The earth is saturated. Birds sing most joyously then, especially after months of no rain. The sun's return begins a new ceremony. Out in my woods, that rain brings the banana slugs and, eventually, if we've had enough winter rain, a plethora of mushrooms push the soil out of the way and provide those same banana slugs something to feast upon. Each rain is different, but there is a pattern of behavior to rain showers that has special significance. Not that the rain "thinks" of what is happening as a ritual, but I wonder if the birds might.

My writing ritual is simple and quick, but serves my imagination. Some days, it's as basic as enjoying a hot cup of coffee. Certainly making coffee fits into the definition of ritual—from the grinding of the beans to the first sip that confirms it really is morning. Just sitting with the night's dream helps me to incorporate that other way of knowing into my work, making it part of my ritual as well.

Other days, when imagination is lagging, I'll put fresh flowers on the Altar of My Dead Before Me. I sit down there, light a candle, close my eyes, ask for inspiration. This homemade altar fills a corner of my office. On top of an old Guatemalan chest I placed photographs of my best beloveds who've gone before me, both those who traveled in human form and those who embodied the form of cat. Surrounding these photographs are a bird sculpture and one of Quan Yin, the East Asian goddess of mercy. There are several favorite stones, a note to myself that says, "Let the thing you love be what you do," and a candle I light when I meditate there. It's easier for me to settle down in front of that altar when I look up and see those old friends. Each whispers yes.

The mind likes to be reminded; the imagination and the soul respond well to familiarity and ceremony. Ritual's repetition serves as an invitation to the powers beyond our own and invokes the larger truths held by them, and can help us feel less adrift when out on the sea of imagination. I'm not one for elaborate rituals because my imagination's work is in what comes afterward. My work isn't served by an intricate preparation process. A ceremony can be as simple as lighting a match—one repeated occurrence signals another. A walk in the fresh air can do it. Schedules may sound mundane, but they, too, get us ready.

Consider creating an altar for yourself, to honor your imaginative spirit. You might include, like I did, photographs of those who have gone but supported you before going. Objects from nature walks, too, I find encouraging. Perhaps a painting done in your own hand.

Take a look at Mason Currey's book *Daily Rituals: How Artists Work*, filled with glimpses into the ritualistic side of making art across mediums and eras. Louis Armstrong's ritual included arriving early to his engagements so he could leisurely bathe and dress beforehand, demonstrating that even an ordinary act can serve symbolically. What might your rituals be?

Mason Currey, *Daily Rituals: How Artist Work* (New York: Knopf, 2013).

ELEMENTAL ART

Some artwork is decidedly elemental—like an extension or an augmentation of the earth herself. Such is the sculpture of English artist Penny Hardy. Her enormous, airy metal pieces are treelike figures that appear to have been caught by the wind and easily bend into it. Some appear to be spinning. Others, which look like up-blown leaves, make me think she'd sculpted the wind itself.

Hardy said, "My work is mostly figurative: the energy and flow of a line that is so well described by nature is an element I strive to capture, and the physical forces of the natural world also influence my work."[16] I find nature's resilience, her ability to adapt, to overcome obstacles, enviable. I, too, want to bend and jut, to reach and fall, to run stream-fast, then get up and do it all over again.

There's an old-time, traditional children's poem that concludes, "We'll weather the weather,/ Whatever the weather/ Whether we like it or not."[17] Oh, and don't we know it! Lately, there's talk in the news about trying to control weather, beyond "seeding" clouds. May it never succeed, that's my hope. I feel cautious about manipulating weather and the unforeseen effects of doing so. Don't we manipulate enough? Not that I wouldn't love a long, sluicing downpour right about now.

Ever been inspired by a thunderstorm? Discussing his debut mystery novel, *The Kept*, on NPR, James Scott remembered the weather at his grandparents' home when he was a young boy: "When those storms gather over the lakes, and they come in, the sky is just so oppressive. It's just this steely gray mass that just weighs down on you."[18] Dark weather sure can lead an artist to unexpected places and unexpected weathers within.

A destructive earthquake came to my town some years ago. It closed roads, businesses, and schools for many days. Several lives were lost. When Gault Elementary School opened again, the children weren't only eager to talk about what happened to their house or to their friend's house, but equally eager to write poems about it. The poem writing made way for them to articulate a level of memory, feeling, and detail that the chatting didn't. Second grader Midio wondered, "Maybe it was God throwing down big boulders on Santa Cruz . . ." Writing about the earthquake, the children discovered that they could interact with the thing that scared them. Their imaginations helped them to gain an active role in what was beyond their control. Like nature, these kids overcame the obstacle in their path, finding inspiration in an unlikely, elemental place.

OPEN, SHUT: LIGHT AND DARK

Envision a dark room in which a large group of people is sitting. It's not a dimmed room, not a room into which light shines through the cracks beneath the doors, but a shut-eye-dark room though everyone's eyes were open. That was the scene in New York City's Lincoln Center's Clark Studio Theater for Georg Friedrich Haas's Third String Quartet in November 2013. The piece takes over an hour to perform and the audience is kept in total darkness for the duration. In order to prepare them for it, the lights are turned off gradually so that anyone who's too freaked out can get up and leave. According to *The New Yorker*, "it's like being buried alive." The sounds coming from the musicians include "musical cries, whispers, songs, and sighs—gradually allowing the ears to map a space that the eyes cannot see." Listening to this music in complete darkness is transformative. "What begins as an experience of deprivation becomes one of radically heightened awareness." If we deprive ourselves of our primary way of knowing the world, which for most of us is sight, we have to become reliant on our other ways of knowing.[19]

Some of us make art in darkened rooms or outside, in the night. In the early mornings, it's as if I'm in a tunnel of darkness. Awareness that is shy and reluctant may more easily approach in a muted light. The essence of darkness is its vast mysteriousness. It's a place that holds its wonders close; we humans only get so far into its secrets. Might time in darkness allow us access to a covert realm of imagination? By the time it's light outside, I've usually obtained entrance into my imagination, so the hidden, the tender, the possibly wrong, and the hesitant have permission to approach. Even then the light through the window can feel intrusive when it comes—"Too soon! Too soon!" I say, squinting my eyes.

Poet Theodore Roethke writes, "Deep in their roots/ all flowers hold/ the light."[20] I like that idea, especially on mornings when all I've been able to do is to brood in the darkness, throwing arrows of fear at it. I like knowing that even in their deep wending mulchy darkness, the roots of the flowers hold their blossoming into daylight.

From darkness and light to the subtlety of spirit, from earth's mutability to water's determination, each of the elements can be a teacher. Many of us are drawn toward one more than the others. Maybe it's because of my quick-to-flare temperament, but fire was my go-to element, until the northern flickers caught my heart, infusing my art with bird and spirit. An exploration of the elements will give your art its broadest, wildest stroke.

13

ANIMAL PRESENCE

SWOOPING OWL AND BOUNDING FOX

What is this joy? That no animal falters,
but knows what it must do?
—Denise Levertov

An owl: not near enough that his wings touched me, but near enough that I was startled. His force was unmistakable. It's not every day that an owl swoops down low and slow and flies a few feet ahead. He continued along the trail till the next bend carried him out of sight—wings bright against the forest's foggy, early morning darkness. I stood still, taking it in.

I've often heard owls conversing high up in the trees, calling across the canyon, but for this, there'd been no warning. Owl feathers are covered in a substance that makes their flight nearly silent. Many traditions place symbolic meaning in these raptors. To some they connote wisdom, and others see them as harbingers of doom. I'm sure the owl knew I was there—the hearing center in an owl's brain has a lot of cells designed for hearing prey moving along the ground; they're particularly good at directional hearing, and though I try to walk quietly, I'm hardly silent. It made me unsettled. I took the owl's presence as a suggestion to stay more alert than usual, to be attentive to possibility—whatever kind.

A few days later, driving to the less visited, more primordial, east side of Jacks Peak Park, where lichen hangs from the trees and the trail drops deep into the narrow canyon, I heard a loud sound—not thunder, not gunshot, not a sonic boom. I've walked in the woods long enough to know that sound: a tree was about to fall, and this one was close by. The predominant tree species at Jacks Peak Park is the Monterey pine. They have a shallow root system; it's not unusual for them to fall, and when a big one does, it's very loud.

In my head there was an agitated voice, as if someone were yelling at me from the backseat of the car, "Drive faster!" I don't know where that came from, but I stepped on the gas, heard a loud groan—a *hurrumph* that sounded like regret—followed by a splintering crash. Down went that tree, across the road just behind my car, blocking my exit from the park. It took a few hours before the park workers could arrive to remove the tree. While waiting, I enjoyed a long contemplative walk, thanking the owl who, days earlier, had warned me. For weeks afterward, my step had more bounce to it. At night, the stars were brighter.

The incident with the owl reinforced a connection to and a regard for ancient ways of knowing. If people who lived on the earth long ago believed that an owl's presence might serve as a warning because it was demonstrated to them, might I, who know so much less about owls and the earth, consider this possibility? And by doing so, might I add a missing dimension into my life? Would my imagination gain depth? Could I become more responsive to the natural world? When I experience vital relationships with the earth and her creatures, my imagination has a more secure place from which to create stories.

The animals in particular contribute to my belief in the primal and innate world that is beyond the modern human realm of understanding. Animals can be trusted to act authentically, to know what matters; whereas the manmade world and our human relationships are sometimes full of potholes.

When asked why people have such need to tell our stories, Native American writer Leslie Marmon Silko answered, "You cannot stop it. The land speaks to you."[1] If a squirrel is having a conversation with me, a squirrel is having a conversation with me, and it's verifiable and easy to recognize. If I can't tell you exactly what he's communicating it doesn't matter; what does is the engagement with a wild being. When I watch and listen to the animals interacting with each other I'm reminded of how much there is I can't comprehend but am enamored of and delighted by.

Animals remind me that part of what I am after is relationships, and how much of that desire is a part of my imaginative process— connections between person and form, the artist and her materials, the author and his imagined audience. Much about relationship precedes language. Through using language, writing this book has been more a process of falling into memory and experience, of listening and responding. The animals, who don't overthink a thing, have been great teachers in that.

A chimp was being released into the wild after being brought back to health following an illness at the Tchimpounga Chimpanzee Rehabilitation Center. His name was Wounda, and he was taken by truck and then by boat to a remote, safe island where he could live a free life. The cage door was opened and he climbed on top of it, looking around. Wounda looked at the small group of people gathered, turned to Jane Goodall and jumped into her arms, put his arms around her neck, laid his head on her shoulder and hugged her tightly and, just as tightly, she hugged him back.[2] Could any expression be more universal than that? Because animals and plants communicate differently, we often discount them and the wisdom of their ways. Watching and being around animals, I wonder how I might be a more authentic person with less artifice, how I might be more thrifty and less wasteful, live in integrity with the environment? In this chapter, we'll look at experiences and relationships between animals and people and consider how those connections can deepen our imaginative lives and restore our spirits.

THURSDAY, JULY 15: ENCOUNTER WITH A DUSKY-FOOTED WOOD RAT

Toward the end of my walk up the hills of Rhus Ridge Trail, past the spot where the yellow ladybugs are flying, where there's always a breeze even on the stillest days, I suddenly yelped, startling myself, not conscious of why. I had come a few inches from stepping on a rat. This rat was sweet to look at, about six inches long. Her snout was rounded. She had a mouse-like demeanor. I was confused—what's a rat doing on the path in the middle of the day? Why didn't she run after hearing my yelp and watching my foot come too close?

Backing away, giving both of us space, I stopped, looked carefully. The fat little creature was shivering in the hot sun, swaying slightly from side to side. Her eyes were barely open. I thought I saw a cut on the side of her body, looked closer. Yes, a wound, upon which flies were gathering. One fly touched the rat's nose, but she didn't flick it away.

I got down on my haunches a couple of feet away. Sunlight caught a glint in the rat's now fully open eyes. We looked at each other, slowly. I saw no inclination on the rat's part to flee, and was surprised to feel none myself (despite that I don't like rats). I began talking to the little creature, trying to make of my voice a lullaby.

"I'm sad that you're hurt," I said in a whisper. I was aware that if someone walked by they'd think I'd lost it, but I didn't care. "I'm so sorry." At which point, surprising myself again, I began to cry.

Here's what I took home with me: The image of light in the rat's eyes, her look of sorrow, the slight sway of her body, and the knowledge that one being suffering is the same as any being suffering. That brief interaction has infused my life from then on, making my empathy bigger.

How does empathy feed your creative process?

DROP THAT BIRD!

In the living room, engaged in writing, I ignored the occasional thumping sound coming from our indoor/outdoor windowed sun room that serves as our summer dining room and my year-round art studio. The cats came in for supper and, before I'd realized what was going on, they'd cornered a little bird who'd been unable to distinguish the windows from the sky. He banged his head repeatedly on the glass, unable to find a way out.

The younger cat had the bird in her mouth in no time, and was beginning to maul him, but when I rushed in, saying, "Drop that bird," she did. I covered the bird with a dishtowel and carried him outside to the big pine, sure I ought to be taking him to the garbage can or digging a hole in the ground.

Lifting the towel I saw that the little bird was alive, breathing roughly, feathers damp and mussed. He appeared stunned (who wouldn't be?), but he looked at me, and his eye held what only the eyes of the living hold—glimmering light that says, "I am here. This is me." Until recently, I did not assign personality or unique identity to wild creatures. If I had not come to my senses previously, the presence of that little bird would have quickly righted me. Carefully, I placed my palm around him, bent to settle him onto the dirt and, with a force that caught me off-guard, the bird pushed against my hand and flew off, up and up, past the boughs of the great pine tree, into the sky.

That day had its frustrations, as days often do, but none of its difficulties could be compared to the joy I received from that small, determined bird's flight. In that moment, a flurry of reminders came to me—the indisputable clarity of life force and the desire to live; that no being replicates another being; that I can have a role in this. Emily Dickinson wrote, "Hope is the thing with feathers."[3] That little bird hadn't given up for a second; he hadn't relinquished his hold on life—the strength of his wings against my hand was irrefutable. Hope was firm and vital beneath his feathers.

UNCANNY INTERACTIONS WITH ANIMALS

In response to my question posed on Facebook, "Have you had any unusual experiences with animals?" came a bunch of replies from people eager to share the unexpected. Bhavananda wrote, "When I came into the living room, my eyes were riveted to the apple tree just outside my window, where, stretched out on a limb, was a coyote eating an apple! I still find that moment hard to believe."[4] Her few words make a picture—smart and hungry, animals were the earth's first foragers. Meredith, who lives in Big Sur, said,

> I met a ringtail cat twice on Coast Ridge Road. Same place but months apart. It was so cute, just sitting on a log about twenty feet away off the road. It seemed totally relaxed so, on our second encounter, I started to walk towards it to get a better look. At about ten feet, the docile-appearing animal bared its fangs and let out a nasty growl. I retreated post-haste and have never seen one again.[5]

I love that Meredith said she "met" the animal. But a ringtail cat? What's that? I'd never heard of one. Smaller than a house cat, their tails are thick, striped like a raccoon's and nearly the length of their entire bodies. The small face has big eyes and ears resembling a bat's. The ringtail is a member of the raccoon family, not actually a cat.

Next John wrote, "I was feeding pieces of my sandwich to a wild baby raccoon. After the sandwich was gone, I held out my hands to show the raccoon I didn't have anymore. The baby took one of my fingers with its hand, stuck my finger in its mouth, and started sucking on it."[6] Just as a human baby would! And then this from my friend Robin, which made me chuckle: "Does getting charged by a domestic cow in a thicket of aspens and suffering a head injury count? Also, there are bears in my backyard that do not pick up their pace if I yell at them. And my mom has a jay that knocks at her window for peanuts."[7] Lastly, Susan wrote, "Once I helped a mama seal give birth because the baby was stuck."[8] How many people can say they've done that?

In Jonathan Cott's book, *My Dinner with Lenny*, Bernstein said,

I am frequently visited by a white moth or a white butterfly. Quite amazingly frequently. And I know it's Felicia. [His deceased wife.] I remember that when she died, her coffin was in our living room in East Hampton . . . and just a few of us were there . . . And then this white butterfly flew in from God knows where—it just appeared from under the coffin and flew around, alighting on everybody in the room . . . and then it was gone.[9]

All of these experiences expand my understanding of animals and the natural world and they prove to me that we are not as separate from the earth as it may sometimes seem.

CARYL'S LION

Of all the responses I received to my query, the one from Caryl raises the hackles on the back of my neck. The day before leaving on a three-day vision quest—an ancient way to seek healing and spiritual guidance—Caryl pulled a medicine card from the deck. Who was pictured there, whose spirit would she take with her on this journey? The mountain lion.

Have you, too, had uncanny interactions with animals? Have they tilted your worldview?

Out in the dry summer hills, Caryl, using corn kernels, cast a circle in which she would live for three days and nights; she wouldn't step outside it. Within the circle there were two large trees that she told me felt like guides—a mother and father oak.

"Soon as I sat down in the dirt of the circle," said Caryl, "a mountain lion approached. She slowly walked the perimeter of the circle, going in and out of the brush, showing and hiding herself. We looked each other in the eye. Once I was in the circle, I didn't feel she was a threat, wasn't afraid she'd hurt me."

During her days there, Caryl was, in fact, more bothered by the ticks. "It was July; there were lots of them." The lion would appear sometimes and at other times Caryl could hear her a few feet away. "It's movement they go after," Caryl told me, "and I was pretty still. I was going to be there for three days; I couldn't be afraid, and, anyway, I'd lived alone in the woods in a small cabin with no electricity for five years and saw mountain lions often. They hadn't scared me then. Why should one now?" I pointed out that maybe the reason to be afraid would have been because the lion was so close, frequently present, and she had no shelter. Caryl seemed surprised by my response. "I was too busy with the ticks and making friends with the birds and the two oaks to think too much about her. It was a time when I was learning to be my own leader. When the lion showed up, I saw her as just another solitary being."[10]

Maybe what we fear isn't so scary, after all. Might I learn to love the animals who I'm afraid of? How would that affect my imaginative life? The German poet Rainer Maria Rilke wrote: "Love consists in this, that two solitudes protect and touch and greet each other."[11] I wonder if that lion was there, in part, to protect Caryl. As *two solitudes*, they certainly greeted each other and bridged an interspecies separation.

The Santa Cruz Puma Project is a partnership between the University of California at Santa Cruz and the California Department of Fish and Wildlife. Their website includes mountain lion photos, videos, and a very lot of compelling content—a good way to get up close and personal with some of nature's more imposing felines without risking some serious scratches!

The Santa Cruz Puma Project: santacruzpumas.org

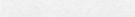

ABOUT A DOG?

I couldn't go to the Esalen Institute in Big Sur some summers ago to offer a collage workshop due to awful forest fires. I'd set aside a week for that workshop; suddenly my time opened up, feeling like a cavern, not an expanse. What would I do? There wasn't much I could do for the fires except offer my prayers to the wildlife and the humans. Just because I wasn't teaching collage didn't mean I couldn't spend the week cutting and pasting by myself and playing with my two-month-old kittens. An eerie time, the smoke-weighted sky hung low. But the kittens didn't know there was trouble; they romped around the backyard while I made art. They were exploring the world for the first time, jumping for butterflies—and missing. They hid behind bushes and leaped out at me and at each other, reminding me of the childhood rules of hide-and-seek.

One day, paste on my fingers, I sat watching the cats and the July garden, mesmerized by the small beauty out my window, when I heard a rustling by the back fence, looked over to see a creature curiously peer over—a pointy reddish nose; she looked in each direction. Must be a dog. I said, "Hello, there."

The animal took that as an invitation and jumped over the fence, stood still, looking at my kittens and at me, and slowly, step-by-step approached them, causing my breath to stop, but I didn't move. Not at first. What was a dog doing in my yard, anyway?

Wait a minute, that's no dog. That is a fox! A fox, really? I stood, watching. She came up slowly to the kitties and they hissed. The fox backed away. The paste dried on my fingers. The fox came closer and the inquisitive kittens went closer too. Then I did—all of us moving in slow motion. The fox didn't snap up one of my babies in her mouth and take off to enjoy a luscious lunch, as I was afraid she would. She came nearer to me, looked me in the eye. I bent down, spoke calmly. She cocked her head but didn't run away. Nor did the kitties. I sat down. The fox sat down. The kittens scampered. Then the fox got up, walked to the fence, jumped back over.

I went back inside to pry my fingers apart. A few minutes later, having safely deposited the kittens inside, I went back to the yard. I called out, "Fox!" And over the fence came the fox; she walked right up to me. We could have touched each other. A few times, over the course of the day, the fox left and I went back inside, waited awhile, then came out to the fence and called, "Fox!" Each time, she came.

About the time I began falling in love with her, I did what I know you're not supposed to do with wild animals. I did what you are supposed to do for guests: I gave her something to eat. She ate the snack and left. A while later I called again and she returned, only this time my kittens were outside too. The three of them approached each other and then retreated. It became obvious—the fox and the kittens were playing! I wanted to invite the fox in, offer her a bed next to our bed. But I knew better. Or, I knew otherwise, anyway.

The next day, the fox returned, and again the day after that. But when she stood at the back door, as if waiting for an official invitation to come in, I realized this needed to stop. So I explained, "I'm sorry, Fox," I said, "I'm falling in love with you in a way that makes me want to offer you some of all that I have. But I can't do that because that kind of arrangement is against your nature. You're a wild one. It's time for you to go." She stood there and we watched each other. There was no hurry. The fox turned on her heel, went back over the fence. I didn't call for her again and she never returned.

The fox gifted me with her presence. In *A Language Older Than Words*, Derrick Jensen wrote about a cat: "What if . . . I pet her because I like to, and because I know she likes it? I can still pay attention, and I can still learn from the relationship. That's what happens with my other friends. Why not with the cat too? But the point is pursuing a relationship, not gathering information."[12] It was a brief relationship I had with the fox; we each reached out of our familiar reality and got closer to the other. My imagination was dazzled; everything within me was.

BRETHREN VS. UNDERLINGS

The encounter with the fox is the most surprising one I've ever had—it fell far outside my frame of reference. My brief interaction with the dying rat is the one that made me feel most tender. Perhaps that shouldn't be unexpected when, after all, my best friends aren't human. (I hope Michael and my best human friend, Gina, won't take this the wrong way.) My two cats are those with whom I'm the closest, especially the six-year-old female named Ace. Born to a feral mother in my backyard, she's timid. Some nights Ace will jump into bed with me, slip under the covers, curl her small self up, place her head on my arm, and look up; at which time I have no choice but to close my book. We stare into each other's eyes like new lovers. I get happily lost where I feel welcomed.

Do you have what you consider to be close relationships with animals? Do animals come to you in dreams? How do you interact with the animals in your life during your waking hours?

We tend to be surprised by our encounters with wild animals because those interactions are far outside the norm. For a lot of us, animals live at a remove from our lives, subsumed by our lack of need for relationships with them and by our actual, physical distance. How often do we communicate with animals, listen to their speech, or feel the warmth of their bodies against ours? Do we stand still long enough to watch a spider build her web from start to finish; or witness a bee gathering so much pollen that she appears to be wearing yellow bloomers; or see a mother-to-be rat carry grass from one side of the riverbank for her nest on the other? Relationships with animals provide particular opportunities to witness resourcefulness, recognize other ways of solving problems, and, in a not-human way, to know reciprocity firsthand.

Naturalist Henry Beston said, "We need another and a wiser and perhaps a more mystical concept of animals. . . . [T]hey move finished and complete, gifted with extensions of the senses we have lost or never attained, living by voices we shall never hear. They are our brethren, they are not underlings . . ."[13]

I'm confused and disturbed by the need for supremacy that human adults have, the tendency to lord over—particularly over animals and children. We perform this act of distancing and separation with such finesse that it often goes unquestioned. This behavior can distance us from our imagination, too; anything that closes us off can. And in the end, what people do is remove themselves from the world. That creates an environment whose basic tenet is fear—thinking that what we don't know and what we don't understand will hurt us. According to a brochure for a collegium at the University of Helsinki, called "Encounters with Animals in Graeco-Roman Antiquity: the Historicity of Experience," the ancients recognized the differences between humans and animals, "but prior to Aristotle," philosophers "did not see the reasoning faculty as the essential distinction between human and nonhumans. Moreover, they included in their discussions continuities and affinities between humans and animals, and thus saw human beings as a more or less privileged class or caste among other living beings—not different in kind, but in degree."[14] That's more closely aligned with how I think of animals, or most of them (I do eat some meat and kill mosquitoes and have, in the past, crushed my share of spiders, as I'm sure many of us have when we've found them crawling across the bed at night). On the whole, however, our domination of animals has lessened who we are. We tend to think of animals as "others," which points out their difference from us and also demotes their stature. We live in symbiosis with every living creature on the planet; in light of that fact, the golden rule has never seemed more relevant and real.

A LOVE OF BEES

The Russian poet, Osip Mandelstam, was imprisoned for speaking out—writing out—against Stalin, and died in Siberia before he was fifty, yet had the tenderness to write, "For our joy take from my palms/ a bit of sunlight and a bit of honey . . ." Mandelstam's wife, Nadezhda, memorized most of her husband's poems—there's no flammable paper in the mind, so a memorized poem can't be taken away and destroyed. Here it is, translated by the Russian-American poet Marina Romani:

For our joy take from my palms
a bit of sunlight and a bit of honey,
as Persephone's bees would have us do.

You can't unmoor a boat free floating,
nor hear a shadow whispering in its furs,
nor overcome the fear that burrows into life.

All that is left for us is kisses,
the downy ones like little bees
that perish once they've left the hive.

They rustle in the crystal labyrinth of night,
their home is the dense forest of Taigetos,
their sustenance is cowslip, mint, and time.

Accept then my wild gift of joy,
this simple necklace made from withered bees
that died while turning honey into sunlight.[15]

When she was five, Ella, a neighborhood child, said, "It's okay to pet the bees, but they don't like being held." She found that out the hard way, and now she knows and won't forget. There's an old tradition from a time when people recognized and cherished the centrality of bees in their lives, called Telling the Bees. Beekeepers would share news with their bees. If there was a wedding or a birth, the keeper would leave the bees an offering—such as wedding cake or, for the birth of a child, small sweets. If the beekeeper died, the bees would be told this, and on the day of the funeral, their hives would be covered in black cloths. Bees were also known to show up at the funerals of their keepers; how they got the directions and the time, nobody knows.[16]

I'll bet on the day Ella discovered bees don't like to be held, she, too, was telling them what she wanted them to know, what was important in her life. That a bee would need to know such things matters to the human spirit and imagination.

Poet Carol Ann Duffy, in her book, *The Bees*, wrote, "bees/ are the batteries of orchards, gardens, guard them." Only a poet would say something like that (notice the gurgling, alliterative guarding of gardens.)[17] To whom, other than an artist, would the idea occur? Might the scientist think that? Sure. But she might stop herself from writing it down. The poet sprinkles her words onto the paper, then shakes the page like a picnic blanket to free it of the crumbs; the words that stick, the ones that shine, are those that belong.

My friend Jim was a very large man; he towered over and around me. He was as large in his body as he was in his kindness. A bee-keeper, he invited me along once to attend a pollination. When I arrived at his place, I saw stacked white boxes on the back of his flatbed truck, ready to go. Alive! Inside those boxes was bee busyness; the boxes buzzed with it, honey-makers inside. Jim and I drove a few hours southeast, outside the town of Los Baños, to deliver the bees to their place of employment, an almond orchard, newly in bloom—those spindly trees anointed in white-pink blossoms. The bees would take their fill of pollen, stuff it onto their legs, make love to the flowers and make honey—all, more or less, at the same time; and they made Jim some money too. Writer William Longgood said, "The bee is domesticated but not tamed."[18] Handing me a crude metal contraption in the fading light of late afternoon, Jim taught me how to smoke the bees into docility. They smelled good. I never knew that the smell of honey is in the bees and their hives, but it is. Jim's laughter was like a buzzing hive; it was that good, making me think of these words by Eloise Greenfield: "Oh, Honey, let me tell you that I LOVE the way he talks . . ." Oh, honey, indeed![19]

Consider that the honeybee has been around for thirty million years—what a lot of honey that is. Each time bees go pollen hunting, they'll each visit a lot of flowers. When a bee returns to the hive after pollen-gathering, it communicates the location of the flowers it found by doing a waggle dance! If the bee waggles facing up, it means the flowers will be found in the direction of the sun. The speed at which the bee dances informs the others just how far away the flowers are.

Beekeeper Lynn sells honey at the farmers' market. Once upon a time, she was an opera singer. Her voice has a force and beauty to it that makes me wonder, but does not let me ask, why she stopped singing. When I ask Lynn about the problems with the bees these days—colony collapse and more—there's a deep, dissatisfied sigh in her words. "The bees, bees, bees. Well, GMOs, systemic pesticides, and fungicides are the culprits. Then, to keep them alive, we human idiots give them more chemicals. And then, there is no nectar, because there is no rain and the flowers are dry, so they get fed high fructose corn syrup. Just poison on top of poison."[20] Lynn knew my friend Diana, who died last summer. Diana bought honey from Lynn as I do, and always stayed long enough to visit. Diana's hair was the color of honey. After Diana's death, Lynn sang me a plaintive song; she sang like honey, like honey from the very bottom of the jar, always the best part.

I pay homage to the fruit of the bees' labor: the almonds, apricots, and plums. Here's to sunlight in a jar, languorous gold on my breakfast bread; the ultimate sweetness that reaches our most sensitive taste buds; honey's good medicine when you take it on a spoon if your throat hurts, especially laced with a bit of cayenne pepper. It also has an uncanny ability to dissolve sadness, even for a little while. Who can turn down the tawny thickness of it? Even its name reverberates with tenderness and protection, "Oh, honey, I love!"

Just as the fruit of the bees' labor adds literal and metaphorical sweetness to our lives, might a connection with the animals add to our imaginative lives? Might we dance like the snake marking the soft ground as he goes? Listening to the call of the hawk descending on its prey, isn't music there? Isn't there poetry in the voice of all the animals we've ever heard or dreamed of?

14

ALONG LOWER RIDGE TRAIL

THE SUSTENANCE OF SOLITUDE
AND SILENCE

I never found a companion that was so companionable
as solitude.

—Henry David Thoreau

Walking down from Lower Ridge Trail to Loma Alta Road, a back entrance to the park, I met a man and woman walking up. He was particularly friendly. She just wanted to walk.

"I'm walking with my sister because I don't want her to walk alone," he said, as if to caution or criticize me for not being with a companion.

"I love walking alone," I said. The woman's eyes lit up.

"I used to do that," she said wistfully, "I lost thirty pounds walking on these dirt roads and trails by myself."

I hope she'll go back by herself and that she'll feel, not necessarily physical pounds falling off her frame, but the weight of daily conversation and responsibilities, the heaviness of our organized, partitioned lives lifting.

Being alone in nature is the truest way to experience it. Alone, I notice the relationships between earth's plant and animal beings. Conversation muffles the experience because it gets between the *real* world and you or me. Chatting about our lives, important as that is, is a distraction in nature and diminishes firsthand interactions and observations. Time alone feeds my inner life. It restores my spirit. Not that I don't love walking in nature with others, but for me, that has to be in addition to the time I spend on the land alone.

"Hey," the accompanied woman said after we parted, causing me to turn around, "I'm going to walk alone again here, soon, real soon!"

SOLITUDE'S DWELLING

Most art is initiated in solitude. A lot of art depends on it. The ability to dwell in solitude—through its peaceful and less-than-peaceful times—creates an atmosphere that, for the imagination, is elemental. In our "Do it now!" culture, periods of aloneness can be harder to come by. The imagination thrives on contemplation and pondering. We can get lost from our essential selves when, amidst hurried days, we leave them behind, opting for necessary action over reflection. A little solitude is a way to get back what's gone missing. Some writers I know, parents of young children, stay up later or rise a bit earlier, stealing time. Others block out an hour here or there in their calendars and treat it with the seriousness of keeping a doctor's appointment.

Contrary to what one may think, having an imaginative practice doesn't have to mean reserving hours and hours of every day. Often we resist doing something new because we think we have to completely change our lives to make it happen. Not so with solitary art-making. And anyway, it's contagious and comes complete without immunity or resistance—once you've got it, you keep getting it!

My student Alice has lived alone since the death of her husband a few years ago. When I called her the other day to confirm workshop plans, she sounded unlike herself. Had I woken her from a nap? "No, I just got back from a few days at the retreat. I go to the convent down the road to revise my poems. I can't do it if I stay home. Too many dishes, too much mail, the telephone rings, and then the garden needs watering . . ."

Where solitude is concerned, you might start out with fifteen minutes. Soon you'll want thirty of them, once a day or a few times a week. Go to the beach or the corner park and leave your phone behind—there'll be less distraction and more inspiration at every turn.

For many years when I, too, lived alone, I'd go away, not so much for revision, but for writing and long inspiring walks, traveling north to the California hill country to a hot springs along a dirt road, surrounded by acres and acres of raw, unfettered nature. Sure, there were other guests, sometimes plenty of them, but I rarely spoke to anyone. I'd write and walk for hours, soak in the hot water. I liked the days and days of not only being alone, but being out of my own element, away from the familiar. I liked not needing a car to go walking and the freedom from a ringing telephone in a place without cell phone reception.

I don't go there so much anymore. Now, solitude is incorporated into my daily routine; my sense of it has gotten sturdier. Time in nature helps. Living with Michael, who's gone at work all day, and our two cats, my sustenance is here with the woods and the sea nearby. The best compliment I ever gave Michael (though I'm not certain he took it as such, even though he got my drift) was, "Being with you is almost as good as being alone." What I meant was that the ease I feel with him nearly equals that which I feel when by myself.

The amount of solitude a person craves changes, depending on what's happening in the rest of life. Though I benefit from occasional periods of round-the-clock solitude, I don't so much find myself seeking it. Of course, the amount of alone time you wish for may not be in proportion to the amount you may be able to obtain. And there can be value to an imaginative life in wanting and not getting, that "grist for the mill" thing. These days, I'm not teaching as much as I had for many years of my life, so my days are less peopled. In order to drop down into imagination, I don't need first to recover from an onslaught of human contact. Having satisfied my need for solitude over time, I'm also a bit better at finding that state of mind within, even when the externals don't offer it; I know how to retreat with myself. I think it's worth remembering how fluid an imaginative practice can be, that what it calls for at one time may change at another, and that our imaginations and our spirits are resourceful and tenacious.

In his book *A Year on the Wing: Journeys with Birds in Flight*, Tim Dee writes, "[T]here is no unknowing the kind of knowledge that birds bring."[1] The same is true of the knowledge that comes through solitude. Time alone is the best way for imagination's generative knowledge to become securely imprinted in the very sinew of self.

VARIETIES OF SOLITUDE

Recently, I went to San Francisco alone for an overnight visit. Cities are second nature to me. Having been raised in two as a child—New York and Chicago—I'm comfortable there, know the protocols, feel adept at getting around. It's easy for me to eat out, flag down a cab, and enjoy a concert solo, feeling lucky that I've got the cash to do so. As I shared earlier, it took time to feel comfortable alone in the woods. But, despite my city comfort, poems and pictures don't come to me there, even when I'm alone, with the same readiness that they do in nature, where nothing feels crimped. Nature's unpredictable is, generally, less jarring than city unpredictability.

If I am in a city, I crave a natural spot within it—Central Park or the Embarcadero; a walk along Lake Michigan, where the hubbub of busy places feels farther away. That said, the Metropolitan Museum of Art, Saint Patrick's Cathedral, the de Young and Field Museums, and some libraries, provide indoor locations in which to find solitude. In certain ways, they mimic aspects of nature—their high ceilings don't show us the sky but do provide a sense of spaciousness. John Fowles said, "Even the smallest woods have their secrets and secret places, their unmarked precincts, and I am certain all sacred buildings, from the greatest cathedral to the smallest chapel, and in all religions, derive from the natural an aura of certain woodland or forest settings."[2] Museums and libraries are sacred places too.

As a child, I loved to curl up on the couch alone when the house was quiet, to read or draw or just be, or to sit in front of my bedroom window watching the light-fairies flit; my thoughts softened then and I felt at ease. Alone and quiet at Jacks Peak, my thinking softens in the same way. There's fluidity to the movement between thoughts. Nothing's held tightly nor feels captured; I'm less likely to beat my thoughts or myself into the ground. Juan Ramón Jiménez, the Spanish poet, in his poem "Silence," said, "You find in solitude only what you take to it . . . Noise shatters my day and brain into a thousand irreparable little pieces."[3] What a relief to know that this is a shared sensibility.

The French novelist, Marguerite Duras, said, "Solitude was that too. A kind of writing."[4] Alone, we may talk silently (or not-so-silently) to ourselves, and that talk isn't at all the kind we have with other people. It's less censored, less formal and mannered, and in that way, just being alone can be an imaginative experience. Words, images, and thoughts come to me in the same way they do when writing or making a collage. Much of my art comes to the surface simply, spontaneously, when I am alone.

Driving long distances in the car is a perfect opportunity to write—I never drive off without slipping a notebook onto the passenger seat. Duras also said, "The solitude of writing is a solitude without which writing could not be produced, or would crumble, drained bloodless by the search for something else to write."[5] A recent fortune cookie read, "Continue your present conversation for some valuable insight." I think it's referring to this talk-writing that I do silently or in a whisper when I'm out among the trees or alone in my garlic-scented kitchen, preparing dinner for Michael.

What are your earliest memories of solitude?

"WHEN MORNING CAME, IT BLEW MY MIND"

In the spring and fall of 2012, jazz musician and composer Bill Frisell visited Big Sur's Glen Deven Ranch, an 860-acre property that sits on a ridge above the Pacific Ocean. It abounds in abundant woods, coastal river lands, grasslands, and wildlife. Big Sur is that stretch of rugged land south of the village of Carmel, along California's central coast—stunning and untamed. On one side of Highway 1, there's acre upon acre of grasslands beside the wild Pacific, and across the road, back, beyond, and through the hills are dense redwood forests. In the past, Glen Deven Ranch was used for cattle and had hives for honeybees. It was given to the Big Sur Land Trust; now, environmental education as well as an artist-in-residence program are held there.

To get to the ranch, you have to leave the highway, head up through the redwoods, and then go along a dirt path. That's what Frisell did when he was commissioned by the Monterey Jazz Festival to write music inspired by this land. His compositions premiered at the 2012 festival. Describing waking up there, Frisell said, "When morning came, it blew my mind. You're surrounded by redwood forest, and there's a trail that you can walk to the bluff's end, where the land just drops off and you see the whole panorama of the coast and the Pacific Ocean."[6] To compose this work, Frisell spent ten days at Glen Deven Ranch alone.

He wrote music that conveys the physical and spiritual sense of Big Sur. That's what I heard, over and over, listening to the CD and that what is I more-than-heard when I attended his Big Sur Quintet concert at the San Francisco Jazz Center. The music entered my body and took me back to my own times along that stretch of coast, the wild and ragged ones, the contemplative ones. The music conveys a sense of place—there's a distinct melodic connection between one song and the next; it is symphonic in that way. But it also gives the listener a singular sense of Bill Frisell, and isn't that partly what we want from music, for it to embody its composer?

Sitting at the show by myself, my thoughts and images wound around the music—if you have an art form, are you ever entirely alone? Isn't art an actual companion? A conversation between the artist and the form is an ongoing one. At times that evening, the quintet played quite loudly (too loudly for me), and I wondered how such volume could come as the result of solitude. Then, quickly, I recalled how loud some of my times alone are. There was a lot of gesture in the music, to my ears—I heard waves at a distance and gently falling oak leaves, the sway of wind. If the trees could sing in a guitar's voice or the voice of viola or violin, might this be their tune? If the rocks spoke melody along with the rhythm of rolling, might these drums be what we'd hear? Does the night sky play the cello to the stars?

A number of the Big Sur pieces have a haunting quality. In an interview about his experience at Glen Deven Ranch, Frisell said, "When you're alone, you put the idea out into the air, and in the beginning I was in a panic to think of something else right away— just the silence was deafening. Now, I'm actually beginning to enjoy it."[7] Outside the walls of the house at Glen Deven, wild animals live and roam, forage and hunt. That land is home to bobcats, coyotes, foxes, and mountain lions, along with blue jays, squirrels and rats, lizards, rattlesnakes, and snails, to name a few. In some of Frisell's songs, I could hear their footsteps. Emily Dickinson said, "Nature is a Haunted House—but Art—is a house that tries to be haunted." Frisell's Big Sur music doesn't have to try.

I wonder what you may be alone with when you hold that brush in your hand or take a curious, if tentative, step onto the dance floor. In solitude, we're better available to receive whatever's coming forward and more able to determine what fits in this piece and what's best left for another time. What will you find?

BUILDING A SAFE PLACE

Somewhere outside of Chicago, there was a swath of land where the annual science camp for fourth graders at my school was held. Never had I spent a night in a cabin with a small group of girls, let alone five nights. I wasn't enamored of the idea, but off I went on the school bus with the rest of the kids. I had no choice. We arrived at the bleak, cold place, for a week of rain. One of the projects we were given was to build some sort of structure with our cabin mates in a place of our choosing on the property. I'd never built anything out of natural materials—at that time, I didn't like to get my hands dirty. But there I was with these girls, gathering detritus along the bank of the creek in the unpleasant weather. We stuck sticks into the damp ground and crudely tied them together at the top to make the ribs of a structure; took wet leaves, small sticks, and mud and closed in the spaces between the sticks. During our hours working together, I forgot that I was miserable and wanted to go home; I even forgot about the other kids with whom I was building, and became immersed in the act of making this small hut.

Later, I went back to the creek by myself and continued to work on the hut, adding wet leaves to spots that needed them. We'd left an open space to serve as a doorway; I crawled in and sat down in the middle of the tiny room, into which late, misty afternoon light filtered. It was silent except for the talking of the creek—a sound I'd never heard alone before, and I took it in, reveled in the aloneness beside rippling water. My imagination felt flush and true; and it felt big, really big. The parts of my life at home that were challenging lost their prominence in my psyche.

Gaston Bachelard said, "Even a minor event in the life of a child is an event of that child's world and thus a world event."[8] In my small nine-year-old world, that experience was a world event. It has remained as a strong, viable memory, but as more than memory, as evidence of the truth of my belonging to the natural world. John Fowles, in his book *The Tree*, wrote, "I was really addicting myself, and beyond curability, to the pleasures of discovery, and in particular of isolated discovery and experience. The lonelier the place, the better it pleased me: its silence, its aura, its peculiar conformation, its enclosedness."[9] That long ago place remains here, and encloses me yet. It's part of what makes up the place that my writing comes from.

THE LIFE OF A HERMIT

Curious as I am about solitude and solitary lives, I look up "solitary animals." There are a lot of them. There's the blue-tongued skink, a ground-foraging omnivore. The polar bear who, for thousands of years, has been important to the Arctic indigenous peoples, is one of the few large carnivores who still live in their original habitat. Until doing some research, I'd never heard of the solitary clouded leopard, another animal whose numbers are decreasing. The pattern of her fur is a patchwork of black, tan, and white. There's the crown-of-thorns starfish, who prefers to be on his own. His "crown" is brilliantly colored; if I had a spiky crown like that, my friends would stay away too. Even the common frog, who lives throughout much of Europe, is solitary. I suppose that means he never gets to turn into a human prince, and maybe that's just as well; his nonhuman existence may be as authentically prince-like as life gets.

Observe the animals in your life and their solitary and communal habits. What might their behavior say about the nature of solitude?

There are many human hermits or hermit-like people who are content in their own company and who prefer that to the company of others. For five years, Neil Ansell lived a hermit's life. Beginning when he was thirty, through all weathers and each season, Ansell lived alone in a cottage in the deep middle of nowhere, without electricity, a telephone, or running water. Nor did he have a car. In his book *Deep Country: Five Years in the Welsh Hills* and in an article in the *Guardian*, he wrote about his experience, "I was never bored; there was always too much to be done. Chopping wood, fetching water, foraging." He saw this time as a challenge: "I would learn to stay still; I would learn to be alone. Perhaps, like Thoreau 150 years before me, I wanted to know just how little I needed in order to lead a fulfilling life."[10] He said he wasn't lonely because loneliness was the result of unchosen isolation; whereas he chose this, wanting to learn to rely exclusively on himself.

What I found most interesting in Ansell's book is that he didn't find retreat to be, contrary to his expectations, an introspective time. At first, he kept journals; then, gradually, he didn't. He wrote: "I am an absence, a void, I have disappeared from my own story. I could have stayed forever; becoming, no doubt, steadily more reclusive and eccentric." He said, "Alone, there was no need for identity, for self-definition."[11] I wonder if that would happen to any of us in a similar situation. Would nature so engage and entrance me that I'd not need to respond? Would the need for the conversation that is at first between self and self be uncalled for when living away from other people? My comparatively limited experience in nature often invites in me a response: questions or observations spark my imagination, and off I go on a riff of image and thought. Ansell's book is full of his surroundings. His descriptions of the birds are unhurried and detailed: "My days were spent outside, immersed in nature, watching."[12]

I've often had fantasies of being a hermit, but as a happily married woman—with no regrets—that's not what I've chosen. The speed of daily life can overwhelm me; its tasks can feel daunting. An introvert by nature, I'm more inclined to stay home than join a party. Walking in the woods almost daily is my antidote to the demands of life.

The great Chilean poet, Pablo Neruda, in his poem "Keeping Quiet," written in 1958, after he had moved to his beloved Isla Negra, says that if we weren't so determined to do so much, maybe we could focus on one thing and experience a silence that "would stop this sadness/ of never understanding each other . . ."[13] He imagines that then the earth would be able to show us that not even in winter is everything dead. Neruda's poem concludes with a request for silence as the poet goes on his way.

THE GULF BETWEEN SILENCE AND SILENCED

There's more than one type of silence. Don't we know a host of them? During the silence of a warm summer afternoon everything is still and easy. Henry James said, "*Summer afternoon—summer afternoon*; to me those have always been the *two most beautiful words* in the English language."[14] One of the best things in life is to lie down in a summer meadow and look up at the clouds— such enormous, silent beings moving slowly across the sky. The silence of incubation is weighted but not oppressive. Discovery can include long stretches of quietude. Enthralled with the process of uncovering, it's not time to speak. I love the quiet of my early morning writing best. The silence before a thunderstorm is as loud and heavy as the one that followed my father's frequent flares of temper when I was a child; the cats would hide under the bed; I would retreat where I could. The quiet that descended right after the Loma Prieta Earthquake in 1989 was ominous—not a single singing bird, not the merest tremble of breeze—a hush fell over the city. The silence of fallow times, too, is its own unfriendly kind of quiet.

Then there are the silences that are imposed through violence or political oppression. These deny people the right, and close off their opportunities, to speak their truth. An enormous gulf exists between chosen, contemplative silence and the slammed-door of being silenced. One enriches the imagination and one can stifle it. It's human nature to imagine, reflect, and respond. American author,

Tillie Olsen, who didn't publish until she was well into middle age (and yet went on to do important, beautiful work), wrote a book on the subject. In *Silences*, Olsen said, "Literary history and the present are dark with silences: some the silences for years by our acknowledged great; some silences hidden . . . What is it that happens with the creator, to the creative process, in that time? What are creation's needs for full functioning?"[15]

In 1973, Augusto Pinochet led a coup d'etat (with American backing) against his country and the democratically elected government of Salvador Allende. Pinochet ordered some of his countrymen and women rounded up and "disappeared" or killed. One of them was the famous poet and singer-songwriter Victor Jara. What follows is a story that I've heard repeated for years—by Chileans and non-Chileans alike. His wife, Joan Jara, who retrieved her husband's body, is said to have recounted that before he had been killed, the soldiers first broke his guitar and then his guitar-playing hands, and taunted him, challenging him to play. Through it all, Jara continued singing.

My friend Margaret went with her husband to Chile years after the coup, not long after the curfew and effective code of silence had been lifted. They noticed how oddly quiet it was everywhere they went and, when they asked about it, were told that, yes, the people had been through a long period of hardship and had been silenced. The coup itself was in the past, but as long as Pinochet was in power the danger remained real. Silence was life preserving.

Not only can people be silenced by others; sadly, we can do it to ourselves as well. When we have a need to speak but—for whatever reason—feel stymied and unable, beginning with the smallest and simplest of words is a way to break our own code of silence. It doesn't matter which words. Such a silence may be the result of distrust in our own point of view or vision or a fear of speaking what we feel we ought not. Once silence is lifted, bit by bit, what most needs saying can come forward. William Gass said, "What is unutterable? Utter it."[16] What matters is breaking the lock secured at the throat, so your voice may be set free.

Have you lived through one of those times when you were unable to speak, unable to make art? What got you through it? How did the experience, as well as the experience of gaining back your voice, change you and influence your life?

ART AND SILENCE

Solitude, stillness, and silence like to hang out together. Silence is wise because it holds all possibility—the violin's bow held in the hand that has yet to touch the strings; the paintbrush hovering above the blank canvas; the singer's mouth open but not a note yet sung. Anything is possible, until we leap and plunge forward into the saying. Then, something has happened; we've said yes to this arc and no to that one. We've made our mark. No longer is the paper blank. No longer are we silent. And though our bodies may appear still, what's happening within us is anything but.

The Swedish Nobel Prize–winning poet, Tomas Tranströmer, in his poem "Allegro," wrote about sound holding silence. I love that thought. Don't we all know such silences, the moment before the next comment or the electric moment between notes? Tranströmer wrote, "After a black day, I play Haydn . . . The sound is spirited, and full of silence."[17] Another musician, Billie Joe Armstrong, lead singer and guitarist of the band Green Day, said, "I love the power of playing quiet."[18]

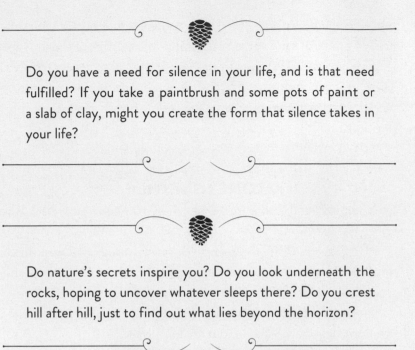

Do you have a need for silence in your life, and is that need fulfilled? If you take a paintbrush and some pots of paint or a slab of clay, might you create the form that silence takes in your life?

Do nature's secrets inspire you? Do you look underneath the rocks, hoping to uncover whatever sleeps there? Do you crest hill after hill, just to find out what lies beyond the horizon?

SELF AND LIBERTY FROM IT

In a piece titled "Tomorrow to Pastures New," Verlyn Klinkenborg wrote about looking out the window at his horses grazing. He said, "They draw me out of myself. My thoughts turn into the cowbirds wandering among the horses' hooves."[19] I would like my thoughts to be like a cowbird wandering among horses.

My self can be like a pebble in my own shoe or a loaded wagon I work hard to lug behind me as I go. There's that old adage about being unable to see the forest for the trees. Well, sometimes I can't see myself for myself. Writing at times like that can be difficult because I'm too mired in my own muck, which may manifest as anxiety or an inability to focus. As my cousin Lorraine says, "Sometimes it's hard being me." That's another time when I find being solitary in nature restorative and soothing. If I get out and surround myself with millions of grains of sand at the beach, millions of drops of water by the river, or thousands of trees in the forest, my balance gets restored. There, my ego and essential self balance out and come down to a nice size—acorn-like—a change that often brings poems and pictures with it.

ALONE TOGETHER

I was headed out the door for a walk when my phone rang. Alisa was calling, so I answered.

"Hey," she said, "I'm in your neck of the woods and want to go for a hike at Jacks Peak. Could you remind me how to get there and suggest a good walk?"

I took a deep, considering breath, before saying, "Alisa, I'm heading there right now. Want to join me for a walk?"

I was unsure that I wanted company. But this was Alisa, after all, someone I knew I could walk with, if not silently, then quietly. Alisa Fineman is a well-known singer-songwriter with a luminous voice. Several years ago, we reconnected following the death of a mutual friend; we stood in the middle of a dress shop, holding each other, crying. Someone I can cry with is someone to walk quietly with.

Alisa knows solitude too. For three years, she spent summers manning a fire lookout in the River of No Return Wilderness in Idaho. Perched high above the Salmon River, Butt's Point sits at an elevation of nearly seven thousand feet. From her lookout fifteen feet above the ground, Alisa could see north into Montana's Bitterroot Mountains and west to the Oregon border. To get to her post, she had to walk in and wait for the cowboys to arrive on horseback with supplies that always included her guitar. Her job was to get to know the land. For water, she had to hike to a spring and haul it on her back. Alisa says, "The Mormon cowboys were very kind. I was shy, appreciated their help. But when I bid everyone goodbye, I finally had the quiet I'd dreamed of. And it was very quiet." After a couple of days, Alisa became "remorseful for thinking I didn't need another human being. There were at least two of everything, except me—lodge pole pines embracing the wind, butterflies in pairs passing through the air, wildflowers growing in clusters. But only one of me." She decided to give herself two weeks to either adjust or leave, but much like Neil Ansell in Wales, soon became busy with her tasks, enamored of the land and the creatures, "Two weeks came and went, and I stayed."[20]

Poet Ellery Akers said, "Trees are solitary companions."[21] They never butt in on my silent reveries, yet, standing upright as us humans do, offer companionship. Few people are as welcome as the trees are when I'm out walking. Alisa, though, has tree-like qualities; she, too, stands tall and bends with the breeze. We walked for an hour, talking and not talking, quietly together in an easy way. No, I didn't do any writing out there that day, but a few days later in my email, there was this from Alisa:

> Spur of the moment
> She is free to walk with me
> Right now, the trail is ours[22]

Art may come out of solitude, but ultimately it calls to others. My poems never feel complete until I've read them aloud to someone. For most artists, their work is meant to be part of a conversation. In workshop settings, though everyone is engaged in their art-making alone, we're fed by the joined spirits of solitude and community. It's like we're all a part of the same biome—a large geographical area made up of particular plants and animals who have adapted to live there. Within a biome, there are many ecosystems. All living things are connected to their specific environment. Might we be members of the biome of imagination, imaginers in nature?

My father-in-law and I were clearly members of a particular biome; we both liked solitude. He was more of an introvert than I am. Just like Roy, I'm not so comfortable at a party. There were a number of times, in the midst of an extended family gathering, that he and I would find ourselves standing together, having both retreated toward the edge of the group, and one or the other would say, "Want to go for a walk?" We might chat while walking, or just as easily not. I was always content to be in the presence of that kind and quiet man. I remember most one hot summer afternoon, following his granddaughter's wedding, when Roy and I slipped away, unnoticed, and walked side by side down an empty country road. Being with Roy never took away from my own experience of a place; his silence and my silence walked companionably together.

Who in your life can you be alone with? How different is it to be alone, compared with being alone together? What do you feel comfortable sharing with these people, emotionally, artistically, and intellectually?

TO WALK ALONE

The happiness of walking alone in the woods is unlike any other happiness. It's communal, but not a town hall. It's celebratory, but there's no clinking of glasses. It's incantatory without priests. Much in the way the happiness of art-making or falling in love enthralls us, so can this. But I don't feel the swell of joy every time that I walk alone; it's not predictable. This solitary happiness surprises me with its suddenness.

Yesterday I went past the park's boundary. There is something mysterious about this that affects me—to go beyond where one is authorized to go, to ignore the "No Trespassing" sign that hangs from a forbidding line of barbed wire. When I get to the other side, there's an ephemeral magic afoot that I think has to do with the fact that people rarely walk in that place. Joy extends far beyond the boundaries of myself.

Go past the bench by the trees on the hill that used to afford one an ocean view. Now, due to the growth of the trees, you have to stand on the bench to get that view. Let your vision soften while looking to the left, and you'll see the mere hint of a trail extending past the rusty fence. Lie down on the ground and carefully shimmy underneath the wire; walk through the dense undergrowth and the closely clustered trees to where the trail opens up. This is the place where, looking from a distance, I once saw a cub and mama bear. I like walking where I know the bears have also walked.

This is a ridge top. Old dirt roads go off through the trees in a few directions. But here is where I go straight ahead toward the point, and here is where that happiness gets bigger. It becomes like an unexpected conversation that bounces from the trees to me and every other growing thing in these woods. There is happiness in the crunch of dry leaves beneath my feet. Joy gets caught on the ground along the line between shadow and sunlight, and it rises, reaching up to the treetops. Happiness is welcomed by the currents of the wind, gets swooped up by the birds and, through their voices, gets distributed farther. It doesn't recoil at the sound of gunfire from the distant rifle range; it listens in on the conversations of the feasting flies.

By this time, I'm nearly at the point, the very tip of land, and the trees are mostly behind and below me. The first day of winter sun is hot against my neck. From here I can see up and down Carmel Valley, across to the other ridge and all the way to Point Lobos, where the sand-crashing waves hit down hard again and again. Happiness greets stones and squirrels, jays and juncos, bends down to the near-to-the-ground yellow flowers blooming in December. Though this happiness is something I have, it isn't mine. Knowing it isn't better than any other thing, it thanks the pines for their sweet, pungent scent, holds its face up to the sun, and is blessed. Not a word has been spoken. The happiness comes back along the trail with me, and we head home.

CONCLUSION

HOW THE LIGHT GETS IN—
THE NATURE OF METAMORPHOSIS

It's not every day that the world arranges itself into a poem.
—Wallace Stevens

Casually sorting the mail, a handful of words from a brochure jump out at me: "Optimism is a political act."[1] That's what Alex Steffen, an American futurist and speaker on sustainability, said. And though I'd written for hours, was tired, about to begin making dinner—my favorite expression of optimism, one I perform most every evening—those words moved me back to these pages. I feel a sense of joy when chopping and slicing, reaching for the sauté pan; I like the smooth weight of an unpeeled onion in my hand; but I never considered that my optimistic feelings might indicate anything political. Mulling it over, I can see it that way. Rarely do I forget how lucky I am to be able to pay for our food; wash the lettuce leaves in clean water; blend olive oil, mustard, and balsamic; set the wooden bowl down on the table. My mother-in-law, Barbara, says, "I want to be there for whatever available joy the day has to offer." Although often quiet and seemingly subtle, optimism can be a revolutionary and revelatory act.

Some of us are born happy; I'm one of those—an anomaly in my family. Pessimism was not the underlying family dictum, but the one next up the ladder. The most basic one was, "We're here, better make the best of it; and, okay, let's be glad enough;" a kind of hesitant aliveness that pessimism often thwarted but never entirely undid. The times my mother heard a jig playing and moved the chairs out of the way, she pleased me with her fast-paced feet, her bent knees. Happiness is transformative; it can recreate a moment, an hour, a day.

Art is optimistic. No matter what emotions a piece of art may convey, art-making itself is a refusal to be plowed under by doubt, political systems, poverty, or any number of other things. Making art—this expression of belief in the act of creation and a desire to converse with spirit and imagination, to give an inner conversation form—celebrates mystery, and we get to make something that never existed before.

Even when shaky, the act of art-making is confidence in the color red; it's a few dollars deposited into the hat of the baritone busking at the busy corner. It's a writer's faith, the writer who doesn't know beforehand what will happen when the words sit together for possibly the first time: "clank" beside "riverbed," is one thing, and "closed" beside "open," is another. Even the saddest poem is a praise poem because the poet has spent time with that sorrow, held it up to the light, saying, "Here's what happened," or "This is what I'm afraid of; this, too, is my story." Then the difficulty, whatever it is, has not won out; art has, the artist has! Art can transform the ordinary into the extraordinary because the act of making allows the covert dimensions of perception and experience to come to the fore and to crystalize. Connections are made that would be impossible for the artist to arrive at from the outset.

In her novel *Beloved*, Toni Morrison, wrote, "Freeing yourself was one thing, claiming ownership of that freed self was another."[2]

By claiming and verifying that we're more than we may appear to be, art frees us—we're all who we dream to be. We go beyond limitations, debunking them. We're not held back or silenced by fear.

How does art-making contribute to your sense of freedom?

German modern dancer and choreographer Pina Bausch said, "Snow is falling—it might also be blossoms. . . ."[3] It *might* be. There's that sense of "what if" again. It's in the not-knowing, but moving ahead anyway; even gingerly, step by step, with curiosity at the helm. The spirit of optimism urges us into the next wild and ravenous moment, alert to possibility, open to all that doesn't slay desire, to all that isn't a roadblock along the path to an enlightened, dynamic, earth-infused imagination. In this closing chapter, we'll delve into the optimistic and transformative qualities unique to both art and nature.

WHISPERING, GROW, GROW

Resilient, relentless nature isn't a pessimist. Determined plants push up between the slivery cracks in the concrete, making their leafy way to the light where they thrive. If nature is curtailed in one way, it does its best to find another—over and over again. One way to maintain the spirit of optimism, in addition to making art, is through being on the land, out in the uncurtained elements. In the Talmud it's written, "Every blade of grass has its angel that bends over it and whispers, grow, grow."[4] Wherever I go in the natural world, I see evidence of such angels in the perpetuation, continuation, and in the cycles of return. I am convinced of the spirit of optimism by light, its daily return, and the sun's ability to warm my back on the coldest winter day.

In Derrick Jensen's book *A Language Older than Words*, he introduces readers to the Maori concept of *kaitiaki*—to be caretakers of the place where we live. We can extend a personal optimism to our communities by dedicating ourselves to that which sustains us. In the Maori tradition, a family would be responsible for the land where they lived. According to Maori writer Bruce Stewart, who Jensen quotes in his book, "In the old days . . . one family might look after a river from a certain rock down to the next bend." They were guardians of the land, the water, the animals, and plants. Stewart continued: "They knew when it was time to take them to eat, and when it was not. When the birds needed to be protected, the people put a *rahui* on them, which means the birds were temporarily sacred."[5] If we feel we have a larger place—larger than our individual selves and families—that is inclusive of the land where we reside, and if we contribute to the health and well-being of that land, which requires no less imagination than making art does, we have greater reason for optimism. To take responsibility for the entire earth is a daunting proposition, but what about being nurturers of a particular place? I've brought children out to Jacks Peak Park to walk and observe, to write poems and draw pictures of earth and sky. Their curiosity led them to art that surprised us all. They got to know the place better that way. In downtown Monterey, there's a mural along a tall wooden fence that covers the gaping hole where a building burnt down. Along the Embarcadero in San Francisco, there are poems about the city engraved in metal and set down along the sidewalk that stop me each time I walk there. From the personal to the communal, making art in honor of a place will increase our understanding and regard for that spot.

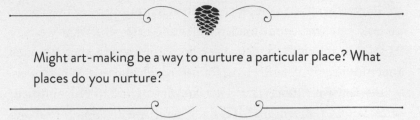

Might art-making be a way to nurture a particular place? What places do you nurture?

FILLING THE CRACKS WITH GOLD: MATERIAL TRANSFORMATION

Art is a form of alchemy. In an interview, the Turkish novelist Elif Shafak, said, "Language for me is not a tool, not an instrument. I am not a writer who uses language. I breathe inside language. I write within language. It's the laboratory of language that makes it possible for me to imagine writing. I'm in love with the letters, the meaning and muscle of letters."[6] Shafak breathes *inside* language—her memory, interpretations, dreams and desires, spirit, her world—all of it. Ah, there's that notion of inspiration again. Whatever the basic materials are—metals, paint, the human body in motion—art makes a way for us to enter our medium, alter it, transform it and, in turn, ourselves. The alchemy between artist and materials occurs when the soul enters the conversation. What a thing to have faith in, what a place to put the optimism of belief.

When traditional Japanese ceramicists mend broken pots they fill the cracks with gold. This is not to mask the break, but to accentuate it—the idea is not to hide the suffering. The otherwise unmarred object doesn't lose value, but gains. The crack demonstrates that life has happened to that pitcher or teacup, much as life happens to us, showing up in our visible and invisible scars. The Japanese term *wabi sabi* refers to a sensibility that an artist brings to her work that accepts loneliness and invisibility, as well as imperfection and transience, and allows them to manifest like shards of lightning.

For our art to flourish, it's important to not shy away from what we may perceive as our inadequacies and errors or what we may think of as dumb ideas. Our very human mistakes make for art's imperfect beauty, genuine in its foibles, rough and real. What is perfection, anyway? It's certainly not art, but tight and unblemished; perfection is uniform and lacks a playful spirit. Those aren't the qualities I'm after, either as a viewer or a maker. If we welcome some recklessness, abandon, and have a mind accepting of imperfection—an open curiosity—we'll find new approaches to our imaginative lives that will help them prosper. Watching how nature does nature, we'll find acceptance, understanding, and infinite variety there too. I want to feel the artist in his work, to see where Matisse's brush slipped, oh, the tiniest bit. Where a few of an artist's failures and frustrations show, the magic slips in.

Whatever you may learn about art-making from a class or a teacher or a book, ultimately it comes down to experience, to a relationship with the materials of craft, self, soul, and mystery. In his Nobel Prize acceptance speech, Pablo Neruda said, "I did not learn from books any recipe for writing poems."[7] There are no recipes; each of us makes it up as we go along. Tom, my chef brother-in-law, may follow a recipe when he cooks, but his food is delicious because of how he improvises, even with his own recipes. When inspiration hits, he slams shut the cookbook—adds a pinch more of this or one less tablespoon of that.

LORCA'S DUENDE

Shortly after getting married, Michael and I went to Andalusia, in southern Spain. Ever since being introduced to the poetry of Federico García Lorca, I'd wanted to go there. There was the city of Granada, and the Alhambra where, as a boy, Lorca freely wandered, but also the nondescript village of Lorca's birth—Fuente Vaqueros.

We were lucky to arrive on one of the days when his former home, now a museum, was open. Seeing the bed that Lorca was born on and the piano on which he learned to play brought the poet close.

Have you experienced "mistakes" or failures in art? Looking from another angle or brushing with gold, have you found examples of your own brilliance? How have they led to transformation?

In Lorca's short life, he produced a large amount of poetry unlike what had been written before. It's a lively, physical, imagistic poetry grounded in place, full of the myths of the people. In his poem "Sleep-walking Ballad," he wrote, "Green, how I want you green./ Green wind. Green branches," grabbing nature by the collar to pull her near.[8] This is enchantment and more. The Spanish verb, *querer*, can have a dual meaning, depending on how it's used: to love and to want, to love so much you want and to want so much you love. It makes love physical, not always erotic, but definitely in the body. If you say, "*Te quiero,*" to someone, you've got more than your eyes on them.

A constellation of things led Lorca to view nature as intrinsic to creativity. Inspired by the Gypsy music called *cante jondo*, "deep song," everything he wrote about bore the mark of passion, curiosity, and wonder. Even the many small things of nature—crickets, snails, cherry blossoms—caught his attention, and he wove them into poems. In his poem, "It's True," Lorca wrote about a girl picking olives,

> with the wind's gray arm
> clasping her by the waist.[9]

He had abundant access to the natural world, spent hours in the countryside, and was possessed of a passionate temperament, as well as a preoccupation with death—particularly his own.

Lorca brought to poetry a quality called the *duende* that had previously more typically been connected to flamenco dance and music. When a flamenco dancer is most fully possessed by the wild, dark spirit of the dance, it's said that she is in possession of the transformative quality of the *duende*. Not a smooth, easy thing, not neat and kempt, *duende* is complex and multilayered; it's art that's not been polished to the point where the edges of despair have been rubbed off, but is inclusive of life's difficulties. I went to Spain looking for the *duende*.

In his essay, "The Play and Theory of the Duende," Lorca wrote, "These 'black sounds' are the mystery, the roots fastened in the mire that we all know and ignore, the fertile silt that gives us the very substance of art . . . I have heard an old maestro of the guitar say, 'The *duende* is not in the throat: the *duende* climbs up inside you, from the soles of the feet.'"[10] He saw *duende* not so much the result of skill but coming from the earth's spirit and the poet's soul.

My Spanish is anything but great; I get by. Curious to know what local people in the small towns we were traveling through thought of the *duende*, whenever I had the chance, I asked. Standing in a tobacco shop, having purchased bunch of stamps for my stack of postcards, I'd begun licking them when the shop owner offered to help. We stood there together licking and pasting, so I asked, "What's *duende*?"

There are actually two definitions of the word; the shop owner thought I was referring to the most common one. "A small person," she answered. "Yes," I said, "but isn't there another meaning also?" She muttered something under her breath to a local browsing in the shop. "No!" she said, emphatically, "That's all, a small person, a dwarf." I thanked her, deposited my stamped cards in the postbox, and went on my way. Clearly I'd caused her to feel uncomfortable, and I left feeling that way myself.

Later, at a restaurant over tapas, I asked our young waiter, "Que es el *duende*?" His answer was the same as the tobacco woman's, but without the emphasis. He was lighthearted; I felt invited to press on. "There's another definition; I'm sure of it," I said. "I'll ask the cook," he said, "but I don't think so." When our waiter returned, he had two glasses of a local liqueur on his tray that he set in front of Michael and me. "Ah, the American is right—for once!" he said playfully. "You are correct; the cook knew. *Duende*, it's the darkness in art, the daemon."

Anytime we make something out of more or less nothing, from an idea or out of questions and possibilities, we enter a space larger than ourselves, and the end is unknown; it can't be; that's the journey of art. How this transition, this transformation, happens is mysterious. Engaging the *duende* is one part of channeling a field of possibilities.

Lorca's own life was cut short when he was only thirty-eight. Although he had committed no crime, at the outset of the Spanish Civil War, Lorca was murdered by Franco's firing squad. He was shot for no reason other than that he was a poet and a gay man who'd inspired the Spanish people through homegrown traveling theater and poetry.

THE MAGIC OF NAMING

Once upon a time, I had a friend whom I'll call Willow. Of all the people who've ever lent me an ear, no one quite listened the way Willow did. Not only were her ears upon me but her eyes, her hands, and, most especially, a divinity that coursed through her. She listened like a nun prays. If I was sad, she honored the truth and beauty of that sorrow. Having twice suffered through cancer, Willow knew more than a little about sorrow herself.

Once we took a holiday together, drove out toward the Santa Lucia Mountains, a few miles and whole worlds away from town. It was late spring, and the flowers were dressed in their best attire. What were their names? Willow knew them all. Standing in front of an orange tubular flower, Willow pressed her thumb and forefinger together, pursed her lips, and acted as if her fingers were stuck together. Then she made an *ee ooo uu* monkey noise, her face gesturing along with her voice. I bent over laughing at her charade, but, being a bit dense, I hadn't the vaguest idea of the name of that flower growing aplenty on bushes everywhere. She relented, "sticky monkey flower!" Because of the way she gave me the flower's name, I've never forgotten it. No matter how many years away from her I am, the flowers that return each spring bring her back.

The eighteenth-century Swedish botanist Carl Linnaeus is considered the father of taxonomy—the name giver. He created a system for naming plants and animals that is still in use today. Linnaeus might be considered a secular Adam. As a boy, he loved flowers. When he was sad, his parents gave him a flower to make him happy again. I wonder how that would work on children today?

If we don't know the name of something, do we see it more clearly because we can't fall back on its name? Do we look with an eye toward remembering the details of what we're seeing—flower, tree, person? A name allows us to distinguish one from another but it also stops the process of inquiry. Who are we without our names? Which are your favorite names? Mine are those that wildflowers and birds have—nightcap and thimbleweed, whorled wood aster, titmouse, striated pardalote, fairy bluebird, and olive-sided flycatcher, the bird who impatiently sings what sounds like, "Quick-three-beers! Quick-three-beers!"

In making art, we're engaged in our own form of transformative taxonomy. We're naming our perceptions and experiences, celebrations of the color blue, joy in the sound of that small bird's voice—the one up in the peach tree—and grief in life's losses. Nobody will name this color the way you will; nobody will listen to that bird in quite your way. The stories you will write, nobody else will, because nobody else can.

These pages are my exploration in naming the vicissitudes of the imagination, spirit, and nature. Might we share in the naming of this world, call out to it in ways new and varied, optimistic and splendored, claiming the blades of grass and the hawks as our brethren?

THE SKY IS A MIRROR

Julius Lester wrote ". . . When I want to see my face, / I use the sky as a mirror. . ."[11] *Who I Am* has been on my shelf everywhere I've lived since I bought it at the Barnes & Noble in lower Manhattan in 1974. It was a hot summer day, and when I walked out of the bookstore I knew I'd gotten a lot more than I'd paid for. I always know where to find the book, with its orange cover. When I grabbed it last night to mull over what I wanted to write this morning, it opened to the just-right page. Yes, the sky is a mirror, the stars reliably wink back at me when I look up.

When out walking in the woods, the ground holds me and so do the trees, every growing thing and the animals who've never shooed me out; the sky encases me from above. Something's shifting within me; the forest has entered in. When I leave the forest, the forest is where I left it. But it's also here, inside me, wherever I am. More than the dirt I carry away in the crevasses of my shoe soles, I feel myself holding the forest. Does sap now run through my veins, along with blood? Eventually, will my hair become branches and leaves? If roots grow beneath my feet one day, will my shoes no longer fit? I will never live at Jacks Peak Park, yet whenever I am not there I am still in those very woods, strolling along the shaded winding paths, along Iris or Rhus, taking in the views from Lower

Ridge Road, enjoying the deep darkness through the canyon while walking on Madrone Trail—the light flickering in, bright cracks between the branches.

May the earth get under your skin. May you, too, make your own path into nature's places. Perhaps feathers are inching their way out, down the length of your arms, unifying your spirit with that of the bird, that of the wind. I hope your imagination has found its wings and that, more and more, art is finding its way into your life; that you trust its place, have secured it with shells, pinecones, and dreams. Any day that arranges itself into a poem or a scuttle-dance across the stage is a good one. May faith in your place along the shore, on the cliffs, and beside wind-washed trees grow certain. May a sturdy, imaginative connection to the source, to the earth, be well rooted. May you find that your story starts out sacred and stays that way, and along the way, discover yourself anew, irrefutably linked to the natural world. May you kiss the ground.

ACKNOWLEDGMENTS

My beloved friends Diana Wertz and Don Rothman died just before I began writing *Step into Nature*; I've missed them in the writing and listen for their voices still. I'm remembering also my cousin Joe Hurley, and writer and student Paula Walling. Everyone at Copy King makes my life easier and better and does such beautiful work!

Charlotte Raymond: there's a damn good reason her name appears on the dedication page; she has my eternal gratitude! Anna Noak is the steward of this book—her July phone call rings like a chime in my life; what a privilege to work with such a fine editor. This book became itself through the care the manuscript received from developmental editor Sylvia Spratt; her smart attention brought the essence of my ideas onto the page. Managing editor Lindsay Brown didn't even let a major computer glitch get her down! She's steady and smart and offered my book her expertise, and I'm grateful. Emmalisa Sparrow not only has the most beautiful name in the world, but her kindness and fine work are lovely too. Everyone at Beyond Words gave their best; thank you to Leah Brown, Whitney Diffenderfer, Jackie Hooper, Karen Preston, Bill Brunson, and Devon Smith. My gratitude to Marci Bracco, publicist at Chatter Box Public Relations, who always goes the extra mile.

Margaret Goldsmith listened to me read nearly the entire manuscript and graciously offered immediate feedback, hot tea, and friendship. Upon the book's completion, not only did Julie Brower read the book out loud to me, she brought me flowers and gave me her love. Naturalist and biologist Nikki Nedeff walked in the woods with me, shared her knowledge, and led me to new stories. Readers Julie Olsen Edwards, Anna Paganelli, and Jerry Takigawa greatly helped this book find its way. They carried my thinking past where I thought it could go. Marion Silverbear, dear friend, was the rarest of readers; she read and reread and asked questions and listened with all of who she is. Out to lunch with Elliot Ruchowitz-Roberts, when the check came he'd always say, "It's my turn to pay," even when it wasn't. Melanee Barash said, "I'll do anything I can for you," and then she did. Marina Romani, Adele Negro, and Raymond Isola made the poem translations possible. Mary McKenna reflected what needed reflecting and kindly gave her invaluable perspectives. Nanda Current helped me to frame this book long before it was this book. Edward Jarvis led me back to my body when I'd gone astray and also offered wisdom.

For the presence and their words that I've quoted here or in conversation, thanks to Kathleen Blount, Amy Brewster, Eleanor Carolan, Marguerite Costigan, Erin Gafill, Donald Hall, Penny Hardy, Daniel Horowitz, Ed Jarvis, Paul McFarland, Rachel McKay, Elliot Ruchowitz-Roberts, C. Kevin Smith, and Briar Winters. Jodi McClean graciously extended herself to me. Despite his own deadlines, Robert Sapolsky generously offered me his comments. Monica Larenas expanded my understanding about Chile.

Thank you to the Monterey Public Library, and in particular to reference librarian (and poet) Victor Henry. Diana Vela, Associate Director of the Cowgirl Museum and Hall of Fame went out of her way to help me source material. Each and every one of my writing students greatly inspires my work. Thank you especially to longtime students Dorothy Bailey, Eleanor Carolan, Laura Caldwell, Ellen Coulter, Bill Deeb, Lois Epel, Diane Grunes, Cynthia Guthrie, Jennifer Hall, Lorraine Kinnamon, Margaret Larson, Annie Lynn, Lisa Meckel, Jane Murphy, Joan Myers, Marina Romani, Persis Rooth, Sarojani Rohan, Richard Sullivan, and Alice Tao. Rachel McKay, who led me to important sources, always offers me her dearness. Alisa Fineman walked with me and told me about her fire lookout days. Thank you to the children and faculty at Captain Cooper and Robert H. Down Schools.

Friends Martha Cervantes Fasnacht, Suzanne Laurens, Pamela Nichter, Barbara Stark, and Gina Van Horn help to make my life sturdy and its sky bright.

To the ones who purr—Ace and Stella—if I could purr, too, I would.

This book could only have become itself because of my home-away-from-home, Jacks Peak Park. My gratitude to every tree, beetle and bird, squirrel and rat, the unseen bobcats, foxes, and lions, and each swoosh of wind, the ground that holds my steps.

And most of all, my gratitude goes to the two men in my life who are everywhere in these pages. My father, Nick Vecchione, showed me the light and, beginning when I was very young, he initiated in me a love of art; still, at ninety-two, he teaches me how to see. My husband, Michael Stark, best beloved, man of red roses and firewood, companion on the journey, and diviner, brought home much more than the bacon so that I could devote myself to writing this book—he brings home the love.

NOTES

Chapter 1

1. Brandon Stanton, *Humans of New York* (New York: St. Martin's Press, 2013), 120.
2. Charles Montgomery, *Happy City: Transforming Our Lives Through Urban Design* (New York: Farrar, Straus and Giroux, 2013), 120.
3. Elizabeth Marshall Thomas, *The Hidden Life of Deer* (New York: Harper Perennial, 2010), xiii.
4. "Stories of Hope: Healing Gardens Nurture the Spirit While Patients Get Treatment," American Cancer Society, July 24, 2002, http://mstage.qa.cancer.org/treatment/survivorshipduringandaftertreatment/storiesofhope/healing-gardens-nurture-the-spirit-while-patients-get-treatment.
5. Leslie Marmon Silko, *The Turquoise Ledge: A Memoir* (New York: Penguin, 2011).
6. Willa Cather, *O Pioneers!* (New York: Houghton Mifflin, 1913), 257.
7. Richard Louv, "Using Nature May Make You Smarter, Healthier, and Happier," *The Vancouver Sun*, Tracy Sherlock, May 7, 2011: http://www.vancouversun.com/health/Using+nature+make+smarter+healthier+happier/4744876/story.html.
8. Rory Stewart, *The Places in Between* (New York: Houghton Mifflin Harcourt, 2004), 28.
9. Alan Watts, "Ear," *New Wilderness Society*, vols. 9–10, 1984.

10. Annie Proulx, *Bird Cloud* (New York: Simon & Schuster, 2011), 184.
11. Wallace Stevens, *The Collected Poems of Wallace Stevens* (New York: Random House, 2011), 386.
12. Arturo Perez-Reverte, *The Seville Communion* (New York: Houghton Mifflin Harcourt, 1999), 195.
13. Jean-Jacques Rousseau, *Jean Jacques Rousseau: His Educational Theories Selected from Emile, Julie and Other Writings* (Hauppauge, NY: Barron's Educational Series, 1964), 173.

Chapter 2

1. Gore Vidal, *The Selected Essays of Gore Vidal* (New York: Random House, 2009), 57.
2. Antonio Machado, *Border of a Dream: Selected Poems*, trans. Willis Barnstone (Port Townsend, WA: Copper Canyon Press, 2004), 333.
3. Theodore Roethke, "The Waking," *The Collected Poems* (New York: Anchor Books, 1932), 104.
4. Gary S. Breschini and Trudy Haversat, "Hands: A Unique Esselen Indian Artform," Coyote Press, 2002, http://www.californiaprehistory.com/reports02/rep0034.html.
5. Robinson Jeffers, "Hands," *Dear Judas: And Other Poems* (New York: Horace Liveright, 1929), 128.
6. Bill Brubaker, "In Haiti, the Art of Resilience," *Smithsonian Magazine* (September 2010): 3, http://www.smithsonianmag.com/people-places/in-haiti-the-art-of-resilience-53519464/?no-ist.
7. Annie Dillard, *Pilgrim at Tinker Creek* (New York: HarperCollins, 2009), 11.
8. Hans Silvester, "Ethiopian Tribal Fashion," *Departures*, May 2010, http://www.departures.com/fashion/style/ethiopian-tribal-fashion.
9. Marguerite Costigan, "Resolve," used by permission of the author.
10. Patrice Vecchione, *A Woman's Life In Pieces*, 2009.
11. Zbigniew Herbert, *Elegy for the Departure*, trans. John Carpenter and Bogdana Carpenter (New York: HarperCollins, 1999), 50.

Chapter 3

1. Else Holmelund Minarik, *Little Bear* (New York: Scholastic, 1985), 8–10.
2. John Berger, *Here Is Where We Meet: A Story of Crossing Paths* (New York: Random House, 2007), 195.

3. *The Georgia O'Keeffe Museum Announces Winners of First Annual Photography Competition*, press release, Georgia O'Keeffe Museum, February 5, 2013, accessed July 21, 2014, prweb.com/releases/2013/2/prweb10405741.html.

4. Ellery Akers, "On Writing: Feeding the Lake," *National Poetry Review* 36, no. 2 (2007): 1.

5. Lucille Clifton, "February 11, 1990," *Quilting: Poems 1987–1990* (Rochester, NY: BOA Editions, 1991), 11.

6. Maira Kalman, *The Principles of Uncertainty* (New York: The Penguin Press, 2007), 25.

7. Peter Stark, *The Last Empty Places: A Past and Present Journey Through the Blank Spots on the American Map* (New York: Random House, 2010), 8.

8. Robert Macfarlane, *The Wild Places* (New York: Penguin, 2008), 140.

9. Ibid, 140.

10. Wallace Baine, "Jenny Offill's new novel 'Dept. of Speculation' takes unusual approach to storytelling," *Santa Cruz Sentinel*, February 5, 2014, http://www.santacruzsentinel.com/entertainment/ci_25071468/jenny-offills-new-novel-dept-speculation-takes-unusual.

11. John R. Platt, "Soon the Only Place to See This Nearly Extinct Bird May Be on Samoan Currency," *Scientific American* (October 6, 2003), http://blogs.scientificamerican.com/extinction-countdown/2013/10/16/samoa-manumea/.

12. Eric H. Chudler, "Neuroscience for Kids: The Blood-Brain Barrier ('Keep Out')," accessed July 23, 2014, https://faculty.washington.edu/chudler/bbb.html.

13. Paul Rogers, "California Drought: Past Dry Periods Have Lasted More than 200 Years, Scientists Say," *San Jose Mercury News: Science and Environment* (January 25, 2014), http://www.mercurynews.com/science/ci_24993601/california-drought-past-dry-periods-have-lasted-more.

14. "Typhoon Haiyan Death Toll Tops 6,000 in the Philippines," CNN (December 13, 2013), http://www.cnn.com/2013/12/13/world/asia/philippines-typhoon-haiyan/.

15. Kate Wolf. "Here in California," Another Sundown Publishing Company, 1980, CD.

16. Patrice Vecchione, "Sing for Your Supper," *The Knot Untied* (Monterey, CA: Palanquin Press/Community Publishing, 2013), 42.

Chapter 4

1. Carole Maso, *Ava* (London: Dalkey Archive Press, 1995), 66.

2. Paula Gunn Allen, *The Sacred Hoop: Recovering the Feminine in American Indian Traditions* (Boston: Beacon Press, 1986), 119.

3. Edward Sharpe and the Magnetic Zeros. "I Don't Wanna Pray." Community Music/Vagrant Records, 2012. CD.

4. Barry Lopez, *Crossing Open Ground* (New York: Open Road Media, 2013), 67.

5. C. Kevin Smith, "Pear Orchard," used by permission of the author.

6. Gary Lopez and Debra Gwartney, eds., *Home Ground: Language for an American Landscape* (San Antonio: Trinity University Press, 2013).

7. Robert Macfarlane, *The Wild Places* (New York: Penguin, 2008), 216.

8. Ibid.

9. Ervin Laszlo and Allan Combs, eds., *Thomas Berry, Dreamer of the Earth: The Spiritual Ecology of the Father* (Rochester, VT: Inner Traditions/Bear & Co., 2011), 35.

10. *Harry Potter and the Deathly Hallows*, directed by David Yates (Burbank, CA: Warner Home Video, 2011), DVD.

11. Lydia Davis, *The Collected Stories of Lydia Davis* (New York: Macmillan, 2010), 49.

12. Joyce Carol Oates, "The Writer's Room," *The New York Times Blog: T Magazine*, February 14, 2014, http://tmagazine.blogs.nytimes.com/2014/02/14/the-writers -room/?_php=true &_type=blogs&_r=0.

13. Ibid.

14. Julie Zeveloff, "Maya Angelou Always Rented A Hotel Room Just For Writing," *Business Insider*, May 28, 2014, http://www.businessinsider.com/maya -angelou-writing-process-2014-5.

15. D. A. Powell, Twitter post, December 8, 2013, http://twitter.com/powell_DA.

16. Norma Bhaskar, in discussion with the author, October 12, 2013.

Chapter 5

1. Henry Beston, *The Outermost House: A Year of Life On The Great Beach of Cape Cod* (New York: Holt Paperbacks, 2003) 24.

2. Kahlil Gibran, *The Prophet* (New York: Alfred A. Knopf, 1923), 32.

3. E. E. Cummings, "I will wade out," *The Complete Poems: 1913–1962* (New York: Harcourt, Brace, Jovanovich, 1972), 189.

4. Donald Hall, "Marianne Moore, The Art of Poetry No. 4," *The Paris Review* 4, no. 26 (1962): 1.

5. "Georgia O'Keeffe and the Faraway: Nature and Image." Exhibit. The Georgia O'Keeffe Museum, May 2012–May 2013, http://www.okeeffemuseum.org/ georgia-okeeffe-and-the-faraway-nature-and-image.html.

6. Ibid.

7. Mary Street Alinder and Andrea Gray Stillman, eds., *Ansel Adams: Letters and Images, 1916–1984* (New York: Little, Brown and Co., 1988), 98.

Chapter 6

1. E. E. Cummings, "maggie and milly and molly and may," *Complete Poems, 1913–1962* (New York: Harcourt, Brace, Jovanovich, 1972), 682.
2. David Wagoner, "Lost," *Traveling Light: Collected Poems* (University of Illinois Press, 1999), 10.
3. Peter Plagens, "Don't Stop, Just Paint," *The Wall Street Journal*, March 7, 2012, http://online.wsj.com/articles/SB1000142405297020460300457726732169338 3832.
4. Priscilla Frank, "Richard Diebenkorn's Berkeley Paintings Light Up the de Young Museum," *The Huffington Post*, June 28, 2013, http://www.huffingtonpost .com/2013/06/28/richard-diebenkorns-berkeley-paintings-de-young-museum -photos_n_3512505.html.
5. De Young Museum Tumblr, accessed July 23, 2014, http://deyoungmuseum.tum blr.com/post/53291013036/words-to-paint-by-richard-diebenkorns-notes-to.
6. Steven Nash, Emma Acker, and Timothy Anglin Burgard, *Richard Diebenkorn: The Berkeley Years, 1953–1966* (New Haven, CT: Yale University Press, 2013), 20.

Chapter 7

1. Wallace Stevens, *The Collected Poems of Wallace Stevens* (New York: Random House, 1990), 95.
2. Dore Ashton, *Picasso on Art: A Selection of Views* (Cambridge, MA: De Capo Press, 1988), 10.
3. Michael Cunningham, in discussion with the author, April 22, 2014.
4. John Keats, Keats' Kingdom website, keatsian.co.uk/negative-capability.php.
5. Frank O'Hara, *The Collected Poems of Frank O'Hara* (Oakland, CA: University of California Press, 1995), 197.
6. Mary McKenna, in discussion with the author, July 23, 2014.
7. Jonathan Safran Foer, *Extremely Loud and Incredibly Close* (New York: Houghton Mifflin Harcourt, 2005).
8. Jan McGeorge, in discussion with the author, December 16, 2013.
9. Louise Bourgeois, *Destruction of the Father / Reconstruction of the Father: Writings and Interviews, 1923—1997* (London: Violette Editions, 1998), 114.

Chapter 8

1. Forestiere Historical Center homepage, accessed July 23, 2014, http://www .forestiere-historicalcenter.com/.

2. Donald Hall, *Goatfoot Milktongue Twinbird: Interviews, Essays, and Notes on Poetry, 1970–76* (Ann Arbor, MI: University of Michigan Press, 1978), 126.

3. Donald Hall, *Life Work* (Boston: Beacon Press, 2012), 54.

4. *Pina*, directed by Wim Wenders (Berlin: Neue Road Movies, 2011; New York, The Criterion Collection), DVD.

5. "Music Fueled By Desire: Hector Berlioz and the Symphonie Fantastique," *San Francisco Symphony: Keeping Score*, 2011, http://www.keepingscore.org/ interactive/pages/berlioz/score-idee-fixe.

6. Henri Matisse, *Tout l'oevre péint de Matisse: 1904–1928* (Flammarion, 1982), 5.

7. Italo Calvino, *The Path to the Nest of Spiders*, trans, Archibald Colquhoun (New York: Ecco Press, 1957); *By Way of an Autobiography, from The Uses of Literature*: uky.edu/neusne2/parares/calvino/ca/auto.html.

8. Diana L. Vipond, ed., *Conversations with John Fowles* (Oxford, MS: University Press of Mississippi, 1999), ix.

9. Catherine Craft, *Jasper Johns* (New York: Parkstone International, 2012), 93.

10. David Rothenberg, *Survival of the Beautiful: Art, Science, and Evolution* (New York: Bloomsbury Press, 2011), 51.

11. Jane Smiley and Kurt Brown, *The True Subject: Writers on Life and Craft* (Graywolf Press, 1993), 21.

12. Barbara J. King, "The Amazing Snow Art of Simon Beck," *NPR Arts and Culture*, December 22, 2013, http://www.npr.org/tags/251615358/simon-beck.

13. "Tracey Emin: Angel Without You," Museum of Contemporary Art North Miami: Knight Exhibition Series, December 4, 2013, http://mocanomi.org /2013/12/tracey-emin/.

14. Anna Swir, "Happy as a Dog's Tail," *Talking to My Body*, trans. Czeslaw Milosz and Leonard Nathan (Port Townsend, WA: Copper Canyon Press, 1996), 91.

15. John Maloof, Maloof Collection, Ltd, 2014 www.vivianmaier.com.

16. Bonnie Raitt. "What Is Success." *Streetlights*, 1971. Lyrics by Allen Toussaint. CD.

17. Susan Farrell, *Critical Companion to Kurt Vonnegut* (New York: Infobase Publishing, 2009), 242.

Chapter 9

1. Eleanor Carolan, excerpt from haiku, used by permission of the author.

2. "How One Day Everything Could Be Recycled," Biomimicry NYC Facebook page post, July 1, 2013, https://www.facebook.com/BiomimicryNYC/posts /519088624823557.

3. Jay Harmon, *The Shark's Paintbrush: Biomimicry and How Nature is Inspiring Innovation* (Ashland, OR: White Cloud Press, 2013).

4. Stanley Kunitz, *Passing Through: The Later Poems, New and Selected* (New York: W. W. Norton, 1999), 11.

5. Paul McFarland, in discussion with the author, December 28, 2013.

6. Ibid.

7. *American Beauty*, directed by Sam Mendes. (Los Angeles: DreamWorks, 1999) DVD.

8. Jarbas Agnelli, "Birds on the Wire," Vimeo video, 1:25, 2009, http://vimeo .com/6428069.

9. John Fowles, *The Tree* (New York: Ecco, 2010), 7.

10. Abby Callard, "Restoring Artwork to its Former Glory," *Smithsonian*, October 2009, http://www.smithsonianmag.com/arts-culture/restoring-artwork-to -its-former-glory-140029173/.

11. Erin Lee Gafill, from a conversation with the author, January 5, 2014.

12. Ibid.

Chapter 10

1. Helen Keller, *The Story of My Life—Helen Keller* (Ramona, CA: Cherry Hill Publishers, 2012), 23.

2. Brad Gooch, *Flannery: A Life of Flannery O'Connor* (New York: Little, Brown & Co., 2009), 13.

3. Annie Paul Murphy, "Your Brain on Fiction," *The New York Times*, March 17, 2012.

4. Ray Magay Tshuma, *uMthwakazi Review*, quoted in Alan August, The Underline website, January 21, 2014, http://www.theunderliner.com/2014/01/when-himba -woman-decides-to-have-child.html.

5. Ibid.

6. Ibid.

7. Rosemary Mahoney, *For the Benefit of Those Who See: Dispatches from the World of the Blind* (New York: Little, Brown & Co., 2014), 231.

8. Kathleen Blout, "A Shattering," used by permission of the author.

9. Charlotte Latvala, "Developing Baby's Five Senses," *Parenting*, Accessed http:// www.parenting.com/article/developing-babys-5-senses.

10. Elizabeth Svoboda, "Scents and Sensibility," *Psychology Today*, January 1, 2008, http://www.psychologytoday.com/articles/200712/scents-and-sensibility.

11. Anne Sexton, *All My Pretty Ones* (New York: Harper & Brothers, 1961), 11.

12. Robert Macfarlane, *The Wild Places* (New York: Penguin, 2008), 203.

13. John Hamilton, "Seeing Less Helps the Brain Hear More," *NPR Blogs: Health*, February 5, 2014, http://www.npr.org/blogs/health/2014/02/05/272092118/see- ing-less-helps-the-brain-hear-more. Two of the study's authors, both quoted in

the NPR piece, are Hey-Young Lee from Johns Hopkins and Patrick Kanold from the University of Maryland, February 5, 2014.

14. Denise Levertov, *The Collected Poems of Denise Levertov* (New York: New Directions, 2013), 53.

15. Simonetta de Filippis and Paul Eggert, eds., *D. H. Lawrence and Italy* (New York, Penguin, 1972), 168.

16. Audrey Carlsen, "Some People Really Can Taste the Rainbow," *NPR Blogs: The Salt*, March 18, 2013, http://www.npr.org/blogs/thesalt/2013/03/12/174132392/synesthetes-really-can-taste-the-rainbow.

17. Stacey Conradt, "Vladimir Nabokov Talks Synesthesia," *Mental Floss*, March 19, 2013, http://mentalfloss.com/article/49442/vladimir-nabokov-talks-synesthesia.

18. Penny Lewis, "The Colour of Sound," personal webpage hosted by the Trust Centre for Neuroimaging, University College London, Accessed July 23, 2014, http://www.fil.ion.ucl.ac.uk/~plewis/other/synaesthesia.pdf.

19. Julia Alter, in conversation with author, January 20, 2014.

20. Sylvia Plath, *Letters Home* (New York: Faber & Faber, 2011), 211.

21. Jean Cocteau, *Opium: The Diary of His Cure* (London: Peter Owens Publisher, 2001), 137.

22. Bill Benson, "Hospice patient and former forest ranger visits outdoors one last time," *Heroes Memorial Foundation*, June 12, 2014, http://www.heroesmemorial.org/content/hospice-patient-and-former-forest-ranger-visits-outdoors-one-last-time.

Chapter 11

1. Samuel Taylor Coleridge, *Biographia Literaria* (Oxford, England: H. J. Jackson, 1985), 314.

2. Joyce Carol Oates, *The Faith of a Writer: Life, Craft, Art* (New York: Ecco, 2004), 75.

3. John le Carré, "Staring at the Flame," *The New York Times: Arts & Leisure*, July 20, 2014, http://www.nytimes.com/2014/07/20/movies/john-le-carre-on-philip-seymour-hoffman.html.

4. Donald Hall, *The Unsayable Said, An Essay* (Ann Arbor: University of Michigan Press, 1982), 141.

5. Jonathan Cott, *Dinner with Lenny: The Last Long Interview with Leonard Bernstein* (Oxford: Oxford University Press, 2013), 68.

6. André Breton, *Mad Love*, translated by Mary Ann Caws (Lincoln, NB: Bison Books, 1988), 114.

7. Patrice Vecchione, *Writing and the Spiritual Life: Finding Your Voice by Looking Within* (New York: Contemporary Books/McGraw-Hill, 2001). 96.

8. Franz Kafka, *The Blue Octavo Notebooks* (Cambridge, MA: Exact Change, 2004), 98.
9. Edward Jarvis, in conversation with the author, February 12, 2014.
10. Edward Jarvis, "Fool's Gold," used by permission of the author.
11. William Stafford, *The Way it Is: New and Selected Poems* (Minneapolis: Graywolf Press, 1998), 32.
12. Walt Whitman, *Song of the Open Road, Leaves of Grass* (New York: New American Library, 1955), 141.
13. Susan Sontag, "Vassar College Commencement Speech" (Poughkeepsie, NY: May 25, 2003).
14. James Knapp Reeve, *Practical Authorship* (Ridgewood, NJ: The Editor Company, 1905), 143.
15. Terry Gross, "Paul Thomas Anderson, The Man Behind 'The Master'" *NPR: Fresh Air*, October 2, 2012, http://www.npr.org/2012/10/02/162153952/paul-thomas-anderson-the-man-behind-the-master.
16. Wallace Stevens, *The Necessary Angel: Essays on Reality and the Imagination* (New York: Vintage, 1985), 6.
17. Ibid.
18. Mary Szybist, "National Book Award Acceptance Speech" (New York, NY, November 20, 2013), Gray Wolf Press, https://www.graywolfpress.org/blogs/mary-szybists-national-book-award-acceptance-speech.
19. Elliot Roberts, in conversation with the author, April 10, 2014.
20. Elizabeth Marshall Thomas, *The Old Way: A Story of the First People* (New York: Macmillan, 2007), 178.

Chapter 12

1. Jonah Weiner, "The Impossible Body: Storyboard P, the Basquiat of Street Dancing," *The New Yorker*, January 6, 2014, http://www.newyorker.com/reporting/2014/01/06/140106fa_fact_weiner.
2. Thomas Berry, *The Sacred Universe: Earth, Spirituality, and Religion in the Twenty-first Century* (New York: Columbia University Press, 2009), 71.
3. Rachel McKay, "Diplomacy," used by permission of the author.
4. Holli Riebeck, "All Dry on the Western Front," NASA, January 23, 2014, http://earthobservatory.nasa.gov/IOTD/view.php?id=82910.
5. Joseph Serna and Veronica Rocha, "First Six Months of 2014 Were Warmest in California's History," *LA Times*, July 21, 2014, http://www.latimes.com/local/lanow/la-me-ln-warmest-weather-california-20140721-story.html.
6. David Spangler, Facebook status, Facebook, January 6, 2014, https://www.facebook.com/david.m.spangler/posts/10201303241038160?fref=nf.

7. Michael Prager, interview with Janine Benyus, November 20, 2008, http://michaelprager.com/green_hero_janine_benyus.

8. H. H. Mitchell, et al., "The Chemical Composition of the Adult Human Body and Its Bearing On the Biochemistry of Growth," *The Journal of Biological Chemistry* 158, (1945): 625–637, http://www.jbc.org/content/158/3/625.full.pdf+html?sid=f51ce105-b21d-4744-b034-af17722d8520.

9. Ezra Pound, *The Pisan Cantos* (New York: New Directions, 1948), 98.

10. Thomas Berry, *The Sacred Universe: Earth, Spirituality, and Religion in the Twenty-first Century* (New York: Columbia University Press, 2009), 74.

11. Dotson Rader, "Alvin Ailey American Dance Theater's Robert Battle: 'I Was a Boy Surrounded By the Arts,'" *Parade*, December 5, 2013, http://parade.condenast.com/238951/dotsonrader/alvin-ailey-american-dance-theaters-robert-battle-i-was-a-boy-surrounded-by-the-arts/.

12. Lewis Henry Morgan, *The Indian Journals, 1859–1862* (Houston, Texas: Courier Dover Publication, 1993), 220.

13. Edna O'Brien, *Country Girl: A Memoir* (New York: Little, Brown and Co., 2013), 134.

14. Daniel Horowitz, in discussion with the author, January 20, 2014.

15. Mary McKenna, in discussion with the author, January 20, 2014.

16. Penny Hardy, in discussion with the author, January 15, 2014.

17. "Weather," *Weather: Poems for All Season*, ed. Lee Bennett Hopkins (New York: HarperCollins, 1995), 59.

18. Jeremy Hobson and Robin Young, "James Scott's Bleak Novel of Revenge Set in Upstate N.Y.," *WBUR Boston: Here and Now*, January 13, 2014, http://hereandnow.wbur.org/2014/01/13/the-kept-novel.

19. Alex Ross, "Darkness Visible: Georg Friedrich Haas Arrives in New York," *The New Yorker*, November 11, 2013, http://www.newyorker.com/arts/reviews/2013/11/11/131111goli_GOAT_classical_ross.

20. Theodore Roethke, *The Collected Poems of Theodore Roethke* (New York: Anchor, 1974), 193.

Chapter 13

1. Ellen L. Arnold, ed., *Conversations with Leslie Marmon Silko* (Jackson, MI: University Press of Mississippi, 2000), 149.

2. "Wounda's Journey: Jane Goodall Releases Chimpanzee Into Forest," YouTube video, 4:33, posted by Jane Goodall Institute of Canada, December 17, 2013, https://www.youtube.com/watch?v=YzC7MfCtkzo.

3. Emily Dickinson, "314," *The Poems of Emily Dickinson*, ed. R. W. Franklin (Cambridge, MA: Harvard University Press, 1999), 140.

4. Bhavanada, Facebook post, July 7, 2013.
5. Meredith, Facebook post, July 7, 2013.
6. John, Facebook post, July 7, 2013.
7. Robin, Facebook post, July 7, 2013.
8. Susan, Facebook post, July 7, 2013.
9. Jonathan Cott, *Dinner with Lenny: The Last Long Interview with Leonard Bernstein* (Oxford: Oxford University Press, 2013), 99.
10. Caryl, in conversations with the author, January 30, 2013.
11. Rainer Maria Rilke, *Letters to a Young Poet*, tr. M. D. Herter Norton (New York: W. W. Norton, 1934), 59.
12. Derrick Jensen, *A Language Older Than Words* (White River Junction, VT: Chelsea Green Publishing, 2004), 25.
13. Henry Beston, *The Outermost House: A Year of Life On The Great Beach of Cape Cod* (New York: Holt Paperbacks, 2003), 24.
14. "Encounters with Animals in Graeco-Roman Antiquity: the Historicity of Experience," Helsinki Collegium for Advanced Studies, December 9, 2013, http://blogs.helsinki.fi/shc-helsinki/2013/11/01/encounters-with-animals-in-graeco-roman-antiquity-the-historicity-of-experience/.
15. Osip Mandelstam, Marina Romani, trans., "For our joke take my palms," used by permission of translator. Originally published in Russian, 1922.
16. "Telling the Bees," *Northern Berkshire Beekeepers Association*, December 12, 2010, http://nbba.wordpress.com/2010/12/12/telling-the-bees/.
17. Carol Ann Duffy, *The Bees: Poems* (London: Faber & Faber, 2013), 21.
18. William Longgood, *The Queen Must Die: And Other Affairs of Bees and Men* (New York: W. W. Norton & Company, 1988), 230.
19. Eloise Greenfield, *Honey, I Love and Other Love Poems* (New York: HarperCollins, 1986), 22.
20. Lynn, in conversation with the author, February 6, 2014.

Chapter 14

1. Tim Dee, *A Year on the Wing: Journeys with Birds in Flight* (New York: Free Press, 2010), 45.
2. John Fowles, *The Tree* (New York: Ecco, 2010), 56.
3. Juan Ramón Jiménez, *The Complete Perfectionist: A Poetics of Work,* edited and translated by Christopher Maurer (New York: Bantam Doubleday Dell, 1997), 56 - 57.
4. Marguerite Duras, *Writing* (Minneapolis: University of Minnesota Press, 2011), 241.
5. Ibid.

6. Nate Chinen, review of "Big Sur," *The New York Times*, June 24, 2013, http://www.billfrisell.com/discography/big-sur.

7. Ibid.

8. Gaston Bachelard, *Fragments of a Poetics of Fire* (Dallas: Dallas Institute of Humanities and Culture, 1997), 33.

9. John Fowles, *The Tree*, (New York: Ecco, 2010), 56.

10. Neil Ansell, "Neil Ansell: My Life as a Hermit," *The Guardian/The Observer*, March 26, 2011: www.theguardian.com/environment/2011/mar/27/neil-ansell-my-life-as-hermit.

11. Ibid.

12. Ibid.

13. Pablo Neruda, *Extravagaria*, trans. Alastair Reid (New York: Farrar, Straus and Giroux, 1974), 27–29.

14. Susan Ratcliffe, ed., *Oxford Book of Quotations* (Oxford: Oxford University Press, 2010), 518.

15. Tillie Olsen, *Silences* (New York: The Feminist Press at CUNY, 2003), 6.

16. William H. Gass, *Tests of Time: Essays* (Chicago: University of Chicago Press, 2003), 163.

17. Tomas Transtromer, "Allegro," *The Great Enigma: New Collected Poems* (New York: New Directions Press, 1987), 65.

18. Jon Pareles, "Anomalous Harmony, Present and Past: Norah Jones and Billie Joe Armstrong Sing Everly Brothers," *The New York Times*, November 22, 2013, http://www.nytimes.com/2013/11/24/arts/music/norah-jones-and-billie-joe-armstrong-sing-everly-brothers.html?pagewanted=all&module=Search&mabReward=relbias%3Ar.

19. Verlyn Klinkenborg, "Tomorrow to Pastures New," *The New York Times*, May 21, 2011, http://www.nytimes.com/2011/05/22/opinion/22sun3.html.

20. Alisa Fineman, in conversation with the author, December 2, 2013.

21. Ellery Akers, "On Writing: Feeding the Lake," *The American Poetry Review* 36, no. 2 (March/April 2007), https://www.aprweb.org/article/on-writing-feeding-lake.

22. Fineman, in discussion with the author, December 2, 2013.

Conclusion

1. Arnie Cooper, "The Bright Green City: Alex Steffen's Optimistic Environmentalism," *The Sun*, April 2010, http://thesunmagazine.org/issues/412/the_bright_green_city.

2. Toni Morrison, *Beloved* (New York: Vintage, 2004), 111.

3. *Pina*, directed by Wim Wenders (Berlin: Neue Road Movies, 2011; New York, The Criterion Collection), DVD.

4. Talmud, Think Exist.com: http://thinkexist.com/quotes/like/every_blade_of _grass_has_its_angel_that_bends/149773/.

5. Derrick Jensen, *A Language Older Than Words* (White River Junction, VT: Chelsea Green Publishing, 2004), 162.

6. Terry Gross, "Elif Shafak: Writing Under a Watchful Eye," *NPR: Fresh Air*, February 6, 2007, http://www.npr.org/templates/story/story.php?storyId=7217653.

7. Pablo Neruda, "Nobel Lecture: Towards the Splendid City." *Nobelprize.org*, Nobel Media AB 2014, 15 September 14, 2014, http://www.nobelprize.org/ nobel_prizes/literature/laureates/1971/neruda-lecture.html.

8. Federico García Lorca, Christopher Maurer, ed., *Selected Verse: Revised Edition* (New York: Farrar, Straus and Giroux, 2004), 177.

9. Ibid., 451.

10. Federico García Lorca, Christopher Maurer, ed. and trans."The Play and Theory of Duende," *In Search of Duende* (New York: New Directions, 2010), 49.

11. Julius Lester, *Who I Am* (New York: The Dial Press, 1974), 6.

BACKBONE BOOKS:
SUGGESTED READING

This is a list of my backbone books—formative works that have made conversations with the worlds of nature, art, and literature, the inner and outer worlds, more possible and true. Some I read many years ago while others are more recent treasures. Here are books of essays, fiction, memoir, poetry, and children's picture books. As books that dwell in my psyche, they led me to writing *Step into Nature*. May they find a place to dwell within you too.

The Poetics of Reverie: Childhood, Language, and the Cosmos, by Gaston Bachelard, Beacon Press, 1971.

Here Is Where We Meet, by John Berger, Vintage, 2006.

The Artist Who Painted a Blue Horse, by Eric Carle, Philomel, 2011.

The Songlines, by Bruce Chatwin, Penguin Books, 1988.

The Collected Poems of Lucille Clifton, edited by Kevin Young and Michael S. Glaser, BOA Editions, 2012.

The Complete Poems of Emily Dickinson, edited by Thomas H. Johnson, Back Bay Books, 1976.

Pilgrim at Tinker Creek, by Annie Dillard, Harper Perennial, 2007.

The Book of Embraces, by Eduardo Galeano, W. W. Norton, 1992.

Goatfoot Milktongue Twinbird: Interviews, Essays, and Notes on Poetry, 1970–1976 (Poets on Poetry series), by Donald Hall, University of Michigan Press, 1978.

Who I Am, by Julius Lester (author) and David Gahr (photographer), Dial Press, 1974.

Vintage Lopez, by Barry Lopez, Vintage, 2010.

The Collected Poems: A Bilingual Edition, by Federico García Lorca, translated by Christopher Maurer, Farrar, Straus & Giroux, 2002.

Last Child in the Woods: Saving Our Children from Nature-Deficit Disorder, by Richard Louv, Algonquin Books, 2008.

Times Alone: Selected Poems of Antonio Machado, translated by Robert Bly, Wesleyan University Press, 1983.

Ava, by Carole Maso, Dalkey Archive Press, 2002.

The Names of Things: Life, Language, and Beginnings in the Egyptian Desert, by Susan Brind Morrow, Riverhead Hardcover, 1997.

Journal of a Solitude, by May Sarton, W. W. Norton, 1992.

This Is a Poem that Heals Fish, by John Pierre Simeon (author) and Olivier Tallec (illustrator), Enchanted Lion Books, 2007.

The Turquoise Ledge: A Memoir, by Leslie Marmon Silko, Viking, 2010.

The Hidden Life of Deer: Lessons from the Natural World, by Elizabeth Marshall Thomas, Harper Perennial, 2010.

The Old Way: A Story of the First People, by Elizabeth Marshall Thomas, Picador, 2007.

Georgia O'Keeffe: The Poetry of Things, by Elizabeth Hutton Turner, Phillips Collection, 1999.

The Branch Will Not Break: Poems, by James Wright, Wesleyan University Press, 1963.